PETE ROSE

An American Dilemma

KOSTYA KENNEDY

Also by
Kostya Kennedy

56

Joe DiMaggio
and the
Last Magic Number
in Sports

PETE ROSE

An American Dilemma

KOSTYA KENNEDY

For Kathrin Perutz and Michael Studdert-Kennedy.
For each and for both.

Contents

Contents

Pete Rose, age 31.

Introduction

"Pete, you're the greatest. In our house you're already in the Hall of Fame."
—Harriet, customer at The Forum Shops, Las Vegas

"People who want him in the Hall, they don't understand. If he gets into the Hall of Fame there's nothing that means anything."
—Goose Gossage, pitcher, Hall of Fame 2008

MORE THAN a quarter century has passed since Pete Rose swung a bat in the major leagues, and nearly that long since he filled out a lineup card as a major league manager. He has been banned from baseball since Aug. 23, 1989. Yet even now, 25 years into exile, he remains a figure who stirs uncommon passion, righteousness, indignation. He remains the subject of perhaps the most polarizing and provocative question in sports: Does Pete Rose belong in the Hall of Fame?

The Rose debate, of course, transcends statistics and performance. This is not a sports discussion on the order of "Who was the greatest quarterback ever?" Or, "Should the American League abolish the designated hitter?" This is something larger than that—unique in its weight and its parameters, a moral conundrum that over the course of its long and changing life has burrowed through every level of the game and expanded far beyond sports talk.

Rose got more base hits, played in more games and came to bat more times than anyone in baseball history. He played with an abandon—a singular and unquenchable joie de vivre—that riled some but endeared him eternally to generations of fans, teammates and opponents. No one, not even Rose's fiercest detractors, questions his on-field credentials for the Hall of Fame. That would be absurd, like asking whether John Glenn belongs on the list of alltime astronauts or whether Bugs Bunny deserves a place among the cartoon elite.

Rose is also a lifelong gambler and during his time in baseball he bet often and illegally on the game—flouting its explicit prohibition, committing baseball's cardinal sin, endangering the integrity of the sport. For years Rose denied, often dismissively and defiantly, that he had ever bet on baseball. Then, in 2004, he admitted that while managing the Cincinnati Reds he had wagered not only on the game but on his own team. Rose has often revised details of his recollections along the way. He may say one thing today, something else tomorrow.

So Rose's story has shifted and still shifts in its particulars, even as the debate around him has slipped and continues to slip into new frameworks. The conversation changes not just as Rose's story changes, but as the game changes, and the times change, and as our perceptions of athletes evolve.

Most pointedly to the Rose case, the Steroid Era has wreaked a complicated havoc on baseball and on how players are seen and judged. Dozens of ballplayers have now been suspended for using performance enhancing drugs, receiving punishments that to many seem paltry when held alongside Rose's permanent ban. And several superstars known for steroid use have been made eligible for the Hall of Fame, having committed a different sin from Rose's—cheating. Although steroids have twisted player legacies and darkened the hallowed records and results that sit at baseball's core, those drug users have been granted something that Rose, rightfully or not, was never granted: a place on a Hall of Fame ballot. This, even though Rose did not stain the game in the way those drug users did. Or did he?

So, what do we think of Rose now, in this new era, in this redefined world? What do we think of him now, in his 70s and deep into a strange, sometimes slapstick postbaseball journey that has led him to prison for tax fraud; to the pro wrestling ring; to the dog track; to divorce from his second wife; to a reality television series pinned in part to the surgical fate of his young girlfriend's breasts; and to so many instances of hawking one thing or another, selling his signature, his story, himself? What do we think of him now, the Hit King who still adores and reveres baseball—its nuances, its history—as he adores and reveres nothing else? What do we think of Pete Rose today, in the noisy twilight of his remarkable, original, powerful and wholly American life?

The Rose predicament leads to big questions. What is the price of sin? And, What price is just? Should forgiveness be granted only to the contrite? Does someone deserve harsher punishment for having coldly let down his followers, for having fallen from especially great heights? Should a false apology carry more weight than none at all?

Does it matter whether or not we approve of Rose? Does it matter whether he is selfish or generous? Does the continually indulged gambling compulsion that has shaped him deserve our sympathy or our scorn?

What drove Rose so forcefully to greatness and to his demise? Why has he denied himself his own redemption? Rose could have carried out his extraordinary life in any number of ways. He could have been any kind of hero. Why this?

From the start, and increasingly over the years, the Rose dilemma has tested not only our ethics and our view of morality, but has also led us to the measuring of a man. What would each one of us have done along the jagged path from exposure to banishment to judgment had we been hustling around in Rose's shoes? What do we think of Pete Rose now?

Chapter 1

Cooperstown, 2012

RIGHT ABOUT at the center of Main Street in Cooperstown, N.Y., diagonally across from the old Cooperstown Diner, next door to the Doubleday Cafe and 396 feet from the three wide stone steps that lead to the entrance of the National Baseball Hall of Fame, sits one of the village's numerous baseball merchandise and memorabilia shops: Safe At Home Ballpark Collectibles. Here you can purchase all manner of items summoning baseball's past as well as its present: There are scores of ball caps (a Cubs one with a Wrigley Field logo stitched onto it, a Mets cap from '69, numerous Red Sox variations) and even more player jerseys (Mays, Musial, Pujols, Jeter . . .). You can choose from an array of bobbleheads and figurines, wristbands and socks, pens, autographed baseballs and photographs, a trove of miniature helmets. The store sells panini presses that can imprint a team logo onto the toast ("I'll have a turkey and Swiss on whole wheat, with the Cardinals' interlocking STL branded into it please."). This is one of several Cooperstown shops that carries a series of three Abbott and Costello jerseys, each with a respective name and number on the back to honor the duo's famous routine: "WHO 1", "WHAT 2" and "I DON'T KNOW 3."

The retail space at Safe At Home runs narrow and deep, and after sidling past many rows of hanging jerseys and T-shirts you come—on Hall of Fame induction weekend, the busiest weekend of every year—to a make-shift partition: a rack of pennants and key chains and other knickknacks. Beyond that there's some carpeting on the hardwood floor and then a folding table covered by a bright blue cloth, at which, for several shifts throughout the weekend, you can find, sitting and joking and signing for a fee, Pete Rose.

The proprietor of Safe At Home, Andrew Vilacky, is a pal of Rose's. "When Pete first came up here in the 1990s, there was a lot of controversy—and excitement," says Vilacky, a wiry, streetwise sort in his mid-40s. "He would step out of his car on Main Street and people would cheer and throw up their arms like someone had just scored a touchdown."

"There were also a lot of people who were bothered by it, like, 'What is he doing here?'" recalls Bill Francis, a researcher at the Hall of Fame. "People found it distasteful. There is still some of that."

Rose, like numerous other baseball stars, has been signing for dollars during induction weekend off and on since 1995, when he debuted at a modern Cooperstown institution called Mickey's Place. He had origi-nally planned to sign there in '93—less than four years into his lifetime banishment from baseball and just two years after he was made ineli-gible for induction into the Hall of Fame. He canceled those first appear-ances, however, after objections from many in the game (including Hall of Famer and former Rose teammate Tom Seaver) who said that Rose's joining the dozens of former big leaguers peddling their autographs in Cooperstown that weekend would, under his particular circumstances, be in bad taste. Upon deciding to stay away, Rose issued a statement say-ing that he didn't want to do anything that would take away from that year's inductee, Reggie Jackson.[1]

---

[1] Jackson, himself not one to begrudge controversy, nor, for that matter, to object to a surfeit of attention, said, "I would have loved to have him there. I would have gone over to say hello." And Bill Guilfoile, then the associate director at the Hall, suggested, somewhat wryly: "If he is here in town, he's more than welcome to visit the Hall of Fame. We have enough of his artifacts here."

After Mickey's Place, Rose moved with Vilacky and Vilacky's mentor and business partner, Tom Catal, to the short-lived Pete Rose Collectibles, and then, about five years ago, to Safe At Home. Still, he has not been a constant fixture. For a while in the mid 2000s, Rose believed, based upon conversations with commissioner Bud Selig and other baseball executives, that he had a chance to gain reinstatement to the game. Rose got the impression from Selig that it would be in his best interest to lie low for a while and not to do things like hold autograph sessions down the street from the Hall of Fame during induction weekend. So for a few years Rose didn't come to town. Reinstatement, though, never happened, and the prospects that it *would* happen seemed to fade.

Rose, impatient and irked—*pissed* in the words of one person close to him—phoned Vilacky and said, "Fuck it. They're not doing what they said they would do. I'm coming back up this year." Over a few days of signing autographs in Cooperstown, depending upon the crowd, Rose might make $30,000 or more.

The arousal that Rose generates by his appearances during induction weekend has abated in recent years, but only slightly. He still attracts a heavy and ardent following—and generates more conversation than the other baseball greats signing their names—and this was particularly true on the late July weekend of 2012 when thousands of Cincinnati fans flooded into Cooperstown to honor the induction of shortstop Barry Larkin, who played for the Reds from 1986 through 2004. As a Cincinnati rookie, Larkin hit his first major league home run in the same game in which Rose, then the Reds' player-manager, swung at his final big league pitch. Larkin played his first four seasons under Rose, becoming an All-Star.

"That first year we had two shortstops, Barry and Kurt Stillwell," Rose recalled in Cooperstown the day before Larkin's induction. "Barry came into my office one day and said, 'Pete, Kurt is a good player, but you may as well trade him. I'm going to be your shortstop here for the next 15 years.' We traded Stillwell the next season." Larkin in 2012 was the first Reds player to go into the Hall of Fame since Tony Perez in '00. (Sparky Anderson, Cincinnati's manager for nine seasons and four World Series appearances, was also inducted that year.) Replica Larkin jerseys hung prominently in the storefront at Safe At Home all weekend, as did T-shirts that read VOTE PETE INTO THE HALL OF FAME on the front, and THE ALL-TIME HITS LEADER NOT IN COOPERSTOWN? *PLEASE* on the back.

Rose, per custom of the trade, commanded varying prices for his signature: on a photo or ball ($60), on a bat or jersey ($95), and so on. A personalized inscription might run an extra $20. To get the autograph you bought a ticket at the Safe At Home register, then were led outside and around back to wait in line in an alleyway behind the store. (The reason for this, as Catal, the store owner, explained while surveying the scene from the store's front step, was so as "not to clog up all this beautiful foot traffic" on Main Street.) Complained one fan wearing a Reds' Sean Casey jersey that Friday afternoon, "I went back there and checked it out. The line is too long, I'm not doing it." But a few minutes later he and his companions, similarly clad, had changed their minds and were standing in the line, items in hand to be signed, partially shaded from the high sun on a beautiful summer afternoon.

To each customer Rose provides generous sit-down time and excellent banter. The few minutes next to Rose is a major part of what people pay for—the monetary value of his autograph has slipped significantly after so many years of signing—and also why the line moves slowly. In effect, Rose is receiving visitors. Burly, quick-witted and genial, he never hurries people along, gently needling ("That's a hell of a wristwatch you got there, what'd it come free with the shirt?"); answering all manner of baseball related questions (Q: "Who is the best player you ever managed?" A: "Me"); and often offering a little something more. ("Do you want to take another photo? Sure, bring both of your kids into this one.") He'll give a young ballplayer advice ("Watch the other team's pitcher the whole time before you come up, you'll learn something"), and at the end of the exchange he will hold a customer's handshake for just that extra moment. When he thanks someone for coming out he looks him straight in the eye.

Rose is not avuncular—he's too crass and not soft enough for that; and although he is advancing deeper into the eighth decade of his life and his children have produced five children of their own, Rose is certainly not grandfatherly. In Cooperstown he wore a lightweight fedora covering up his dyed, reddish hair, and an oversized T-shirt and jeans. Also a thick gold watch. He is prone to telling crude jokes and he is not at all above saying, in mixed and even unfamiliar company, "Right now, I could use a blow job."

There's a scruffy sort of soulfulness about Rose, though, something genuine and to admire, and, because of his many sins and because of the strange company he sometimes keeps, there is an aura of mystery too. The broad strokes of his life story—his inspiring self-propelled rise and his astonishing self-inflicted fall—continue to render him an object of deep curiosity. Customers in the store who aren't waiting to get autographs hover 40 feet away from his signing table, peering over and talking to one another about Pete as a hell-bent ballplayer or about his betting habit or his current romantic involvement with Kiana Kim, a former *Playboy* model who is more than 30 years his junior. "How much money do you think he has gambled away in his life?" someone asks another. "Millions?" There is no need to speak softly, Rose is out of earshot, but the onlookers do, heeding to a sense that they are talking about something they should not be talking about, the details of someone else's iniquitous life. It's a bit like the cocktail party guests standing together at Gatsby's mansion when one woman whispers, conspiratorially, of the host, "Somebody told me they thought he killed a man once."

Rose is hardly the only lure for autograph seekers this weekend (although he is, even now, arguably the most popular). Main Street is lined with choices. Within a single block a passerby might over the span of a few hours have the chance to get the signatures of Hall of Famers Juan Marichal, Lou Brock, Rollie Fingers, Johnny Bench, Frank Robinson, Goose Gossage and others. A restaurant is offering, just off its outdoor patio, a series of sessions with former Reds such as Eric Davis, Dave Parker and manager Lou Piniella. Big Cecil Fielder, the former Tigers slugger, has a table. There are lines for all of them. Farther down the road is a grouping of players meant to appeal to Yankees and Mets fans: Elliott Maddox, Ron Blomberg, Roy White and Howard Johnson. In front of a memorabilia store called Legends Are Forever a young woman hollers out, carny barker style, "Ernie Banks here from 1 to 4 o'clock. A Hall of Famer! Get your Ernie Banks autograph!"

The hawking of things, the sheer volume of memorabilia and all the money changing hands reveals a Cooperstown greatly altered from the quieter heather-strewn hamlet that officially welcomed its first Hall of Famers on June 12, 1939. Fifteen thousand people spilled onto the festively adorned streets that day—onto Chestnut, Railroad and Main—crowding to try to get glimpses of men like Babe Ruth, Napoleon Lajoie, Walter Johnson and Cy Young. Schoolchildren let out early on that Monday hustled about looking for autographs, but there were no signing tables, no price structures, no thoughts of resale or estimations of value beyond that value which is evident to a child holding, or showing to a friend, a scrap of paper onto which Ty Cobb, say, has just scrawled his name. Today's scene, with collectors noisily comparing their wares, is a transformation not only from that seminal day, but also from the Cooperstown of the 1960s, '70s and into the '80s, before the influx of memorabilia shops and before the autograph and collectibles market went haywire.

In another sense, though, in a feeling, the Cooperstown induction experience is at its core unchanged. Baseball remains a community and on this special weekend, everyone is welcome—the alltime greats, the everyday big leaguers, the Sunday adult leaguers, the fans. Just as Yankees manager Joe McCarthy and recently retired Pirates third baseman Pie Traynor ran into each other and sat to chat on a Cooperstown bench in 1939, Hall of Famers Tony Perez and Andre Dawson stopped for an impromptu conversation in front of the Doubleday Cafe in 2012. Just as fans, come from afar and sparked by the heroes mingling among them, called out then—*Hey Babe! Hey Ty!*—so do they now: *Hey Eck! Hey Whitey!* For all its commercialism, induction weekend can still provide a fine measure of surprise and closeness, a commingling of history, legend and memory, and a prevailing spirit that draws its strength from so many baseball lives. The spirit was there when Connie Mack went in in 1939, and Jimmie Foxx in '51 and Jackie Robinson in '62 and Barry Larkin in 2012.

Out on the street in Cooperstown, Rose hears lots of ballpark chatter directed his way. "Whaddya say, Pete!" and "Gotta get you into the

Hall, Pete" and of course, inevitably, "Who do you like in the Reds game tonight?" and "What are the odds they'll win the division?" followed by laughter. Naturally on this weekend there are many references to his hometown, to which he remains so closely associated, and where his idol is most powerful. "Pete, Pete!" a fan calls out. Rose is standing just in front of the glass door outside Safe At Home with Kiana Kim. It is early evening, and he is done autographing for the day. They are going out for dinner with Kiana's kids. The fan is in his late 20s, sinewy and tough, roughened around the mouth, tattoos running along the inside of both forearms. He has on a white tank top and when he sees Pete look up at him, showing a grin and a thumbs-up, the fan raises a fist and shouts in a raspy hoot, "Cincinnati, baby! West Side!"

Chapter 2

Harry Never Walked

THE RIVER there was narrower than it is today, maybe 500 feet across, and much shallower too. In the height of every summer the channel shrank further still, drying up to but a few feet deep, becoming little more than a lazy creek. Native Americans would cross the water there, following after herds of buffalo and elk. Even in the spring and fall, when the river rose full again, the natives would leave their hillside dwellings and paddle across in their bull boats to pick up the trail on the southern bank, passing through the groves of water maples and osiers and entering into chest-high grasses and fertile hunting grounds.

When white men came to this part of Ohio and Kentucky in the late 1700s, they saw the trail and began to use it too, not only for hunting but also as a way across what they had named the Ohio River. The town of Cincinnati was established just up the northern bank. The settlers grew in number and the Native Americans swiftly dwindled and the river widened over the years. In 1817 a businessman named George Anderson got it into his mind to run a ferry service at the crossing, and that service, the Anderson Ferry, has been making trips just about every day for the nearly two centuries since.

At first, the men powered the ferry with long poles and pulleys and then later they deployed horses, blindfolded and made to run on a treadmill that spun the waterwheel that churned the boat across. The vessel carried men with their wagons and women with their pushcarts, and it was this way right through the Civil War and even after the great suspension bridge was built to span the Ohio River from Cincinnati to Kentucky. The bridge was seen as a symbolic as well as a practical connecting of North and South. Some people, the Whig writer and sociologist Harriet Martineau among them, believed that Cincinnati could make a worthy capital for the entire Union, because it was in a sense a truly American city, not so influenced by the motherland as those on the East Coast were, and being Western and still new. By war's end the population in Cincinnati had grown to near 200,000.

The stone ferryhouse on the Kentucky side of the Anderson crossing stood in the small town of Constance and it was in this town that a man named Zachary Taylor Fox lived with his wife, Annie. Fox earned his way as a tanker, transporting fresh water, and a few years after the Civil War he moved his family from Constance and across the river to live on the Ohio side, near the Anderson Ferry road. The Foxes had a daughter they named Laura, and she married Edward Bloebaum, whose parents, like many others, had come to Cincinnati from Germany and Prussia.

The Bloebaum family owned a small house on a short dead-end, Braddock Street, just up from River Road. Laura and Edward had a daughter, LaVerne, and LaVerne in the 1930s married a man named Harry Francis Rose. Together LaVerne and Harry had four children, the third of which—and the first boy—they gave the name Peter Edward Rose. All through the years and generations, from Zachary to Pete, the Foxes and then the Bloebaums lived here on the northern bank, on the West Side of Cincinnati, and all along the family used the Anderson Ferry to go over to Kentucky for one thing or another, for some transporting business or to fish off the far bank or just to take the children on a Sunday ride.

Back in 1867 when the ferryboats had converted to steam power, the new owner of the Anderson route, Charles Kottmyer, began using a line of wooden boats that he named after Daniel Boone. In the 1700s

Boone had laid his stake in the nearby tangle of northern Kentucky, traveling northward on the Licking River into the Ohio as he fought spectacularly with the Shawnees and led epic hunts for big game, fashioning as he did so an American legend in buckskin. Every 15 years or so the Kottmyers built a new ferryboat: *Boone No. 1* was replaced by *Boone No. 2* and so on up until *Boone No. 7*, the first steel boat in the line, 64-feet-by-22-feet and diesel-powered, upon whose red-and-white trimmed deck Pete Rose worked as a teenager in the 1950s, collecting fares and parking cars. The river had been locked and dammed repeatedly over the decades and by the time the '50s ended, the banks were close to 600 yards apart at the Anderson Ferry crossing, and the water was 10 fathoms deep. Pete held the deck job only briefly, being as he didn't much like the leisurely pace of the work.

THE WATERFRONT in Cincinnati is the source of the city's birth and life and of its hard-won history and its legends besides. When those first settlers came to Cincinnati along the river from Limestone, Ky., they came not to find fortune and return to the East, but to take the land from the natives, to plant crops and to live. They arrived on crude barges, steeled for the fight ahead and knowing that because of its place along the river with its nearby tributaries, along what they took to calling the "water highways," this was a crucial region to control. In the 1790s George Washington sent troops, thousands of them, to garrison in Cincinnati. More and more boats came—bateaux laden with livestock and a family's furniture; single-sail pirogues to fish from; keelboats stocked with whiskey kegs. The bigger flatboats crept slowly down the river, fortified against attack by thick-cut side timber that had carved into it portholes through which muskets could be fired.

Settlers' children were captured by natives in those years and people died of sickness and of the struggle, but the city was won—in the way much land in America was won, in a manner of perseverance familiar in the narrative of the nation—and it indeed proved a vital landing spot, situated between New Orleans and Pittsburgh. By the turn of the 20th century, or around the time that Pete Rose's grandparents, Laura Fox and Edward Bloebaum, were marrying, Cincinnati was a thriving metropolis, a busy whiskey market, home to 43 breweries as well as to factories where, in 1901, some 49 million decks of playing cards were produced, more playing cards than were made anywhere else in the world. Some of the decks were designed for everyday games, while others were meant for casino play.

Yes, the great stories in Cincinnati all seem to involve the river: the floods of 1883 and 1907 and '13, and then the truly great, or truly awful, flood of '37. In the last week of January that year the Ohio River rose to nearly 80 feet—79 feet, 9 inches as the marking had it on the side of one downtown building. Homes were swept away and thousands of people were left shelterless. Horses drowned. All of Crosley Field, where the Cincinnati Reds played, was underwater, right up through the lower grandstand. You'd have had to be a crack diver to swim down and touch home plate. Days into the storm the newspapers blared out RIVER STILL RISING! though to see that all you had to do was look out your window, if you could open it, if your house was still safe and you still had a home. Radio WLW quit running commercials and covered the flood nonstop 24 hours a day.

The rain fell and fell and fell. On the West Side of Cincinnati the river washed over the train tracks and over River Road. The water came up into the low lying hills, overtopping cars and sheds and uprooting young trees. It reached then the sloped front yard at 4404 Braddock Street, a three-bedroom house built in 1886 by the landlord who had lived in the manor higher up on the hill, and owned by a Bloebaum just about ever since. This was the house where Pete Rose would spend his childhood and where now, in the flood of '37, his parents Harry and LaVerne were already living and waiting out the storm with little Caryl, their one baby girl.

The river rose right to the edge of the small stone landing at the front of the house, roiling there, seeming ready to rise higher still until finally, abruptly, the rains stopped and an unnatural calm enveloped the January afternoon. There would be time yet before the water would recede and it was LaVerne, looking out off the landing, who saw and seized the opportunity. She went inside for a fishing line and found something in the cupboard for bait and then cast the line off the porch and into the risen river. The Ohio was known for its catfish and its carp and after just awhile—would you believe it?—LaVerne pulled out a fish worth eating.

Though Pete would later tell many stories about his father, this was the one story, and pretty much the only one, that he told about his mother, that saucy broad. Pete liked the fish story because it spoke of a certain can-do-ness on his mother's part. She didn't take what she was dealt but rather made things happen. He liked to see her in that way just as he liked to see himself. Pete enjoyed telling the story because it said something about the history of his life before he was born, about the people who begat him and about the land, and because the story spoke not only of resourcefulness, but also of ingenuity and even humor, a little winking at the gods, a measure of irreverence and wit.

———————————————

WHEN HARRY FRANCIS ROSE shook your hand he did it right. Not a crushing handshake certainly, but firm enough to let you know it *could* be crushing if Harry so chose. Decisive. Authentic. Harry's was not a large right hand, just a strong one, and for the duration of the grip he would look you right in the eye. Harry went about 5'9" and 175 pounds and even at that size he was the kind of athlete that if you played against him you remembered it years later.

He had a thick neck and a straight jawline and a wide nose and his head seemed square because of the way he cut his hair. Harry held beliefs consistent with his handshake: A man should exert himself fully in the things he did, especially when it came to athletics. He should have clarity of opinion and certainty of purpose and he should accept in himself no physical weakness. There was no tolerance for bull. You did not miss a day of work for any reason at all. This, Harry would tell his children, was the real American way. Although Harry had never made it in college football, lacking both the academics and the size, when he was in his 20s he earned a spot on the old Cincinnati Bengals, who played their home games at Crosley Field. Harry had made that team, said the folks around Anderson Ferry, because he'd been so determined to do so.

Harry did not smoke cigarettes or drink hard liquor and while you always knew clearly when Harry was angry, none of his four kids—Caryl, Jackie, Pete and Dave—ever heard him raise his voice to his wife LaVerne. Harry had a keen, ever-present and narrowly defined sense of right and wrong.

"Grab the day that's in front of you," Harry would say, often by "day" meaning the game or the play. He was never one to talk much about his past, about how he had spent his earliest years over in Ripley, on the northern bank of the Ohio and then, after his parents split, moved with his mother Eva and his brother William 50 miles west to Cincinnati to begin a life with Eva's new husband, Harry Sams. After living for a while in Over-the-Rhine, an inland community on the West Side, Harry's family had moved to a house on Southside Avenue, a couple of miles directly east of the Anderson Ferry route and closer than just about anything else to the water's edge. The house stood on the far side—that is, the riverbank side—of River Road, tucked among industrial buildings and local landmarks: the water tower, the Standard Brands malting factory and the sheet-metal car shops. Harry Sams worked as a driver and then a brakeman and for a little extra money, like a number of people around there, he brewed and sold his own beer.

Harry Francis didn't dwell on his past as an athlete either, although others certainly did. He was known at times as Pete—a nickname he had acquired as a child because of his fondness for a local plow horse by that name—and he was a standout champion in local leagues, especially at football. He was extraordinarily tough, hard to bring down as a runner and uncommonly fierce as a tackler. Harry understood the social currency of being this kind of athlete. He played league baseball too, and at one of his weekend games he met LaVerne Bloebaum, the sister of a very good ballplayer named Buddy Bloebaum. LaVerne was a fine softball player herself, and Harry told Buddy right away how pretty he thought she was. Harry's manner was measured and reserved, LaVerne's was sassy, plucky and coarse. When they got married, two years after that first meeting, LaVerne was 18 and Harry 19. Ten years later, on April 14, 1941, they had little Pete—born on the same day, and this is a coincidence impossible not to note, that President Franklin Delano Roosevelt was throwing out a ceremonial first pitch, Opening Day in Washington, D.C.

Harry, or Big Pete or Pete Senior as he would now often be called around the football field, worked at the Fifth Third Bank downtown, tellering and doing some accounting work. Neighbors talked about Harry with a great respect, owing to what he did on the sports field and solidified by the way he held himself. As Pete Rose the Hit King would say throughout the years that he was coming up in baseball and will still tell you today, no one has ever stood larger in his life than his father Harry. "He is the only hero I have ever had," Pete says. Pete and his siblings felt their father was the most important man living anywhere near Anderson Ferry. "The shit," as Pete's younger brother Dave puts it. "My father was the shit."

Harry arrived home from work at just about the same time every night, stepping out of the bus onto River Road at a little before 6 p.m. Always the same thing: he would tuck the day's newspaper under his arm and sprint hard up the steep incline of Cathcart Street and make the sharp right turn down the length of raggedy Braddock to get home. The neighborhood kids all liked to watch this. Harry never just walked.

Sometimes on a Monday or Tuesday if his team had lost its weekend tavern-league football game or if Harry had not lived up to his own expectations, he would sprint further up Cathcart, push ahead for another piece on the punishing hill and then bend left down along crudely paved Allenham Street before turning around and going hard back down the hill to home. He ran this wearing his leather work shoes and on hot days he sweat through the thighs of his slacks, sending himself a message—a reminder that the failure of the previous weekend's game could not happen again, that next time things would be different on the field, that they would go his way.

"He is 41 years old, father of four, still can run 100 yards in 10.5 seconds and after 22 seasons in organized football he still lines up at right halfback every Saturday afternoon." This appeared in a Cincinnati newspaper in 1953, alongside a photo of Harry, known as Pete. "Who is he? The only person in Cincinnati fitting this description is popular Pete Rose . . . now in his third year with the Trolley Tavern eleven in the Feldhaus Major League. 'He is the eldest by at least six years,' says Frank Feldhaus. 'And still one of the best.' " Rose went on playing football until he was 42, twice the age of most guys in the league.

———————————

LITTLE PETE came to the games. He'd scurry around as a gofer or a water boy, eating up the excitement as best he could. He'd see his father get knocked to the ground, then jump up and chase down a man 20 years younger. Once Harry got back up even after breaking his hip. This, on the West Side of Cincinnati in those years, was seen as just about the noblest thing you could do. To the kids on the grass field at Bold Face Park or the baseball diamond at Sayler Park, or wherever the game was that day, it meant much more that your dad played ball like that than what he might do for a job, or even what sort of wheels your parents drove—a dinged-up old Chevy? The new '52 Ford?

On good weekend nights if Harry had led his team to a win, had broken off a run for a touchdown or two, he would take the family out to celebrate. They'd go nearby to get a piece of fish and the tall lemonades at that Trolley Tavern maybe, or else they would all pile into the coupe and drive out to the A&W Root Beer shop in Groesbeck or Harrison. Frosty mugs and double-burgers, ice cream for dessert.

The family didn't often celebrate this way after little Pete's games though, not after his Little League baseball games nor later when he was at Western Hills High or playing legion ball. If Pete went 4 for 6 his father saw not four hits but two missed opportunities, and he would talk about this, harrying Pete all the way home, questioning why he hadn't done this or that and reminding him again that he needed to work harder than the others, especially given his size. When Pete started high school he barely weighed 100 pounds. "Understand that you represent all of us out there, every Rose," his father would say.

Why had Pete not backed up first base properly in the third inning? Why had he tried to haul off and hit that 2-and-0 pitch for a home run—

and Harry from behind the plate had seen that that was exactly what Pete had tried to do—when a single was all the team really needed in that spot?

If LaVerne spoke up from the passenger's seat, "Aw, he played O.K., honey. I think he did real good," Harry just let the words sit there in the hushed car for a moment, and then went right on with it. Why had Pete not tried to make a play on the pop-up that just barely landed into the grandstand? Why hadn't he had his catcher's gear on, ready to go at the start of the fourth inning? Did he understand he needed to go right through the guy to get to second base if that's what it took? What was he afraid of anyway? Throw harder, run faster, take something extra beyond what they give you.

Pete would look out the window as the car rolled down River Road, his turf-stained glove on his lap, silent save for the "yes, sirs" here and there. Maybe one of the other neighborhood boys was in the car with them, Slick Harmon or Bernie. Baby Dave might have been in LaVerne's lap. The older sisters Caryl and Jackie sat on the bench-seat in the back of the car, glaring and sulking, despising all the sports talk all the time, hating even more the fact, as Caryl would say even six decades later, "that Pete got all this talking to about what he was doing and our dad didn't seem to see us hardly at all."

Pete would get out of the car as soon as it stopped on Braddock Street and before the engine had cooled he'd have that old practice bat in his hands again, working his swing against the sycamore at the side of the house. Harry would come over and watch Pete in the late afternoon light, set up a ball on a makeshift tee, and then finally he'd go over to the window and call inside to LaVerne that in just a few minutes they'd be coming in to eat, fish sticks would be fine. After dinner maybe there would be a Reds game for them to watch together on the family's tiny TV. Sometimes Harry took Pete to Reds games at Crosley Field. As Caryl puts it, "Pete and my dad, they were just as close as there is."

Chapter 3

LITTLE PETE played football at Western Hills High as a shifty, stutter-stepping halfback, and behind the Mustangs' smallish offensive line—the five kids averaged 185 pounds—he made the runs that won the games. He wore number 55 and stood in the front row for the team photo, his socks to an even height above his ankles, his uniform snug. It didn't matter that so many opposing tacklers, from Walnut Hills, say, or Newport Catholic or Taft, descended hard upon him. Little Pete (and few were littler on this team) knocked those tacklers off or swiveled past them, his legs churning so that he would be "twisting and turning his way through three defenders on his way to a score" as one yearbook caption read. Another caption noted that "after evading several Elder tacklers [Rose] was finally brought down."

Elder High served as the Hatfield to Western Hills's McCoy and the year that Pete carried the ball most, West Hi (as the name often appeared) scored 31 points in the rivalry game on Thanksgiving Day, winning it going away, 11,000 people in the stands. They finished 7-2-1 that season, ranked 17th in the state. The next year, without Pete, the West Hi Mustangs won three games and lost six and the result on Thanksgiving was altogether different: Elder 12, Western Hills 0.

21

Pete played varsity baseball too, of course. Western Hills had that rich tradition and all. He wasn't the star on those teams though. Not like centerfielder Ronnie Flender—known as Nobbie—who lived over on Beechmeadow, well up from the river and who would later play minor league ball for the Reds. Nor did Pete have the air of a prospect like smooth Eddie Brinkman, pitcher and third baseman. Even when Brinkman was just a sophomore, everyone said he was going someplace, that someplace turning out to be 15 seasons as a major league shortstop.

Still, Pete could play. Unpolished, a little herky-jerky, sure, but coach Pappy Nohr liked his grit and his smarts. Pete pushed his way in at second base, gradually worked his way up the batting order, became the best bunter on the team. He was a switch hitter, and had been since nine years old when his dad and uncle Buddy said that he should learn the skill because it would give him a better chance to keep making teams. He could hit O.K. from both sides, a lot of sharp ground balls, and he was always getting on base. At the West Hi athletic fields on Ferguson Road, the baseball diamond and the football field shared space, with first base smack in one of the end zones—making this a small piece of North American earth on which Pete Rose in the late 1950s spent a lot of happy moments. At the early morning practices Pete's dad, overcoat on, was most often the only dad who had come out to watch.

The boys at West Hi were one crew cut after another, and the girls all had bobs. If you drove a car with any rumble in it (Pete, until the very end of high school, did not drive any car at all) you brought it around so people could hear and see. The school board built roadblocks—speed bumps we'd call them now—into the driveways and into the parking lot out back.

Pete didn't go much for studying. There was hardly a class he could stand, except gym, of course—which had the added bonus of being co-taught by Mrs. Cook with the dimples, the cutest teacher in the school. Pete flat-out flunked his sophomore year, putting himself, he would joke, on the Five-Year High School Plan. He might have made up the 10th grade coursework in summer school, but Harry determined that playing baseball over those months, legion ball and for local sponsored teams, would be a better use of Pete's time.

In what would have been Pete's senior year, the kids at Western Hills devised a class theme and a slogan that appeared on hallway posters and echoed from teachers when they addressed the students en masse, a theme of enthusiasm derived from a Ralph Waldo Emerson quotation. Pete wasn't attending the Bandwagon variety show at the high school gym or mingling at the Hi-Y socials with the other jocks on Tuesday nights. He wasn't hanging around the parking lot listening to Elvis and the Everly Brothers on some kid's Bel Air radio. Yes, he wore his tie to school sometimes, but picture day, no, that wasn't for him. Not that year or any other. Who could sit still that long, anyway?[1] When it came to the social scene at Western Hills, in other words, Pete was not exactly conforming. And yet if there was a student who embodied West Hi's student spirit and its proud new slogan, maybe more than any other among the hundreds in that sprawling school, it was Pete. The Emerson quote read: *Nothing great was ever achieved without enthusiasm.*

"Pete was not fast and he was not strong and for a lot of years he was tiny," says Jim Luebbert, who played ball with Pete at Sayler Park. "I mean tiny. But if you were choosing up sides for a baseball game, and you wanted to win the game, you picked Pete first. There was not any question about it. There was no, 'Maybe I'll take this guy or that guy.' You picked Pete. He'd get in there at catcher and just run the game, have everyone on his team rallying together.

"And we were all guys who could play. We cared about baseball. All that stuff that Pete would be famous for—the way he went so hard with all that energy—he was already like that then, far back as I can remember. You know, there was always a chance you might get hurt by Pete during a game. That was just the truth of it. He wasn't a dirty player but he was balls out. When we were eight years old playing baseball he was like that. When we were 11, when we were 16. Same way all the time.

---

[1] Look today at the rows of headshots in the 1960 Western Hills yearbook, to the right of Evelyn Root (pep club, senior choir, French club) and to the left of Virginia Lee Rosenberry (business club, Red Cross): Peter Edward Rose isn't there. His name's on a short list in the back, under "seniors not pictured."

He had scrapes on his arms, you know, and if you got into a close play with him at a base, well you just didn't want that. That was part of why a lot of guys hated playing against him—and another reason you always picked him for your team."

———————————————

OTHER KIDS liked Pete. He could joke around with anyone, make a sharp remark about a gal or someone's wheels, or some funny comment about an incident in a game, and that was enough, more than enough to win them over, on the ballfields or even on the front steps of West Hi in the early morning before the bell. The school was a tall brick building with arched doorways and an enormous U.S. flag before it blowing in the breeze. Some of the frat-boy jocks at Western Hills, the ones who wore the good clothes and had a mind to go to college, they didn't much like it when the river rats came up and took spots on the sports teams, but the way Pete went about it, they kept quiet. Pete would go over to the track team's practice and bet a guy he could outrun him and, especially if there were a couple of bucks on the line, he would find an extra burst and win the race. The other athletes respected him for stuff like that, and they knew too that Pete was a fighter with an edge to him, a fearless son of a bitch.

When Pete couldn't find a ballgame, when there weren't even enough kids around to play Indian ball over at Bold Face Park, he'd ride to the river, glove hanging off the handlebars of a second-hand bike and slap a rubber ball against the wall at Schulte's Fish Garden next to the Anderson Ferry landing. He'd been doing it for years, like something out of a hokey movie, a kid with bat and glove and ball, bouncing it against the wall all day when he should have been doing his long division. The kid swings his bat, 100 swings right side then 100 swings left, and coaxes some grown-up to pitch to him for a while. He swings until his arms ache and he chases the ball even after the sun drops and the light is lousy from the outside bulbs, and then that kid grows up to become that man, the alltime hits leader of Major League Baseball. Someone puts that in the movie and people watching roll their eyes and shake their heads at how terribly trite it is, just another old cliché of the supposed American life. Only this is really how it was for Pete Rose, banging that ball against the side of Schulte's Fish Garden—the windowless concrete wall with the giant breaching walleye painted upon it. The air there smelled frankly of fish.

He wasn't always alone of course; Slick and Bernie came and played rubberball too. It was just that Pete didn't stop having at it, even after the others went home, and then the next day before the others showed up. At it and at it and at it on bright days or under a lid of heavy cloud, until he himself became a landmark for the folks who lived around there or who lived higher up on Price Hill, folks who might go for a drive with a brother or sister in from out of town, talk them through the scenery a little bit. *And here's the Anderson Ferry I told you about. And that's the fish place where we go to eat sometimes. And there's that little pale-faced kid, some river rat, who is always playing ball against the wall.*

From the Schulte's lot you could see the riverboats floating full of lively passengers on the Ohio. Or sometimes there'd be a long line of commercial barges churning upriver, 15 or more traveling bow to aft, the entire line of them pushed by a single little tug.

IF PETE, or later his brother Dave, ever had a problem with one of the neighborhood boys—and problems certainly arose—Harry had his way of taking care of things. He'd bring out two pairs of boxing gloves and lead the boys to the one flat patch of yard in back of the house and let them settle things that way. He'd wait until things got pretty convincing, one way or the other, before he stepped in to break it up. Harry had been a hell of a boxer himself, having fought 16 Golden Gloves bouts as a featherweight mostly, and 15 times a winner. LaVerne, though, liked to say she was the real champ, undefeated by her count in the public scuffles she was given to have. Once she pulled a woman off a barstool and took her outside, miffed that the woman had said some things that LaVerne didn't like. "I knocked the living hell out of her," was how she described it.

Pete's own official boxing career was brief, lowlighted by an amateur fight downtown at age 15 when he got beaten so badly in three rounds that even Harry could barely stand to watch. Beaten, yes, but unbowed; Pete was proud that though he had been battered so that his face and body stayed bruised and welted for many days, he had hung on to the end of the fight without getting knocked to the mat.

Harry's message in setting the kids up to box in the yard, and it was a message preached again and again by the other fathers in that Anderson Ferry neighborhood—men who worked at the riverside factories, or as car mechanics or postal workers, or other honest jobs, and among them former Army officers and U.S. Marines—was that you were to stand by what you did or said, or what you believed, even to the point of suffering for it physically. Away from the backyard boxing Pete still got into it just the same, and on the street (no gloves; feet and elbows fair to use) he fared well. He never minded if the guy was bigger, that was no obstacle at all. "Pete was tough, and he would never get whupped," says Greg Staab, who grew up a few houses down on Braddock Street. "You couldn't hurt him. He'd scrap. Pete did not take any shit." The next day, often as not, the guys who'd fought would be friends again, more or less, and up to something.

They'd raid Mr. Stadtmiller's vegetable garden down between the train tracks and the riverbank, sneaking over after dusk with a small blade and cutting into the sugar melons and the cantaloupe. They'd bring a salt shaker one of them had pinched from the Trolley Tavern (where LaVerne had now found work as a waitress to help out with the bills) and they'd salt Mr. Stadtmiller's tomatoes and eat them right off the vine. There were gardens and greenhouses all over Delhi Township, a community of green thumbs.

On summer days the boys dived into the dun and rippling waters of the Ohio River and swam across to the sandsoil beaches and the low green hills of Kentucky, or they would "borrow" a johnboat from just downriver, take it for a float to nowhere in particular. When heavy rains came, the Ohio overtopped and the river rats—the real rats, some of them big as raccoons—came rushing out for dry land, and the boys went after them with their baseball bats on raucous, murderous sprees. Staaby's father would sit on his front porch, his .22 in hand, and shoot the rats if he saw them headed across River Road.

They believed in the West Side and in the life they led along the river—"If you have to go downtown stay west of Vine!" went the half-joking caution—shaped as they were by the unflinching blue-collar view, the value of work that was real and plain. The neighborhoods were Catholic in name and ideal, unmistakably so, even if the churches weren't full on Sundays. There was a sense of hardship in life that you accepted uncomplainingly. Maybe you were angling for a way to get up and out of there if you could, but you would never come out and say you had such a thing in mind. You might signal a kind of aspiration by laying too much down on a 10-to-1 horse at River Downs or on a ballgame with a bookie over in Covington. But you didn't show or even feel any true ambition to change things, only, maybe, to have a little more; you were never anything but proud of the life at hand. There remained, for all the folks living down and around the Ohio River there, the simple and relevant geographic fact that to get just about anywhere you had to go uphill.

(There was a clatter too in these parts, a literal clatter, from folks working on their cars or in their yards or fixing up the siding on their houses, and from the traffic speeding by on River Road. Nowhere was noisier than Braddock Street, with the Whitcomb Riley train full of passengers barreling past at morning and night, Chicago-bound or from, and the conductor sounding the horn from far down the tracks, leaning on it sometimes for half a mile at a time just because he could. The noise of the train mixed with the honking of the barges, and with the roar of the planes taking off from the airport across the water. Loudest of all on Braddock were the trucks on River Road, U.S. 50, shifting into gear, starting up again with a great grind and a wheeze—and sometimes a long, bone-shaking hornblow of their own—after stopping at the light at the Anderson Ferry Road.)

The kids from right there around Anderson Ferry or from over on Fairbanks Avenue by Bold Face Park or from further along on Rapid Run or Twain, all shared a certain underlying conviction, passed down from their parents who shared it too. A belief that in the hardest times you would find a way to survive, that when the river rose up or work was hard to come by, you would persevere. Their conviction was tied also to the feeling that if you did really make it somehow you would make it in the manner of this community, by these same bare-knuckled rules. A certain arrogance this was, a defiance even, in the way it showed itself. You knew without saying so that you could whip any kid your age from over in Hyde Park or Linwood or one of the other places where the money lived, on the other side of town, east of Vine.

Each summer, in the slapdash tangle of trees and thickly coiled brush around in back of Braddock and in the cornstalks there, Pete and Dave and the other boys would make their own little ballfields, cutting through the stalks or getting someone to drive a car over the growth, flatten it out. They played Wiffle ball and argued over fair and foul and found wooded places to hide together and plot whatever needed plotting after dark. If these boys were not exactly pricking their fingers and swearing blood oaths to Tom Sawyer's gang of robbers, still they were making their own way on their own river banks. It was later on, during Pete's first years in the big leagues, that a Reds p.r. man took a good look at him and started calling him "Huck Finn's long lost brother."

Even though he didn't get drafted out of Western Hills (still just too small, not enough glove, not enough power), and even if for a while it looked as though his days on the Bentley Post Legion team, playing with guys like Brinkman and Flender, might be the last and the best of it (and that he would not follow Don Zimmer, 11 years before him, out of the West Side and into major leagues), Pete did then get his break with a minor league contract from the Reds, procured for him by uncle Buddy who had been doing some scouting for the team. Pete took the contract and went to Class D Geneva that first summer and when he came back after hitting .277 he had grown to near 6-foot and added 25 pounds. Then he was sent for a season a level up to Tampa, and there he busted his way into 30 triples, most in the Florida State League. "And this was a guy who was maybe 10th fastest on the team," says Dan Neville, a pitcher on that Tampa club. "If that. He made those triples happen. Some of them didn't even look like sure doubles off the bat, but Pete went after it. He'd be turning at first base by the time you looked up. I have never seen anything more amazing in baseball than the way he hustled that year."

Pete came home in the off-seasons and lived at the house on Braddock Street and worked some odd jobs, at the ferry or packing up boxcars for the UPS or any other work he could find. And then, on account of all those triples and that .331 batting average at Tampa and after a season at Macon in the Sally League during which he hit .330 and showed plenty more of that drive, Pete got called up to the big leagues.

He still lived in his boyhood room that rookie season of 1963 and Dave, now 15 years old, still slept in that same room with him too. Pete owned a car then, and a better one than the cramped and ancient '37 Plymouth he'd bought cheap off Ed Blum a couple of years before. This was a '57 Corvette, plenty of wear on it, and with the Rochester fuel injection that gave the car some giddyup but that also meant Pete could never start the damn thing if the morning was even a little cold.

He'd wake up Dave, who was still bleary and remembering that it had been just a couple of hours earlier that he'd opened his eyes for a moment and seen Pete standing in their dimlit bedroom, stripped down before the mirror and once again swinging and swinging the lead-weighted bat uncle Buddy had given him. They'd rouse Staaby and maybe another kid on the block, and they'd all maneuver that Corvette, the Green Bean they called it, down the hill onto flat River Road. The teenage boys would push as Pete, in the driver's seat, popped the clutch and gave some gas until finally the engine caught and with a thanks-buddies beep-beep-beep Pete was off, past the traffic light at the Anderson Ferry Road, and on his way the seven miles or so to Crosley Field, to park in the players' lot and to play baseball for the Cincinnati Reds.

Chapter 4

Cooperstown, 2012

O N THE Friday morning of induction weekend, 2012, word got out in Cooperstown that Rose, along with his girlfriend Kiana Kim and her two children, would be having a midmorning breakfast at TJs Place on Main Street. TJs, a diner, opened in 1990 and was itself a pioneer in Cooperstown's rapidly expanding memorabilia trade, selling from its adjoining retail space autographed baseball cards, vintage ballcaps and other items of the ilk. The green dining tables all have sugar and jam caddies on them, and the walls around the eating areas are hung with old-time baseball photographs, as well as colorful Grandma Moses–style paintings depicting what is ostensibly a sunny Saturday scene near Cooperstown: wide rolling lawns in front of clapboard houses, a man pushing a wheelbarrow, fruit trees, kids jumping rope.

At TJs' front register, where you can settle up for your eggs and also buy a baseball signed by, say, Bert Blyleven, you were likely (until March 2013 when he sold the place) to find the owner, Ted Hargrove, a large gregarious man in later middle age whose typical outfit includes a tall gray top hat, suspenders and loafers without socks. He knew all the regulars—the locals as well as many of the patrons who come back in on one weekend, induction weekend, each year—and he set a mood with his general joviality.

Rose would often stop in at TJs for breakfast or lunch when he was in town—"Pete and I have known each other for almost 20 years," Hargrove says—yet this weekend was different. Normally Rose would just show up. But on this day his table was reserved in an area off to one side and when he and Kim entered the restaurant they were preceded and trailed by a small phalanx of cameramen, directors and assistants, a crew filming an episode for Rose and Kim's then forthcoming reality series on the TLC cable network. From the start, one of Pete's set lines about the show was, "We're just like your family, only we have more base hits."

Reality in the case of this television show is a relative expression, a term of art—that is, things are realistic but not necessarily real. When Pete and Kiana first came in through TJs front door the camera people did not get the shot they were hoping for. "Can you go back out and come back in," asked Mark Scheibal, one of the show's producers. Rose said he got a lot of those sorts of requests throughout the filming: "Take it one more time please, tape one more time please. I went to sleep last night saying 'tape it one more time please,' " Rose groused good-naturedly during induction weekend. He added that he was encouraged by the prospects for the show's success because, "We got a pretty funny and pretty interesting life."

TJs sits on the northern side of Main Street, across from the Safe At Home memorabilia shop, and about 200 yards down from the Cooperstown post office, outside of which on this Friday morning, festivities were being goosed by the unveiling of a line of four first-class postal stamps depicting, respectively, Joe DiMaggio, Ted Williams, Larry Doby and Willie Stargell. At about 10 a.m., sheets of these "Baseball All-Stars" stamps were revealed in a brief ceremony. In the parking lot, tables were set up selling all manner of postal-related, baseball-related collectibles. "This is a great day for the post office and a great day for baseball," said Maureen Marion, a communications manager for the U.S. Postal Service.

The post office provides an important part of the landscape and the lifeblood in Cooperstown—it's directly across from the Hall of Fame and a block west of the village offices and unlike many places in town it stays open year-round. Locals linger and swap jokes at the package counter, and the mail itself plays a crucial, connective part for a small and out-of-the-way community set among mountain foothills. Even in the Internet age, there remains an anticipation about the daily letters and parcels arriving into Cooperstown and it is easy to imagine how it was in the early 1800s, when the state road from Albany was still new and the twice- or thrice-weekly arrival of mail was heralded from a mile out by a postman sounding his horn. The townspeople would hear as well the beating hooves of four galloping horses and by the time the postal wagon pulled in, an excited crowd had invariably gathered. Letters were distributed and torn open in a local tavern, where Cooperstown's first postmaster moonlighted as a barkeep.

The 2012 stamp ceremony, with all the tourists milling around, was not dissimilar to a stamp ceremony at the initial Hall of Fame induction event in 1939, when the post office unveiled a commemorative stamp honoring what was billed as the 100th anniversary of baseball. The very first of these three-cent stamps, depicting a town scene of boys playing baseball, was sold directly by Postmaster General James Farley to baseball commissioner Judge Kenesaw Mountain Landis as a crush of people in town to see Cobb, the Babe, Honus Wagner and the rest looked on. The low brick post-office building remains largely unchanged since then (construction was completed in 1936), and the happy, ongoing union of these social bedrocks—baseball and the U.S. mail—lends to the sense of Cooperstown as a real and quaint American place.

The town occupies the southern shore of Otsego Lake, a clear, spring-fed glacial remnant that runs eight miles long and never more than about a mile wide. In the good weather you can look down Pioneer Street or off Stagecoach Lane from the center of town and see the water sparkling brilliantly, occasionally cleaved by sailboats. The lake is home to brown trout, walleye and smallmouth bass and serves as the headwaters of the Susquehanna River, which was made navigable in 1779 by James Clinton, a Revolutionary War army general sent to the region by George Washington to beat back both the British and the Iroquois who had sided with them. Clinton had the river mouth dammed and then broke the dam apart so that the lake waters spilled into the channel. That summer, as a weathered brick marker by the shore there recounts, "2000 men and 200 batteaux" sailed southward down the Susquehanna.

Clinton's damming is a seminal moment in Cooperstown history and is recounted by James Fenimore Cooper in his 1823 novel *The Pioneers*. The son of the town's founder, William Cooper, Fenimore Cooper remains Cooperstown's most famous citizen—*The Last of the Mohicans* is also among his books—and he's buried along with other members of the Cooper family in a small church graveyard on a shaded street, just off Cooper Park and the outer grounds of the Hall of Fame. The Coopers lived for a while in a log cabin on this site, a flat, tamed piece of land they found rich with fruitful apple trees planted and then abandoned by the routed Iroquois. Tourists now stroll into the park to look at a bronze statue of James Fenimore Cooper seated in thought, as well as at the neighboring statues of Dodgers lefthander Johnny Podres letting fly a pitch to catcher Roy Campanella in a rendering of Game 7 of the 1955 World Series. The baseball statues stand in an open-ended courtyard of the Hall of Fame and the Fenimore Cooper statue is 80 feet away on a grassy island. On the driveway between them members of the Hall of Fame's staff park their cars for the day.

Throughout his *Leatherstocking Tales*, Fenimore Cooper refers to Otsego Lake as the Glimmerglass, a name that stuck. Visitors camp in Glimmerglass State Park and picnic on Glimmerglass beach. The Glimmerglass opera has become one of America's premier opera companies, attracting to its summer festival enthusiasts from all over the world—among them Charles Parsons, a music critic and reviewer for the *American Record Guide*, a bimonthly music publication with its office on the same dead-end street in Cincinnati, Braddock Street, where Pete Rose grew up. Parsons was raised nearby, off River Road, and he attended the Sayler Park School, where from first through fourth grade he was a classmate of Rose's. Parsons is no baseball fan but on his trips to the Glimmerglass opera festival, he might engage with baseball-mad families at the bed-and-breakfast where he stays. When he reveals that he went to elementary school with Pete Rose, noisy excitement follows and "everybody all of a sudden wants to talk to me."

"I was a kind of an intellectual as a child and kids picked on me a lot," Parsons recalls. "But not when Pete was around. He wouldn't let anyone bully me. I don't know why he took a liking to me. Maybe he saw I was vulnerable. I just know that nobody wanted to mess with Pete and so no one bothered me when he was there." This is the kind of thing, both the childhood humiliation and the gallantry of a classroom savior, that a man will remember his entire life. Parsons is 72.

Pete and Charlie were not close friends, though, and after elementary school they hardly saw each other at all. Many years passed. Yet when they ran into each other as adults around Cincinnati—at Frisch's restaurant or at River Downs racetrack, Rose, by then a major league star, recognized his old classmate immediately. As Parsons recalls: "On at least two occasions I was suddenly surprised by Pete with a hearty 'Hey Charlie! Charlie Parsons!' across the crowded room. Peter then barreled over to say hello."

Another time, in the 1980s, Parsons was working at the public library in downtown Cincinnati when he took his evening break and went to the nearby Cricket Lounge for dinner. There in a booth was Rose, sitting with two Cincinnati Bengals, quarterback Ken Anderson and offensive tackle Anthony Muñoz. "Pete hailed me over," says Parsons, "and invited me to join them and I agreed."

For Rose, the notion of asking a local librarian to sit and join a bull session with himself and two NFL superstars seemed completely natural. He was happy to talk with all of them; it would never occur to him that anyone might feel uneasy. Said Parsons, "Sitting in that booth, Pete treated all of us just the same."

Though he has never been to the Baseball Hall of Fame, nor even to a major league game, and though he could tell you little about Rose's baseball career, and even less about Rose's willful violation of the game's prohibition against gambling and the danger that it might violate the integrity of the sport, Parsons view of the matter is, not surprisingly, clear. "And, YES!" he wrote in an e-mail, answering a question that had not, in fact, been asked. "I do think Peter should be in the Hall of Fame."

ROSE MAY have been the only one at TJs Place that morning having a reality series breakfast; but there were plenty of ex-ballplayers around making appearances for Hargrove. At 10:30 Yogi Berra walked in. In his late 80s, and thinned markedly in recent years, Berra had made it a priority to get to Cooperstown for induction weekend. He was accompanied by his wife and one of his sons, and though he moved haltingly, he appeared in high, clear spirits as he settled in near the front of TJs to greet people and exchange a few words. When Hargrove had advertised his weekend lineup in the weeks leading up to induction, the copy read, "Come say hello to a few familiar faces, get an autograph and shake hands with a legend." Berra was the legend.

Among those signing on Friday morning were Hall of Famers Juan Marichal and Rollie Fingers, along with former Black Yankee Bob Scott, and Art Shamsky, who may be best known as a member of the 1969 World Series Mets, but who was also, in '60, a promising 18-year-old outfielder for the Class D Redlegs in Geneva, N.Y., where he spent a couple of months living with Pete Rose. They rented rooms in a family home on a quiet residential street. Both players earned $400 a month and Shamsky, with some speed and good power, was regarded as much the better prospect. At TJs, he and Rose greeted each other warmly and talked for a while.

"There was no way that in Geneva you could have seen the player that Pete would become; just no possible way," said Shamsky shortly after chatting with Rose. "He could hit a little and he ran hard, and he got to the park in the early morning when some of the rest of us were sleeping. That's what you could have said about him. But he was small and very raw on defense and you would not have pegged him for a future big leaguer. The next time I played on a team with him"—two years later at Class A Macon (Ga.), where Rose hit .330 and scored 136 runs in 139 games—"that had changed. He was bigger and stronger and just much, much better. By then there was no doubting him."

Upon first being signed by the Reds and assigned to Geneva, Rose had literally run around Braddock Street shouting, "I'm leaving! I'm leaving! I got a contract to play ball!" But he soon found himself homesick in the small, remote Eastern college town. LaVerne came out and stayed nearby for a couple of weeks to help ease him in. Uncle Buddy visited as well. Harry drove out and met the team when it played a series in Erie. While some of the other players enjoyed the freedom of being on their own and the opportunity to drink beer together in local bars—"I had come from Missouri where the drinking age was 21," says Shamsky. "In Geneva it was 18, so there was that"—Pete did not drink alcohol or go out or do much of anything except get to the park early and stay late. A letter written to him that summer from a Reds scout who knew Pete's father Harry (a letter, incidentally, that Rose included in his 2004 memoir) described Pete as being "down in the dumps" and encouraged him to buck up. There were apple and pear trees in the hills around Geneva and some people grew grapes for wine. On damp summer evenings, mosquitoes dispersed around the Redlegs' Shuron Park, dining on the several hundred fans or more who attended each game.

One Redlegs teammate, the pitcher Dan Neville, whose career faded before he hit the big leagues, said that the homesickness of Rose and a few other teammates was so profound—and this now is a remarkable claim, unique in the long span of Rose's career—that it sapped Rose's determination to win.

"We were lousy [the Redlegs finished 54–75 and last in their six-team league] but four teams made the playoffs and it looked for a while like we might have a chance. Only some guys didn't want any part of that, of having to stay around and play more games," Neville recalls. "There was a *let's get the heck out of Geneva* mentality, and Pete was one of the guys leading that. The idea was not to win at all costs, but instead to make sure we didn't make the playoffs so that we could get home. Pete was an incredibly hard-nosed player when I played with him in Tampa the next season and whenever I saw him before and afterward. But that one year, for maybe two or three weeks, he was not one hundred and ten percent all the time."

In Geneva, Rose committed 36 errors in 85 games, primarily as a second baseman. Manager Reno DeBenedetti complained about the rough, sometimes costly aspects of Pete's game. All in all, the scouting reports on Pete Rose out of Geneva were not strong. Still, he always slid headfirst at a time when no one was sliding headfirst, and he was a conspicuous competitor. At season's end the fans voted Rose the team's most popular player. Still, Geneva had slipped from fifth place to sixth as the summer wore on, and Neville (who would appear in a Reds uniform on the same Topps rookie card as Shamsky in 1965) says, "It was very surprising to me that some other players did not want to win at all costs. And so I have never forgotten it."

AFTER HIS chat with Shamsky at TJs, Rose sat down for the breakfast with Kim and her children. They were joined by Vilacky—Pete's guy from the Safe At Home memorabilia store—and Hargrove. An assistant on the reality show filming crew asked a waitress to remove all the ketchup bottles from the surrounding tables so that the labels would not appear on camera. Pete began telling Kiana and the kids about Yogi Berra, choosing as his touchstone Don Larsen's perfect game in the 1956 World Series. "Yogi is the guy who ran out and hugged Larsen after the last out," he said. "Yogi was short but solid, 185 pounds, and Larsen was holding Yogi off the ground like it was nothing. Usually if anyone picks anyone up it's the catcher picking up the pitcher. It tells you Larsen was a big, strong guy."[1]

---

[1] Rose's baseball talk is invariably elevated by observations like this. He is a student of baseball history and holds many of the players who came before and after him in great regard. It's one reason—along with the more central fact that there is money to be made—that he likes coming to Cooperstown. When he interacted with Berra at TJs Place, Rose became briefly and uncharacteristically quiet, leaning in close to hear what Yogi said, then nodding; he seemed delighted at the exchange. Rose likes to tell of how a few years earlier an elderly woman came through the crowd as he was signing autographs in Cooperstown and said: "My father would have liked the way you played." "Who's your father?" Rose asked. The woman, it turned out, was Julia Ruth Stevens, Babe's daughter. Pete stood and shook her hand, then pulled over a chair and asked her to stay beside him. And so it happened that the daughter of Babe Ruth sat and talked a little baseball with Pete Rose, a bonus sight for the fans queued up to get Rose's autograph.

Scrambled eggs and sausage arrived on thick white plates, and pancakes for the kids. Various people came by to talk with Pete and at one visitor's request he spelled the names of Kiana's children, Ashton and Cassie, at which he made a point of saying with a snicker, "that is Cassie with an a-s-s!" She was 14 years old at the time.

Pete, wearing that fedora and loose aqua T-shirt, laughed a lot, pitching forward slightly in his chair when he did. He said how Ashton, who was then 10 years old, was not really a baseball player yet. "He's a karate guy so far," said Pete, tousling the boy's hair. "I am not!" said Ashton, and Pete chuckled and shrugged. "I'm just their prop," he said, gesturing to Kiana and the kids. Then Rose and Hargrove talked for a while about Pete's prospects for ever getting into the Hall of Fame, winding toward Pete's conclusion: "If I ever get in," he said, "it will be when I'm dead."

There was a pause in the conversation—at the table everyone had turned to their food—and Pete, not eating yet, quickly grew restless, batting the plastic salt-and-pepper shakers back and forth between his forefingers. He looked around and saw at a nearby table a white-haired man wearing a Mets cap. A look of recognition flashed over Rose's face. "Hey, how've you been?" he called out. "You still working?"

The white-haired man looked surprised ("I have never met Pete Rose," he would say later. "I think he thought I was someone else.") but he responded, "No, I'm not working anymore. But it looks like you are."

To which Pete cackled, "Hah. This ain't work! Loading boxcars, that's work."

Rose's talk—which is, in some ways, the essence of the man—is an eternal spatter of language, a ragtime of quips, anecdotes, jokes and memories ever unfolding. Baseball, horse racing, Cincinnati, his wife, his son, a remembrance of running out of gasoline 50 years before, the Los Angeles Lakers, the idiosyncrasies of some small American town, dugouts, clubhouses, breasts, Mike Schmidt, Bud Selig, infield dirt. He has a great talent for humorous detail so that even in rendering one of his stock stories, and by this point in Pete's life there are many, he projects the sense of newness. In banter, Rose has a bright face with bright things in it: a joker's mouth and a rascal's eyes.

For all the goings on, Pete does not ramble, but rather pauses at the end of an observation, takes a cue, and then is off again on a new verbal jaunt tethered loosely to the topic at hand, his salted words rendered in the same yip-and-yap fashion with which he left his mark upon ballplayer after ballplayer from the start of his baseball career to the end. The entire weekend in Cooperstown, indeed the entirety, more or less, of Rose's public life, might be defined as one streaming, bouncing, never-ending, ever-entertaining, rarely filtered conversation—a conversation that Rose has been having here there and everywhere, in some form or another, with those around him and with the world at large, for as long as anyone can remember.

Chapter 5

Black and White and Red All Over

S OON THERE would be baseball again in Cincinnati. The frigid winter had given way to a warm March and now, sweet springtime, the date that Cincinnatians from Westwood to East End, from Sayler Park to Indian Hill, had long since circled on their calendars was nearly at hand: Opening Day, April 8, 1963, a Monday, the first game of the major league season, a tradition there since 1876. As the Reds' yearbook of the previous season had crowed, "Many cities are famed for their particular celebrations—New Orleans's Mardi Gras, New York's St. Patrick's Day Parade, Inauguration in Washington, Philadelphia's Mummers Parade on New Year's Day, etc. But none is more universally accepted than Cincinnati's Opening Day." The yearbook's cover was a design in three colors: red, white and blue.

Down in Florida, manager Fred Hutchinson, in his 11th year running a big league club, looked around him and said, just as the Reds prepared to come north, "This is the best team I've ever managed. Yes, even better than 1961." Those '61 Reds had won their first National League pennant in 21 years before losing in the World Series to the Yankees. So if Hutch thought this '63 team was better, fans reasoned, there was only one way to go. The Vegas oddsmakers had the Yankees (and really, who else?) as the 1–3 favorite to win the American League and the Dodgers at 2–1 in the National League, but the Reds were right there at 4–1, and among the baseball writers they were a popular choice.

The newspapers ran diagrams of the newly finished parking lot at Crosley Field—room for 2,600 more cars—and ruminated, with sketches and analyses, about the traffic that would jam the streets on Opening Day. The city had put up 41 temporary new road signs to help guide folks around. A neighborhood group close to the ballpark, composed of folks living on Sherman, Liberty, Wade and Wilstach, petitioned the City Council to reroute the game-day buses that unloaded and later loaded scores of giddy passengers in front of their homes. For two years running, and this was something that was measured at the time, Crosley Field had led the majors in attendance per capita. Baseball fan per geographical inch was another way to look at it.

"I thought about Opening Day like it was the biggest start of the year, and that's how I prepared," recalled pitcher Jim O'Toole half a century later. He was the lefty who would take the ball for Cincinnati on April 8. "You could feel the buildup and the hoopla and then the game itself came and it felt like such a big deal, so much energy. Especially when it was a nice enough day like we had in '63. Days like that, Opening Day felt like the World Series."

The Reds were coming up from Tampa now, playing the last of their spring training games along the way, traveling through the South and all its seething righteousness from all sides in the Civil Rights struggle. James Meredith had been in school at Ole Miss for just half a year, and still fresh for the country were the images of the federal marshals who escorted him there, and the riots surrounding his enrollment. A determined unrest was gathering strength in Birmingham. John F. Kennedy was 26 months into his term, and the national intelligence agencies were preparing for him a report entitled *Prospects in South Vietnam*. You could make long-distance calls direct, now, from your own home, and you could take your Polaroid pictures in color. People had begun to hear on the radio the breakthrough songs of Bob Dylan.

There had been professional baseball in Cincinnati for 94 years, longer than anywhere else. This was the greatest baseball town in the world.

And if Hutchinson was predicting first place for his team, buoyed to optimism by the pitching and the power (Frank Robinson!), and the 98 games the Reds had won the year before, he was inspired too by another player, an unpolished rookie playing second base. Hutch talked about the kid all spring, about how even with only a few years in the low minors behind him he already had some serious big league sass about him. The kid played baseball harder than anyone Hutch had ever seen. And he could really hit. Reds' owner William DeWitt came down and after watching the kid on the field for a couple of days, he had no uncertainty: "When he makes it, fans from all over the country will want to come out and see him play," he said. "He loves to play baseball and the best part about it is his ability. A fellow like this can spark an entire ballclub."

Some of the fans in Cincinnati already knew about the kid, of course, and some knew him as one of their own, a mulish scrapper out of Western Hills High, raised down around Delhi Township, hard by the Ohio. West Siders knew who the kid's father was too, a tough and square-jawed semi-pro footballer, a star of renown in the tavern leagues. By the time the Reds broke camp the kid already had a nickname, "Charlie Hustle," pinned on him with an air of derision by—and how's this for a stamp upon a player?—a couple of Yankees named Mickey Mantle and Whitey Ford.

Still, he was only 21 years old, and he had plenty of rough edges to his game. The Cincinnati batting coach, Dick Sisler, didn't like the hitch in the kid's swing or the way he held the bat so close to his ear. Maybe he needed another year down in the minors somewhere—in San Diego, say, or Rocky Mount. No. Not on Hutch's watch. A few days into April word went out that the Reds had made their final roster cuts for the season. And the kid was on the team. As it said so plainly in the morning *Cincinnati Post*: "The 28 players, the limit for Opening Day, include Pete Rose."

NINETEEN-SIXTY-THREE WAS by no reckoning an ordinary year in the history and progress of America, neither ordinary in hindsight, nor in the days in which it unfolded—a fact that was clear long before the sudden blow and deep darkness of Nov. 22 when John F. Kennedy was shot in Dallas. During April of '63, as Rose made his way through his first month in the major leagues, slumping and then rebounding at the plate, and with his conspicuous moxie inspiring already much ardor among the fans (and some distaste among the players), the nation shook, reverberating out from Birmingham, where the civil rights movement was rumbling in earth-changing ways.

A daily campaign of demonstrations and marches had begun in Birmingham, peaceable but pointed, led by Martin Luther King Jr. and the Southern Christian Leadership Conference. On the eve of the start of the baseball season, as it so happened, a prayer march made its way through the streets to Birmingham's City Hall, so that the next morning's newspapers in Cincinnati were at once draped in optimism across the front page (WE'LL WIN 1963 FLAG, REDS DECLARE ran the six-column banner across the *Post*) and then blunted by another too familiar story: DOGS, POLICE STOP NEGRO PRAYER MARCH.

Dozens had been arrested in Birmingham that day—most of those taken away as they knelt in prayer, refusing to move on a city street—and dozens more in the days that followed, and then in mid-April, King himself was taken in. From the cot in his cell, starting off on paper scraps, he handwrote his *Letter from a Birmingham Jail*, appealing to the need for persistence and determination in the fight against injustice, the need to barrel ahead through and over those who said "No!" There would not be violence, he vowed as ever, but there needed to be tension to effect change. King's writing, and this was invariably his way, proved precise in its facts and philosophical in its message. Invoking Socrates along the way, he talked about the need for an enlightenment that would indeed pull the masses from the metaphorical cave, that would "help men rise from the dark depths of prejudice and racism to the majestic heights of understanding and brotherhood."

King's words resounded as righteous and defiant, stoic and tide-turning, his drive for integration unbowed in a state, Alabama, where three months earlier, governor George Wallace had pledged as he took office to awful cheers: "Segregation now, segregation tomorrow and segregation forever."

And if Cincinnati, 460 miles to the north, was no Birmingham (and really, that was the most segregated city of all, as Dr. King said) it was a place with its own set of tensions, its own ways and temperaments, a Northern city peopled by Southerners. It was true that blacks and whites would convene in the same setting, might sit side-by-side in a hospital emergency room or stand in line to get a driver's license, might mingle loosely at a public parade. Still, the black man and the white man went home in different directions, to all-black or all-white neighborhoods defined by something deeper and harder than custom. One could have asked Frank Robinson about that. He may have been the Reds' finest player, a Rookie of the Year in 1956, the National League MVP in '61. He may have had them standing at Crosley Field with his long home runs and his hard-nosed play, but when it came time for him and his wife to buy a home in Cincinnati, to try to raise their children in the neighborhood of their choosing, at a level and scale that Robinson had by rights earned, well, that was not possible. That the Robinsons had money and means didn't matter; in some neighborhoods, and there were more than a few, no one would sell them a house, the reason as plain as the skin on their faces. "We knew, or we quickly found out, where we could live and where we could not," says Robinson.

In 1963 a man Rose's age could remember how when he was a boy going to the Sayler Park swimming pool, the water on most days was as pure white as the streets around the Anderson Ferry. Black children were allowed to swim there on just one designated day each week. On the other days they would sometimes pass by and peer over, hot and sullen in the summer sun—until sometime in the late '40s the black families around Sayler Park staged their own small and focused protest and quietly got that swimming pool open to all. Those who lived there might say Jackie Robinson had something to do with that protest; Cincinnati was such a baseball town and all. When Jackie first came to Crosley Field as a Dodger, in May and June of 1947, he was winning over all kinds of fans with the way he played, and he'd made a conspicuous ally in Brooklyn shortstop Pee Wee Reese, a white man, Kentucky-born and bred, and a Cincinnati favorite. If you were a black family down around Sayler Park you could take courage from what Jackie Robinson was doing. You could become determined to make change even if your numbers were few.

Right across the river in Covington, Ky.—where at age 13 a boy could drink a pitcher of beer in the front of the barroom while his dad laid down a little something on the game with the bookie in the back—the train depot water fountains were still labeled with those blistering signs: "White" for one of them, "Negro" for the other. So maybe Cincinnati wasn't so far away from Birmingham as all that, in place and in time. The demonstrations went on down there in Alabama each day in the spring of 1963—the sight of the firehoses being turned on to the backs of black kids barely 10 years old—and were seen and felt all over the country. "I am cognizant of the interrelatedness of all communities and states," King wrote from his cell. "We [in America] are tied in a single garment of destiny."

The hate was neither new nor a surprise to the Reds ballplayers who had seen it clearly while playing in the South, at the team's spring training in Florida, or in the minor leagues when black ballplayers couldn't eat in the same restaurants or use the same restrooms, or were forced to find a family to put them up in this town or the other because no hotel would have them. In 1961, when Rose was a Tampa Tarpon, the team traveled from game to game in big red station wagons. One of the wagons would invariably be driven by the manager Johnny Vander Meer—"Mr. No-no, No-no" they called the former big league lefty for his indelible 1938 achievement of leaving a team hitless for two straight games—and when Vander Meer was not falling asleep at the wheel, as he was given to do, he was always one to stop and get something to eat.

They would pull in to a roadside restaurant and when everyone else piled out, the black guys knew it was better for everyone that they stay in the car. (Lee May, 18 years old and four seasons shy of the first at bat of his 18-year, 354-home run major league career, was on that team.) And even though a carload of hungry ballplayers had now appeared in his damned and sweaty little diner, all of them with appetites and money to spend, the guy who ran the place, aware and attuned, might come away from his grill, toweling off his grease-spattered hands and peer out from the restaurant doorway and say, "Get those niggers out of my parking lot."

Rose could not have cared less what color a guy was. He bounded into the big leagues like a golf ball on hot concrete and if the Reds veterans didn't much like him for all that zip and brashness—oh Lord, the way he could carry on with the cheapest of groupies, with that pliable stripper on the team's trip in Mexico—well, they especially didn't like him taking a job away from Don Blasingame that spring of 1963. Blazer was a former All-Star second baseman, a guy who'd batted a decent .281 in '62, who'd come down and worked as hard as he should have in the preseason, who was a steady guy with his pretty wife Sara (a Miss Missouri no less) and their little girl Dawn. Now, Rose, spraying hits everywhere, busting out of the batter's box like sprung from hell, was just going to knock Blasingame aside. For the decision by manager Hutchinson and the front office, the veterans mused, it didn't hurt that Blazer was making $23,000 a year, Rose only $7,500. If Blasingame could get pushed away like that, they figured, how soon before it happened to them?

"He made us uncomfortable," recalls O'Toole. "We hadn't seen Pete's kind before and a lot of people didn't much like it. He could get under your skin with the way he just went and went. We were not inclined to welcome him in so fast or to make it easy on him. A lot of guys on the team just started to freeze him out."

Pete found friends in the black players: Frank Robinson, Vada Pinson, Tommy Harper—men who knew what it was like to be shunted aside by teammates, to be ignored and derided. "The way Pete was being treated was not something we were going to go for," said Pinson. So when Pinson and Robinson went out to eat on the road, Pete went right along with them. They dressed sharp and never drank a glass of booze, early dinner and back to the room for a little TV: just Pete's style.

In the clubhouse too often that season it was white guys one way, black guys another. Dick Young, writing about the Reds in New York's *Daily News* that summer would describe the friction around the Reds' locker room this way: "The Negro players think they are being picked on, and the white players think the Negro players are getting away with murder, and that is the climate of our time."

It was in that climate—16 years after Jackie Robinson, sure, but "if you think baseball has licked that [race] problem, you're nuts," Young wrote—that Rose ignored Reds management when he was called upstairs and told to stop spending so much time with the black guys. It was in that climate that Rose would sidle over to where Frank Robinson and Pinson lockered and start chattering away, laughing and joking and talking baseball ("Talkin' *jive!*" Pete said gleefully) and figuring out how they could win the game that day. Sometimes Rose would plop down on the floor of the clubhouse and start shining Robinson's shoes. "Another thing that guys didn't like," says O'Toole.

Rose adored Robinson for the way he played, for the very aggressiveness that irked so many around the league. In a game against the Milwaukee Braves a couple of years before Rose arrived, Robinson had come in hard to third base, setting off a fight with third baseman Eddie Mathews. ("He always tries to kick and slap at you when he's sliding in," Mathews grumbled later.) Hearing the story, it didn't matter to Rose that Robinson had wound up battered by Mathews in the brawl. What mattered was that even with his bloodied nose and black eye, with his thumb jammed and swollen, Robinson had come out for the second game of that doubleheader and hit a double and a home run and taken a hit away from Mathews with a catch in leftfield, and the Reds had beaten the Braves 4–0. "The way I look at it, I won the fight," Robinson would say. Rose could not have agreed more. Some old-timers called Robinson the black Ty Cobb, not for the players' similarity of skills—Robinson rode largely on power, Cobb conspicuously on speed—but for their ornery style on the field. (It was an irony scarcely noted that Cobb had been known as a racist.) Rose understood what that analogy meant as well as any player in the game. "Pass the salt, Ty," he'd say to Robinson, grinning across the dinner table.[1]

Rose was no civil rights activist, no high-minded advocate. He would

---

[1] Rose's affinity for baseball's past and for Cobb in particular was clear from the start. On team flights as a rookie in 1963 Rose would often sit beside Waite Hoyt, a 63-year-old Reds broadcaster who had pitched in the big leagues from 1918 to '38. "He'd ask me to talk about Cobb and the others I played with and against," recalled Hoyt years later. "I said to him that now is the time for a player with the similar kind of makeup and ability as Cobb to project himself out front." Hoyt, in this bit of advising, was referring to Rose himself.

make racial jokes quick as anyone, just as he'd make a crack about a "Kraut" or a "Polack," or tell some off-color story at his own expense, whatever might keep the energy purring around him. He was Pete being Pete. It was he who would come up and put his arm around Harper as the players were toweling off in the locker room, fresh out of the shower, and say loud enough for everyone to hear: "Damn, Tommy, you know you are just a big dick with man hanging on the end of it." At such moments any tightness in the room fell right away: There were no black guys or white guys; just a room full of ballplayers cackling together and shaking their heads at what young, smart-ass Pete Rose had said.

"Pete was always my good friend," says Harper. "Not my white friend, my friend. Those first years in the major leagues he was always chirping on me, encouraging me: 'C'mon Harp, c'mon Harp.' He would say we're going to do this and we're going to do that, they're not going to be able to send us back down. It was always 'we, we, we' with Pete. It wasn't 'I'.

"Our wives were friends too," Harper says. "We just liked spending time together. We'd get some stares when we went out to eat together, but stares were not ever going to bother Pete."

In Tampa some years later, spring training of 1967, Pete and his wife Karolyn would often invite Tommy and Bonnie to have dinner with them at a place that remained whites only by custom if not, of course, by law. If Tommy and Bonnie arrived first they took a table in the corner, quiet and to themselves. Then suddenly through the restaurant would come a small but heavy bellow, "Unka Tommy! Unka Tommy!" This being the excited cries of two-year-old Fawn Rose, her voice like a barrel-echo even then, calling out to a man who, in Karolyn's words, "she absolutely loved. She could have played with her uncle Tommy all day." The Harpers would put their heads down and hide their smiles and with the attention now upon them from the other diners, wish they could somehow slip beneath their table and disappear.

IF THOSE restaurant customers frowned at the noisy intrusion—"Here we come, Unka Tommy!" Fawn boomed. "Here we come!"—and if the waiters and waitresses cast a tsking glare at the young black couple that the little girl was calling out for, those frowns turned to forgiving grins when they saw that trailing the girl, bouncing in with his broad face and gap-toothed grin, was Pete Rose himself. Not a superstar yet but by then, the late 1960s, a beloved fixture on the Reds, the heart of the team, a .300 hitter and a gamboling, bristle-topped player—his teammmate Tommy Helms had taken to calling him HH for hedgehead—who, as *Time* magazine wrote in the summer of '68, had with his "flip tongue and frenetic brand of baseball injected fresh breath into an increasingly stale game."

He was a man in his late 20s known for headlong slides and tumbling catches and who never wanted to spend even an inning out of the lineup lest he miss a chance to put his bat on the ball. On the second day of the 1968 season Rose, chasing and then leaping in vain after a ball hit to rightfield, tore open his hand on Crosley's fence. The next day, his hand bandaged, he singled and doubled and started a 22-game hitting streak. "If I had eight Pete Roses we would run all over the league," the manager Dave Bristol said. Bristol, on the Reds job since '66, was a baseball guy who spit tobacco juice through his teeth, often for emphasis. "He hates to be wrong," Bristol said of Rose. "He hates to be beaten."

That was the impression that Rose left with everything he did. As a second baseman his first four years he attacked every ball he could get to (as well as some that he could not) and the aggressiveness led to errors, balls bouncing off his glove and body. He could look like a wreck out there. Although he spent a winter season playing in Venezuela, where on each off day he took hundreds of ground balls, made hundreds of throws and worked for hours, literally hours, on catching the ball at second base and turning to throw to first, he continued to play the position with a profound inelegance. "Technically, Rose was the worst I've ever seen at turning the double play," says O'Toole.

Yet he was indefatigable and unbowed. Along with the errors, he often made improbable diving stops. Rose always seemed to be where the ball was, and always backing up the play, going straight to where he was meant to be. He would run clear across the diamond to pursue a pop-up. On a double-play pivot at second, Rose stayed right at the bag even with the runner from first base bearing directly down upon him. "He is completely fearless," Robinson said.

In leftfield, where he moved in 1967, Rose had little grace and moderate range and no throwing arm to speak of. Yet it wasn't long before Leo Durocher, the Cubs manager, looked out from the dugout and said, "Rose looks like he was born out there."[2] When he led the National League in outfield assists in '68 he did so not with majestic throws from the deep corners but by positioning, savvy and hustle. He anticipated. He charged in hard to field base hits. He found ways to get an out when he had no business getting one. Rose's crashes into the sidewall in pursuit of foul fly balls—during one otherwise unremarkable 6–3 win over the Pirates at Crosley Field, May of '67, he toppled into the stands twice, both times being bruised on the face and both times making the catch—became so frequent that someone in the Reds bullpen down the leftfield line had the designated assignment to keep an eye on Rose, to try to get over and break his fall so that he didn't get hurt. Rose later changed positions again, moving from left to right. He played some centerfield as well when the need arose. In '69 he won a Gold Glove.

Many around the league groused at Pete for his flash and his bubbling confidence. "If you didn't know him you would think he was cocky," said Henry Aaron, greatly understating. Rose strutted on the field, more so after making a good play, and he chirped noisily as he took his lead off first base. When he drew a walk, he took off racing down the first base line. (He had gotten the idea from Enos Slaughter, the Cardinals spikes-up igniter and an All-Star during Pete's youth.) "Let's stick it in Rose's ear, then see how fast he goes to first on a walk," Phillies' manager Gene Mauch called out angrily during Rose's rookie season.

Soon, though, it became clear that beneath Rose's bluster whirred the real deal, an exceptional and deeply committed talent. It was Mauch himself who, after Rose had led the Reds in batting for a second straight season in 1966, declared that given the way Rose elevated the Reds on

---

[2] Durocher also said at that time, "I've got about six players I'd give the Reds for that guy." Charlie Hustle was unmistakably Leo the Lip's type of guy.

the field, he had become a perennial MVP contender. "Rose is now being recognized for what he does, not how he does it," Mauch said with an air of resignation and even surprise. As Rose himself observed: "I sneaked up on 'em. They were so busy calling me Charlie Hustle and Hollywood they weren't looking at the statistics."

He created the most compelling statistics, of course, with his bat, leading the league in base hits in 1965 (209) and again in '68 (210), earning regard as baseball's best switch-hitter even in the years when Maury Wills and Tom Tresh and, yes, the aging Mantle were still making their marks. "Never mind the switch-hitting," said Mets manager Wes Westrum. "This guy is one of baseball's best hitters period." Rose had vowed to become the game's "first $100,000 player who isn't a home run hitter. I gotta. I just gotta." Some labeled him a singles hitter but the singles were just the half of it. He was good for 35 to 40 doubles a year, right near the top of the league, stroking line drives from foul line to foul line and into the gaps. He hit about a dozen home runs each season and invariably finished among the top 10 in triples. Rose stated his goals of 200 hits and 100 runs scored each year. He made the first of his 17 All-Star Games in '65.

Rose was rarely a stolen base threat—raw speed being another in the long list of natural skills he did not possess—but he was unquestionably the best base runner on the Reds, and one of the very best in either league. He carved his way around the diamond with a sense of mission and by smarts as much as intuition. He judged the outfielders before he came to bat, noting who was playing too far off the foul line, or a few strides too deep. He knew every fielder's arm strength and he knew when to put it to the test. It was nothing for Rose to go first to third on a single to leftfield.

"I played with Pete for four years [1963 through '66]," says O'Toole, "and I don't think I ever saw him get thrown out trying to take an extra base. Not once. It must have happened. Of course it must have. But I remember many things and I don't remember that. A lot of close plays, a lot of dirt flying everywhere as he slid in headfirst, but when that dirt settled, Pete was safe."

Rose coveted statistics not least because he knew what statistics could bring. He had a keen affection for money and he delighted openly at how his salary, which began at the major league minimum, steadily grew. After making the All-Star Game, Rose asked around until he had enough information to figure out the average salary of all the other All-Stars—a cast of veteran and well-paid players—and then trumpeted the figure to Reds assistant G.M. Phil Seghi, as a means of bargaining. He earned $25,000 in 1966, $46,000 in '67 and $55,000 in '68, when his .335 batting average led the National League. "I'm one of the two most exciting white guys in baseball, me and Carl Yastrzemski," said Rose. The next season his salary jumped to $85,000, nearly 3½ times the league average and more money than a Cincinnati Reds player had ever earned in a season. After winning the batting title again, in '69, Rose vaulted past $100,000 a year.

"You hear a lot of guys say you can't make any money playing ball in Cincinnati," Rose said in those years. "I don't believe it. All you have to do is play every day and do your job."

To Rose that job included being a kind of cheerleader—for himself, certainly, but also for the Reds and for all of baseball. The press found him accommodating, often solicitous, and he amused them with his frankness and his humor. He was not frugal with his time and once sat for a long game-day interview with an ice dancer who was serving as a celebrity journalist for her hometown paper—in Vienna, Austria. "When someone wants to interview me I've usually got something to say," Rose observed.[3]

Most of Rose's teammates embraced his publicity seeking, considering that he spent much of his time with reporters talking not just about himself, but telling people why a baseball ticket was the best deal in town and extolling Tony Perez or Helms or any number of other Reds. When the Cincinnati ace Jim Maloney said "I'm just glad we have Pete on our side," it was not simply because of all the hits Rose got and all the runs he scored. Rose delivered to the team an unflagging intensity.

---

[3] Rose also understood that having the reporters on his side never hurt at contract time. He was especially close to the Reds beat writer Earl Lawson; if Pete wanted to get an idea out there in the public, he just told Earl.

"He could bring a lesser player up to a higher caliber," is how Reds pitcher Mel Queen put it. "Looking at him running out ground balls and walks and hustling all over the field [a teammate] had to say, 'How can I do anything less than that?'"

He arrived first to the ballpark and he stayed to the last and he did not slow down in between. That teammates never saw him on the trainer's table was not because he never got hurt—diving attempts in the field had caused Rose a broken thumb and a badly bruised shoulder in those seasons; his style of play inevitably produced numerous nagging pains—but because he got to the trainer early and took care of any ailments or rehab work before most of the players had even arrived at the park. He didn't want to miss a thing out on the field. He worked extra in the batting cage, and during the pregame he often fielded balls at several positions. Sometimes Rose volunteered to put on the catcher's gear and warm up a pitcher. All the while his inimitable banter spouted forth. One teammate called Rose "Basil", a play on basal metabolism. "You get tired just being around him," said Helms, Pete's roommate on the road. It was not unusual for Helms to be roused in the first light of day, just as Pete's brother Dave had been roused years before, and to see Pete standing in front of the hotel-room mirror, completely nude, working on his swing.

In the clubhouse Rose organized betting pools, on big horse races or other signature sporting events. Everyone wanted in. Rose had Forward Pass in the '68 Kentucky Derby and Stage Door Johnny in the Belmont—good calls both—and he even won a little something on the Masters and the Indy 500 that year. He went to the River Downs race track whenever there wasn't a game to play ("A lot of us went now and then," says ballplayer Dan Neville. "And you knew that when you went to the track, you would run into Pete.") Sometimes Rose met his teammate Leo Cárdenas over at Jorge's restaurant on Vine Street and they played pool with a few bucks on the line. Rose kept his cash in his right front pocket, he said, so that it was always "right where I can reach it quickly."

There was a lightness about Pete, whether he had lined three hits in a game or none at all. "I was getting to him," he told his teammates shortly after striking out four times against Houston pitcher Don Wilson. "You may not know it but I foul-tipped that last one." He concocted quips that he would use throughout his career: "We were so poor growing up that I had a sister with a tag on her that said MADE IN JAPAN," Rose said. When he made the position change to leftfield, slotting in next to Pinson in center, with Harper over in right, Rose came into the locker room and announced, "Well, we had to integrate the outfield sometime."[4]

That wisecrack was another that thawed the ice in the room, another Roseian flick at racial tension at a time when it continued to run high in America and in Cincinnati. It was the same year, 1967, that race riots erupted across the country, including in Avondale and other Cincinnati neighborhoods. The black families there—men and women and people of every age—raised a fearful hell, angry at their joblessness, their help-lessness and the sense that they were being oppressed. A White House study that year declared that nine out of 10 "Negro city youths" would be arrested at some point in their lives. This was also the year that the Supreme Court ruled it unconstitutional to forbid interracial marriage, as 16 states then did.

That first round of riots in Avondale began a day after Martin Luther King Jr. had visited the simmering city and preached again the impor-tance of nonviolence. But the people of Avondale would not be contained. Plate glass windows were shattered at furniture stores and jewelry shops, and a liquor store got looted. Black shopkeepers taped to their storefronts signs reading SOUL BROTHER in hopes of being spared. White journal-ists covering the riots got roughed up and knocked around. Debris in the streets was set ablaze and from so many vantage points around there, from the outdoor performance stage at the Cincinnati Zoo, for example, one could hear sirens pealing and see smoke rising thickly to the sky. "I don't remember all that much about those riots, I think we were on the road," says Harper. (The Reds indeed were away for nine days.) "I do re-member going downtown to watch a fight—you know, a boxing match—with Pete and his dad a little later that summer. I guess that might have

---

[4] Never mind that a white player, Deron Johnson, had spent much of the previous season in leftfield. Pete wasn't one to let facts get in the way of a good joke.

been a problem for some people, me being there with two white men, but I will never know. No one was going to hassle you if you were with Pete."

Rose had become by far the most beloved Red, a player from Cincinnati's own soil and, the locals loved to believe, from their own mold. Before games, Rose stood near the dugout, or down one of the foul lines, signing autographs and giving away photos of himself and chattering with fans leaning over the railing, arms outstretched toward him. The love affair was plainly apparent at Crosley Field over the last weekend of September 1968, a couple of games against the San Francisco Giants significant only in that Rose was in a fight for the league batting title with the fine Pirates outfielder Matty Alou. Rose had come into September with a 13-point lead, but he had slumped badly, his average slipping from .347 to .330. Alou was at .329. That last week of the season Rose had been visited by ad executives promising endorsements if he were to win the batting crown.

There weren't many in the crowd on Saturday afternoon, just over 5,500, but those who were there were there for Pete. Each time he came to bat they all stood and cheered. No Reds player had won a batting title in 30 years. Rose's at bats went like this: a single to right in the first inning, a single to left in the second, a double to left in the fourth, a single to center in the sixth. Although Pete had gone 4 for 4, word came to Crosley that Alou was not going away. In the Pirates game against the Cubs at Wrigley Field—a ballpark, incidentally, where the fan base had little love for Rose, where earlier that season he had been pelted with garbage as he stood in the outfield—Alou was on his way to getting four hits himself. So when Rose came up in the bottom of the eighth inning with the game well decided (San Francisco led 10–4) but the batting race still unsure, the devotees at Crosley stood in appreciation again. Rose knocked a double to centerfield. 5 for 5.

Each hit had come against Gaylord Perry, the highly effective saliva-dealing righthander whom Pete loved to ride loudly from the dugout. Once Rose stood outside the batter's box staring at Perry, then telling the umpire, "I'm not stepping in until the ball is dry!" even knowing it was no use, that sooner or later, usually sooner, Perry's spitball was coming again. Now Pete was on second base after his fifth hit and Perry, who had a sense of humor himself, turned and called out to him. "Is that enough? Is that going to do it?" And Pete said, "Yeah, that'll do it."

The task though, was not quite finished; Alou was still only a point behind. The next day Bristol canceled batting practice, gave the guys the final Sunday off. Pete came out to hit anyway, enlisting a coach to pitch and a couple of kids to shag. He hit for a full half hour. Then he doubled his first time up in the game, lifting the crowd to its feet once again—this time there were close to 30,000 there—and ending the suspense. Rose .335. Alou .332. Batting champion. Bristol says that he never saw a player want anything more.

The 1960s in Cincinnati provided Rose's major league terroir, the place and the decade that formed him as a player—this was the Beatles in Hamburg, Cassius Clay in the Golden Gloves. There were no World Series appearances in the '60s, no MVP award, no breakout TV commercials. No eclipsing of Ty Cobb, of course, and no lifetime banishment from the game. It was, by the final measure, a quiet decade. Yet these were the years in which Rose found a way of being, a way of seeing himself in the game—a matrix for the '70s and '80s when by dint of his style and great achievement and then of course his disgrace, Pete Rose would become and remain the most famous baseball player in the world.

He saw what he could accomplish by his effort in those early years, and he learned that his core ethos could carry him far. *He hates to be beaten. He hates to lose.* The veteran players forgave his indiscretions (as did his wife Karolyn), and while he was reviled in some towns for his chutzpah and brass, Rose had built himself a deep equity with the fans who mattered most, in Cincinnati. He had thought that certainly he had angered the faithful after one incident in July of 1965. He was arrested in the early morning hours—4:25 a.m.— for running a red light in Newport, Ky., a place many folks went to lay bets on the horses and sports. Pete was driving back to the West Side, to Gilsey Avenue in Price Hill where he lived with his new bride Karolyn and her parents. He paid the $100 bond with the cash he had in his front pocket and the next day, represented in court, he paid $13.50 in the ticket and fees. "This is going to cost me

18,000 boos and a $500 fine for being out after curfew," Rose said. But he was wrong. The team fined him just $250 and the fans did not boo at Crosley Field that night but rather stood and applauded as he came out to receive, as it happened, a free TV set for being the Reds' top vote-getter for the All-Star Game. In the end, the red light incident was a suggestion to Rose that the things he did at the ballpark, his excellence there, could camouflage some of the other things he chose to do in life.

He played his first seasons in the 1960s not only alongside Robinson but also under Hutchinson, a manager with a face and demeanor straight out of casting: craggy and severe. Hutch was steeped in the knowledge and culture of the game, and he would break a clubhouse chair after losing a tough game. He was the first guy with big league sway to really believe in Pete, the man who brought him into the majors even when others wondered if it was too soon. "Pete fuckin' Rose!" Hutch would say in delight, slapping his thigh as he watched Rose pull off another play with his hustle.

Rose and all the Reds witnessed the way that Hutch bore up in 1964 when he was being ravaged by cancer, so weak that he had trouble hanging up his jacket on the hook, so skinny he winced when he tried to sit down. Hutch would disappear from the team for a day or two to see a specialist, then return, a shade paler, clearly gaunter, but still snarling at players about needing to bust their ass, still warning that he would have to make a lineup change if he didn't start seeing what he liked. In early August, Hutch came back after treatment to manage a doubleheader at Crosley but didn't have enough strength to make it past the seventh inning of game one.

Hutchinson died that fall. It was two years later that Dave Bristol would say of Rose, "He doesn't let anything get in the way of baseball. Never." That fact would help define Rose's career but it hadn't been true before he started playing ball for Fred Hutchinson. It had not been true, say, when Rose was in the minor leagues, homesick in Geneva, N.Y.

Hutchinson was in the dugout, and Robinson was playing leftfield on that cloudy, mild Opening Day, April 8, 1963, when Rose made his major league debut. His parents were at the ballpark of course, Harry with his grayed hair neatly squared off and wearing a newly pressed suit, LaVerne with a scarf about her neck. In his first at bat Pete drew ball four and the crowd cheered as he bolted to first base, the same way as he had done in Macon when the derisive cries of "Hey, Hollywood" began. He came around to score the first run of the '63 season and the first run of the 2,165 he would score in the major leagues.

Rose's going 0 for 3 that day didn't bother him much, nor did the ground ball that he muffed for an error in the eighth inning. He was in the major leagues. He had been in on three double plays at second base and the Reds had beaten the Pirates 5–2 before 29,000 noisy Cincinnatians on Opening Day. In the locker room after the game, as the players dressed quickly ahead of a trip to Philadelphia, Rose opened up a box of chocolates he had gotten as a gift from someone, a congratulations for making the team, and with his mouth already full, he leaned over to Harper and said, offering up the box, "Hey, Tommy! Ya want one?"

Chapter 6

Cincinnati, 1970

H E IS leading off second base now, the most popular player from the hometown team, in a brand new stadium that is filled through to the final rows of the highest deck even now, 3½ hours after this game began. Midnight is just a few minutes away. The President of the United States is still in his front row seat, beside the commissioner of baseball, and it is the bottom of the 12th inning of the 1970 All-Star Game, the 41st in major league history and the score is tied at 4–4 with the Angels lefthander Clyde Wright on the pitcher's mound and the Cubs' Jim Hickman in the batter's box. Pete Rose, having started a rally with a two-out single, is bouncing off second base in his shirtsleeves on the clear midsummer's night, looking into home plate alert and covetous. The National League had won seven straight All-Star games and if Rose could come around to score, that would make eight.

For months the city of Cincinnati had been grooming and primping for the game, a gift bestowed upon it by Major League Baseball in honor of the new Riverfront Stadium, the round-as-a-ring Astroturfed replacement for Crosley Field. The park had opened just two weeks earlier and in the 11 games there (the Reds, on their way to a pennant, had won seven of them) plenty of the dirt around the bags at second and third had already wound up on the chest of Rose's uniform. He had hit a triple his final time up at Crosley Field and then gotten the first Reds hit at Riverfront, a single to rightfield. In between those games he had made a wager with his teammate Tony "Big Dog" Perez as to who could christen the locker room john at Riverfront. They put $150 on the line and Perez arrived so early to the stadium on game day—more than eight hours before the first pitch—that the place was empty, cool and cavernous. Perez went right into the locker room, stepped into a toilet stall and sat down; he was feeling good about his wager, until he heard a voice ring out suddenly from the neighboring stall, "Hey Doggie, good morning!" Pete Rose was already there.

So that was one bet that he won.

Officially Riverfront Stadium had room for 51,500 fans, some 22,000 more than had wedged into a sold-out Crosley Field, and all of the seats—and then some, the aisles too—were filled for this All-Star Game. Perez and catcher Johnny Bench had made the National League's starting lineup (Rose was selected as a reserve) and Cincinnati pitchers Jim Merritt and Wayne Simpson were on the staff. The players' wives all sat together, some with kids at their sides, and stood whenever a Red came to bat. Karolyn Rose had her seat right next to Pituka Perez, as usual. They were together a lot in those years, at the stadium or out for a meal or at each other's homes helping to look after the kids.

All the wives, and indeed just about everyone in Cincinnati it seemed, knew Karolyn. She and Pete, now in the seventh year of what would be a 17-year marriage, were in full blossom. Karolyn, all busty and loud about town—cantankerous sometimes, and effervescent—served as a kind of team den mother and leader. If you came to play for the Reds the first thing you did was have your wife call Karolyn Rose. She would tell you where to get a reliable babysitter. She'd recommend a family doctor, set you up with a dentist, tell you the best places to get a deal on a couch. Pituka. Bonnie Harper. Randee Shamsky: They all looked to Karolyn to show them how to maneuver their way around Cincinnati. She was a West Sider too.

"It was just what you did," Karolyn says. "You welcomed people in." She chewed gum and threw her arms around you in greeting, told you exactly what she thought of the shoes you had on and used four-letter words no matter who was in the room, all of that being part of her charm. You'd have said after being around Karolyn that she was much taller than 5' 2" but she was not.

She may have been Mrs. Pete Rose—anyone married to that man in that city had to be that—but Karolyn was herself an engine, from the start and through to the end. They had met at River Downs, at that same racetrack where Pete had gone so often as a child, with his father, or with Dud Zimmer and his son Don from the West Side. (Don Zimmer was about 10 years older than Pete, and went into the Dodgers' organization right out of Western Hills High.) Pete would see Dud, or Mr. Zimmer as the kids all called him, pick a horse just based on a name—*well, Top Hat looks pretty good*—but also see him go through the racing form and break down the splits and the latest workouts and talk about the condition of the track and then place what seemed to be an educated bet. Pete loved that kind of analyzing, the details of it, and he loved the idea that by some diligence with the particulars a bettor could gain an edge. As much as Mr. Zimmer lost, he won sometimes as well and on those occasions he might take the boys out for something to eat, Pete seeing the pleasure and reward of having new cash.

One afternoon in the spring of 1963, early in the baseball season, Pete was at the track when he gazed from the grandstand through his binoculars and came upon a woman who caught his eye, standing jauntily by the rail. Voluptuous would be an accurate way to describe her, and Karolyn didn't waste her time with loose-fitting clothes. She was on a date at the racetrack—then as now that was the way a guy and a girl from the West Side or northern Kentucky might spend some getting-to-know-you time. The grounds were pretty at River Downs, the hedges in the grassy infield cut into a neat RD on one side of the scoreboard and on the other side a heart-shaped pond with squat pine trees planted around it. From the grandstand you could see past the American flag flapping in the infield to the river and beyond to the thickly settled hills of the West Side. Down at the paddock you could just about touch the horses as they passed and then the guy would get in line at the betting window behind the older, rumpled men smoking thin cigars, and buy the girl a $2 win ticket on the chestnut colt with the white diamond on his nose, or whichever horse she'd picked out.

Even on an ordinary day in a sparsely filled little track like River Downs, a sweet low murmur hums through the crowd when a race goes off, building sporadically to the sharp surge of noisy excitement—the varied, random shouts and curses, the exhortations and the pleas—as the field rounds the far turn and heads down the stretch for home. As Pete tells it, he was already up a few bucks the day he met Karolyn.

A kid named Tommie North made the introduction. "Don't you play football on one of the tavern teams," Karolyn asked after hearing Pete's name. It's possible she had his father in mind. "Are you shittin' me?" he said. "I play for the Cincinnati Reds."

And that was how it started. Back home on Gilsey Avenue, Karolyn asked her brother Fred if he knew about a guy named Pete Rose. "Yeah I know him," said Fred. "He's a hot dog. But he can play." Pete called her a couple days later at her job at the American Book Company (Karolyn was coy: "Pete? Pete who?") and on their first date he let her borrow his car to drive over to Crosley for the game. Later, out for dinner up in Clifton, Karolyn pulled out her pack of cigarettes. "You smoke Salems?" she asked, offering him one. And Pete, lying to impress, said, "Nah, I smoke Camels." He took one of the cigarettes anyway, though, and on the first drag his grin disappeared and he came up coughing and spitting and sneezing like his right lung would fly out of his throat, his left lung out his nose, until finally sputtering, "Christ, these are a little strong, ain't they?"

Karolyn fell out—"To this day I think that is the hardest I have laughed in my life," she says—but Pete shook his head. "I don't think it's funny. I don't know how you take these damn things." It was clear that Pete didn't smoke Salems or Camels or any cigarettes at all, that he never had and never would.

They were married eight months later, after the season, and even before the wedding day Karolyn knew what she was getting into. That summer, while the Reds were on the road in California, she had called the hotel room. "Is Pete around," Karolyn asked when his roommate, the pitcher Jim Coates, picked up the phone. There was a pause and then some stuttering, "Uh, um, I'm not sure," said Coates. "Hold on and I'll check."

"So I'm thinking, what does that mean, *I'll check*?" says Karolyn. "It's two guys in a hotel room, what was he going to do, look under the bed?"

"Nope, I checked, and he's not around," Coates said.

"A few minutes later Pete calls back," Karolyn says. "And he's annoyed. He says, 'Aw, Karolyn I knew it was you. Why you calling out here? You messed me up with some girl I had over.'"

So that was Pete, out there in the open with it, an unabashed slave to his indulgences. He was always trying to make some girl. Over the years friends would ask Karolyn in disbelief how she could stand it, but for the longest time she didn't seem to really care, at least not enough to fight it. Each year at the start of the season, Karolyn would give Pete a coin to take on road trips. "It's for the pay phone," she said. "If you find someone you like much better than me, just call and let me know. I won't come pick you up at the airport."

She knew that she could always reach him at his hotel room, at least. Pete wouldn't be out drinking or running around exploring the nightlife or the sights. He liked to get dinner and stay in, put on the TV if there was one and just fill the time until he could go back to the ballpark. If he had a girl over he had a girl over, was how Karolyn looked at it, allowing herself a mental shrug. It was later, deeper into the 1970s, when Pete had the long affair with the woman from Florida, and they had a child together (the paternity suit made the newspapers) that things began to fray for Karolyn. Really fray. And when Pete got serious with another woman, Carol Woliung, and Carol could be seen out and around right there in Cincinnati or Philadelphia, driving Pete's car—"My car!" Karolyn yelled the time in '79 that she accosted Carol at a red light and socked her in the nose with a well-placed fist—and flaunting fine new jewelry at the racetrack or the ballpark, well, then Karolyn truly had enough, had to take the kids and get away. No one alive, save for Pete himself, could have blamed her.

But for many years before that Karolyn seemed easy with it all, and easy too with the life she would lead—her needs a deep afterthought to Pete's, and Pete's needs being first and foremost and almost completely about baseball. At their wedding, after they'd said their vows at St. William church (a photo of the two of them, freshly hitched in front of the church doors, ran on the front page of *The Cincinnati Post*), she had to go over to the Cheviot Fieldhouse and carry on at the reception line herself, the guests complimenting her on her bridal headpiece and asking, "Where's Pete?" It was the night the Cincinnati baseball writers were giving out their year-end awards downtown, and they were honoring Pete as Rookie of the Year. He still wore his wedding tuxedo, carnation in the buttonhole and all, when he accepted. "I'm going for doubles this year. I'm not a singles man now that I'm married," Pete cracked. By the time he made it to his wedding reception, he was more than two hours late.

The whole event seemed surreal anyway, this West Sider and his gal mixing with big league stars. Close to 1,200 people had turned out and for Pete's sisters and little brother Dave and for many others from the neighborhood, there just wasn't much sense of scale. Karolyn had an uncle called Freck, an outgoing guy who had agreed to tend bar at the reception. Many of the guests, hearing the name—"Hey, Freck, how about another"—believed that it was in fact Ford Frick behind the bar. Meaning, that is, Ford Frick the commissioner of Major League Baseball, the man who had served 17 years as National League president, who had cut the ribbon at the opening of the Baseball Hall of Fame in 1939. Sure, that made sense: commissioner Frick serving up drinks at 22-year-old Pete Rose's wedding. For a river rat now suddenly standing for a few hours on an elevated plane, and looking around to see the great Frank Robinson talking to Cincinnati manager Fred Hutchinson, and seeing clutches of Reds ballplayers—O'Toole, Harper, Edwards, Coates—mingling about, well the notion that Ford Frick might have accepted the task of pouring

Cokes and fixing whiskey sours seemed reasonable enough. Each time old Uncle Freck got asked for an autograph that day he was happy to oblige, signing on a cocktail napkin, "Nice to meet you, Ford Frick."

Pete and Karolyn lived for a few years with her parents (the Engelhardts, Fred and Pearl) on the third floor of the house on Gilsey Ave., and then they moved over to the Hilltop Gardens apartment complex on Harrison Ave., and all along Pete, even as his salary grew, was still the kid with the roots. He would go back around to Western Hills High sometimes, play catch with the guys on the baseball team, or stop in with the football coaches to see if they were still showing the highlight film of all the tackles he broke that time against Elder—and they *were*; the coaches showed that Pete Rose run for many years.

Dan Neville lived at the Hilltop Gardens too in those years and he recalls one weekend morning wondering where his son had gotten off to. The boy was about five years old. Outside in the parking lot Dan ran into Karolyn. "Have you seen David?" he asked.

"Yeah, sure. He's upstairs with Pete," she said.

When Neville got up to the Roses' apartment the two of them were watching Saturday morning cartoons.

PETE AND Karolyn went down to Braddock Street only rarely, on Thanksgiving night and on Christmas Day, or sometimes to bring Fawn around to see Pete's folks. The girl was getting bigger now and had a feistiness to her. When Fawn was three, Pete brought her on set to shoot a TV commercial for mustard. A yellow-slathered hot dog had been prepared for filming but Fawn kept trying to eat it before her cue. An assistant kept moving the hot dog out of her reach, until Fawn bellowed out: "You take the wiener away from me one more time, and I'm going home!"

"You had better let her have a bite," Karolyn told the crew. "When she says something she means it." Telling the story later Pete added, "Fawn thinks she's a boy. She wears boys' pants and a baseball uniform. She tells everybody she's Pete Rose Jr."

Karolyn and Fawn didn't sit with Rose's parents at the Reds games, and not at the 1970 All-Star Game either.[1] Harry was there of course, the one of the 51,838 fans at Riverfront who mattered most to Pete. At 58 Harry was vital and involved, still riding Pete to hustle every play. That ethos, he reminded his son, didn't change whether you were in Class D or the big leagues, whether you were hitting .330 or .130. If Pete didn't see Harry at the ballpark for a couple of games in a row he'd pay a visit to the Fifth Third Bank to find out what was wrong. "You haven't visited your mother," Harry would tell Pete sharply. And so that same day Pete would swing by Braddock, eat some dumplings at the kitchen table with LaVerne, and in so doing ensure that for the next Reds game, Harry would be at the park again pulling for his son.

Late that fall, after the 1970 season and the Reds' run to the World Series had come to an end, Harry sometimes went along with Pete when he and other Reds (Bench, Maloney, Bobby Tolan, Jimmy Stewart) played charity basketball games at high schools around Cincinnati. In early December the squad went over to Colerain High, up there by Groesbeck, to tip off against a faculty team. Before the game, during the shootaround while many of what would be an overflow crowd of more than 2,000 were filing in, Harry challenged Pete to a race: there was a 40-yard sprint setup with tape on the polished wood floor. He was always telling Pete

---

[1] Harry and LaVerne never really went for Karolyn and that was partly on account of how she dressed. At that 1970 All-Star Game, Riverfront Stadium security was on the lookout for the spectacularly buxom stripper, Morganna, who was then in the early stages of her illicit career as a self-styled kissing bandit, a career that had begun, incidentally, when she hopped the railing during a Reds game and ran out to plant one on Rose's mouth. (Pete cursed at her then, but the next night brought roses to her pole at work as a means of apology.) Now an All-Star Game security officer, on duty before the game, saw Karolyn arrive in a tight pink top stretched over her own colossal cleavage, along with her eye makeup and a skirt that stopped at the thigh, and he watched the way she strutted into the stadium calling out to folks she knew; the officer pulled her aside to detain her, having confused her with Morganna. Karolyn was only mildly put out by the mistake and observers were quick to empathize with the officer. Said one reporter of Karolyn: "There's no question she looks like a stripper." (The real Morganna, by the way, did indeed crash the field that night, getting quickly apprehended and brought down to District 1.)

he needed to get faster. So Pete took the bait and the pair of them lit out, father and son. The crowd hooted to see that it was Harry who crossed the finish line first—never mind that Pete was 29 years old, exactly half Harry's age, and a big league outfielder in his prime. Harry won the race with a few steps to spare.

He was trim and brisk and he seemed invincible, right up until the day that he died. A week after his victorious sprint in the Colerain gym, Harry was at work at the Fifth Third—he had been at the bank for close to 40 years by then and at the moment was working as a cashier—when he complained that he suddenly felt ill. Harry knew right away that something serious was at hand. He took a taxi home to Braddock Street, and no one could remember him ever taking a taxi home from work, or leaving work in the middle of the day for that matter. He died on the stairs just inside the front door of the house, collapsed. A heart attack it was believed at first, and then later a blood clot. Out of nowhere it seemed. Harry's epitaph could have read: NEVER SICK A DAY IN HIS LIFE . . . AND NOW THIS.

Pete was in the barbershop when the telephone rang and moments later the barber told him his father was dead. Pete couldn't fathom it. "You mean my mother?" he said at first. He wept "for three days," he says, and those around him had never seen him so broken. Not before or since. One obituary called Harry—or rather, in the local parlance, "Pete Rose the First"—the most famous semipro athlete in Cincinnati history and added that "The Pete Rose who plays for the Cincinnati Reds is a 100 percent replica of his father."

And although he would of course regain his wink and his swagger, and although he would keep Harry's hustle about him all his life, Pete Rose would never again feel the demand for accountability the way he had felt it from Harry. He would never again feel that there was anyone else, not a wife or child, not his mother or siblings, not the agents or the associates serving him, who could see through him or tell him what to do. *You haven't visited your mother,* Harry had said, and so Pete did. With Harry gone, Pete did not care who he might disappoint.

"When my father died that's when the family fell apart, and Pete went his way," his sister Caryl would say 43 years later. "Not all at once, not immediately, but that is what did it. Pete and I had a special relationship as kids, but it was my dad who kept us all together." As Caryl spoke, she was at home, in a house in Indiana that Pete bought for her in the 1970s. She said she had not talked with him, however, not even briefly, for more than a dozen years.

What they all believe, Caryl and her brother Dave and the folks who have known him best, is that had Harry still been alive, Pete would not have drifted and fallen as he has, that he would have found it in himself to stop doing what he was doing, to stay away from the trouble he courted, to admit to and rectify his mistakes, to stand up and conduct himself in the way that his father had. Harry would have been 77 in 1989.

When everything went wrong, when Pete got himself banished from the game and then later sentenced to prison; when he was sneering in his lying denials, when he made the women around him feel small, at those times people like Greg Staab from Braddock Street would share a look with Dave and they would ask one another resignedly and rhetorically, "Now what would Harry Francis have to say about that?"

JULY 14. That was the date of the 1970 All-Star Game. In the Cincinnati newspapers that season (much as in the seasons just past) the word *Reds* sometimes referred to the hometown, first-place baseball team and other times referred to the communists in Vietnam. A headline REDS ROUTED or more typically REDS SHOWING RESILIENCE could be (and often was) misread. This was two months after the madness at Kent State, where student protesters had been shot to death on a campus four hours north of Cincinnati; and it was three months before President Nixon announced that he would be bringing 40,000 more troops out of the jungle and home for Christmas. David Rose was still over there in uniform. He'd been there about a year.

Pete had gone to Vietnam, too, although not by way of the draft like his brother. His was a three-week ambassadorship, in the off-season of 1967, a goodwill tour taken with a few ballplayers, including his idol Joe

DiMaggio. The players went around talking to the troops about baseball and the soldiers all asked DiMaggio about Marilyn Monroe—and DiMaggio's face would darken and he would glare them into silence—and all the while as the ballplayers went from camp to camp through the searing hot jungle Pete would lighten spirits with the clubhouse banter he had brought along.

And although it was harrowing at times for Pete, the high-speed helicopter rides just above the treetops ("so they can't get us with gunfire," the pilot said) and the sounds of the distant or not-so distant explosions, and the smell of smoke and fire and most sobering and thudding of all, the sight one hot-moist dawn of body bags—19 of them Pete counted—being unloaded at a camp for transport home, disturbing as all of that was, this was not close to being a soldier's experience. The ballplayers always knew they would be going home soon.

For Pete the trip was indelible most of all for his traveling with DiMaggio, talking hitting and baserunning with him. DiMaggio was a player, Rose long knew, who did not have quit in him. Later and through the years Pete would tell of helping Joe to bathe—that is, in the way bathing went over there, Pete pouring buckets of water through a kind of rawhide sieve over DiMaggio's head while DiMaggio soaped himself behind a partition out-of-doors. "I'm the only guy who ever gave DiMaggio a shower," Rose would say even decades later. "At least I *hope* I'm the only guy." At some point well into his banishment years Pete would in the telling reprise his old Tommy Harper joke, and crack on a radio station that it was the great DiMaggio who looked like a dick with a man hanging off of him, and people would wonder why Pete had to be so crude like that, about DiMaggio.

When his time in Vietnam ended, Pete came home and had Christmas on Braddock Street and got ready for spring training, which was not at all the experience that Dave would have, beginning in the summer of 1969 and running through the fall of '70. Sixteen months in all. And for what he went through and also what he missed, it is clear how very much Dave at the time, and all the more in hindsight, would have rather been at that All-Star Game in Cincinnati watching Pete step to the plate and seeing U.S. flags flapping in open splendor, than where he in fact was, 8,000 miles and an ocean away, wearing combat gear under the blistering morning sun, the flags inside the camp tents there a grim source of pride. Dave was a door gunner in Vietnam.

HE WAS bigger earlier than Pete, more strapping and more athletic. "The fastest white guy in Cincinnati," is how Dave was known. He played football at Western Hills and like Pete before him Dave made highlights, his produced even playing on a god-awful team. DAVE ROSE'S RUNS BRIGHTEN DARK SEASON, read the yearbook spread after West Hi had gone winless in 1966, and there were photos of Dave as he "rambled around left end for a ten yard gain" or "broke through Elder's line of defense to score" or brought back a kickoff 60 yards for a touchdown. Pete's little brother big on game day. Dave made all-city as a halfback and he might have gone somewhere serious to play college ball—Oklahoma liked the looks of him, VMI wrote to him—if the thought of spending four more years in school had held any appeal to him at all. No. Dave would play baseball like his brother. He batted over .300 for Western Hills and tracked down balls in the outfield and had all kinds of home run power. West Hi won the state championship Dave's senior year (he batted .430 down the stretch of the season) and afterward the Reds signed him to a minor league deal. He went off to Wytheville, Va., in the Appalachian Rookie League. ANOTHER ROSE MAY BLOOM read the headline in *The Cincinnati Post* and a photo went out over UPI of Dave in a golf shirt flexing his biceps while Pete squeezed it and Harry, "the proud father of the two boys," stood between them.

"Dave can make it if he gets it up *here*," said Harry, tapping upon his brow. This was now spring training of 1968 and both Rose boys were in Tampa. "He's got to realize the opportunity he has."

That Dave wouldn't hit all that much at Sarasota in 1968 wasn't a lot to go on—he had raw skill as a ballplayer, no question—but what was clear even then, more than a year before he left to fight in the war, was that Dave was never going to hustle like Pete did, would never put himself through that kind of ordeal. The more talented Rose? Well, even the scouts said that was true. But Dave never wanted it the way that Pete did.

Some folks in baseball would wonder why the boys were so different that way, why one left his innards on the field and the other hit the morning alarm and went back to sleep.[2] Really it was not so confounding to those who knew them, the explanation (as if a single one could suffice) boiling down to this: that although Dave was born to the same mother and the same father and although he was raised in the same house and went to the same school and played the same sports as Pete did, it will always be true that just as no man steps into the same river twice no two children are born into same family. By the time Dave came along for the Roses, Pete was already there. When the boys crossed the Ohio as kids, Dave, easily the better natural swimmer, meandered across doing the sidestroke, relaxed. This after seeing Pete thrash across in a clumsy but manic crawl, reaching the opposite bank ahead of the rest.

Dave says he was devastated, left literally shaking, when his draft notice came, and who wouldn't have been? He was together with Cynthia, his high school sweetheart, his first wife who would soon give birth to their boy Shane. At Western Hills High, Cynthia had sung in the choir and played in the band, been on the school paper and done good works in the Sunshine Society. Dave always thought she looked just fine in her glasses and he liked how her thick locks fell to her shoulders. He himself wore his dark hair the way that Pete did, doglegs over the ears, though he let the hair grow fuller on the top and the sides. Dave had the same square-looking skull, high forehead and worthy chin that the other Rose men had.

His extracurriculars were about sports, playing on the teams, of course, and also joining for a while the Maroon W club devoted to character and sportsmanship. The club took on spirit jobs, selling pro-

---

[2] Dave's unsatisfactory reasoning for this marked difference in drive: "Pete had that one off-season loading boxcars and he realized he didn't want to be working a regular job. Me, I don't mind doing work." And Pete's: "Maybe because he was bigger and faster he didn't feel like he had to do much. I always knew I had to work for it."

grams at basketball games, posting event times on the school marquee. ("Pete never did nothin' like that," Dave says.) He also served some months as a lunchroom monitor, the appointment his punishment for fighting in school. Dave was broad and rippling through the shoulders and arms, bore impressive fists and had a temper that just went off, giving him a ferocious and renowned strength. His principal asset as a lunchroom monitor, the way he so effectively kept the peace, was that the other kids knew if you made a crack or acted out in some way as to make Dave's life more difficult, he was likely to kick your mother-loving ass.

Dave and Pete used to wrestle sometimes as brothers do, and Pete having those seven years on him would get the better. But that roughhousing ended for good when Dave got back from Vietnam, and there was now a certain look about him, a smoldering inside. "I'm never going to fuck with that guy again," Pete said of his little brother then, "and I wouldn't recommend that you do either."

In Vietnam Dave learned to hold strong and steady against the kickback when he fired that machine gun—the Pig, they called it—and he learned to bear without effect the racket of the gunfire and the chopper blades, and the force of the wind. They would chopper in ahead of, or just behind the ground troops, and Dave would cover those men as they got down and unloaded. At times Dave got the order to cut loose and strafe an enemy camp. You could never be sure how many, if any, of the enemy you might have taken down, a welcome ignorance because truly you did not want to know.

In some ways he liked working the air better than being on the ground, trudging ahead with that anti-mortar unit, digging in and stacking sandbags at the mouths of those huge culvert pipes, checking the radar and bracing for incoming. It got pretty close one time near Bien Hoa, much closer than anybody liked. Dave was the one who extended his tour to those 16 months, his thinking being that when he came home he could be free of obligation, not have to worry about getting called up and spared from having to put in weekends of duty when he was back playing pro ball. When he finally left for good, October 1970, when the wheels went up off that airbase at Bien Hoa, the 248 men in the plane jumped out of their seats, relieved and giddy to be going home.

There were the things over there that Dave did and the things that he saw and smelled and heard and the way that he felt inside through all those hot uncertain terrible nights, Vietnam becoming for Dave one long dark dream now many years behind him but never fully gone away. If he learned to accept it all, accept the duties and assignments and if he learned to forgive both fate and himself, he never truly accepted nor forgave the time that he lost, coming home to see little Shane for the first time days after the boy's first birthday. He could not get that time back, those many months, as it turned out, right near the end of his father's life. "It's losing out is what it is," says Dave, in his mid-60s now. "My dad was going to set me the right way. He was going to be the manly influence I needed."

It was mid-autumn when Dave got back to Cincinnati, so there would be no continuing his baseball career until the following spring. He had some money saved from his service time, and although Pete and Harry warned him against it, chided him to no end, Dave went out and bought himself a motorcycle. Just something to tool around on, he figured. He loved motors, loved things that *went*, he and Staaby (his great pal Greg Staab) always had. For Dave's 12th birthday Pete had given him a Kurtis Kraft go-kart with a West Bend 580 engine inside. Best present Dave ever got, he says. "And it was Pete who gave it to me!"

Now, he figured, a motorcycle. He deserved it, deserved to treat himself to something after what he had just been through over there. Dave settled on a Honda 175 Scrambler. Popular bike. He wouldn't take it racing or on a track or anything. He'd just use it to get around town, to get up to Scarlato's Italian Inn where he had his first kitchen job, doing dishes as well as a little cooking here and there. Pete and Dave had known the Scarlato kids forever—Jerry was about Pete's age, Greg a year older than Dave—and the family was thrilled when Dave took the job. You could count on him. Maybe Dave wasn't hell-bent on a ballfield, but he showed up early for every day of work and on the job he always did a little more than what you asked of him.

Then came the night Dave wasn't supposed to have been working at Scarlato's Italian Inn at all. He was off that night. Only Greg called and said how he and Jerry had gotten last-minute tickets to see Wayne Cochran and the C.C. Riders over at the Lookout House in Covington—and that was the kind of white soul-slinging you did not want to miss—and could Dave take his shift? Sure Dave would. He would always do a favor or back you when you got into a fix. Badass as he could be with his fists, and badass he truly was, Dave was unerringly loyal, a decent guy. The thing about Dave Rose, his friends said, is that he would pick you up from the airport if you only asked.

It was late that night after work at Scarlato's and Dave was away from the restaurant, leaving downtown, his Honda rumbling loud on the quiet, near empty streets. He merged onto the long sweep of River Road. Maybe it was 12:30, quarter to one. Dave felt the wind whoosh cold around him as he gathered some speed. And then suddenly there were the headlights and the car, swung out over the yellow line, headed straight at him it seemed and Dave swerved hard away and into a parked car, his whole right side scraped and walloped and his right kneecap shattered to bits. Blood everywhere. Right there on River Road, a few weeks back from Vietnam, Dave's life had been reconfigured again.

For a week and half, or maybe closer to two, Dave had to stay in the hospital. Pete did not come to visit him once—that's how ticked Pete was at Dave. Idiot for having bought the motorcycle in the first place, idiot for whipping home on it at night is what Pete said. "Guess he felt he had to make his point," says Dave.

After the hospital Dave went into physical therapy just about every day, driving up to the medical center from the house by Sayler Park where he and Cynthia lived. He was just able to drive with that bad right leg. Dave was on his way to therapy one afternoon when he caught sight of the rescue wagon up on Braddock Street. The leaves were off the trees by then so he could see up there clearly from River Road. Dave turned the car right around, pulled a U-turn across the lanes, and got up to the house, frenzied, and when he pushed past the medics he, like them, could not open the front door yet, for his father was lying motionless on the floor. Dave ran, or really he limped fiercely on that battered leg, forgetting the pain, across Braddock over to the Staabs' stone house, yelling about his fallen father, and this would be another in the sharp series of images in Dave's suddenly upended life—the snarl of the machine gun and the car out on the dark road and now his father on the ground.

Dave's leg was not close to fully healed by the time spring training of 1971 came about, his speed not nearly back. But he went down to Reds camp in Tampa anyway. When you are 22 and you've been away two seasons in Vietnam, and you haven't hit much in your brief stops in the minor leagues, then it doesn't matter whose brother you are, you are running out of time to show yourself as a ballplayer. That's just how it was.

The Reds cut Dave on Easter Sunday, and although he surely could have gone over to St. Louis's spring training camp or one of the other teams down there and said he was Dave Rose and still had plenty left in him, and thus gotten a look-see or more, he did not. He might have kept that thing flickering a little longer, given himself a little more baseball and a chance. But Dave was not up for any of that, not up for the challenge nor the effort it would require. He couldn't have cared less about playing baseball in that moment. He didn't care about much of anything at all, save for finding himself an easier way to get through his every day.

Through the life that followed he would look back on that time and think about what might have been: through his marriages and divorces, through his five children, through the kitchen jobs and learning to be a damn good cook, through living up north of Cincinnati in Blue Ash and in Florida and then back in Cincinnati again, and through the times when his life went paycheck to paycheck and by Tuesday each week the money spent on cocaine and crack. And didn't it then just have to be Greg Scarlato, the kid who went to see Wayne Cochran that awful autumn night in 1970, who gave Dave a job at Popeye's in Cincinnati when Dave really needed it, and Scarlato again who helped put Dave through rehab, those eight months Dave spent away in Rockford, Ill., trying to get himself straight, trying to, as he says, "get my heart in the right place"? Through all of that and through all the chances he had to rise up, to actually manage one of Pete's restaurants, say, or to make a marriage stick for good, he would through all his unsettled nights look back on this time. *What did he deserve in life? What did he deserve to have?* Dave will say out loud that the past is long behind him, although it is with him every day, with him in the gnawing sense of what might have been had those years of Vietnam and the year after it gone differently.

The loyalty remains—in the stands at the ballpark Dave over the years would unleash himself upon hecklers heckling Pete, pound a guy again and again until security took him away—and in that loyalty his dignity. In his early 60s he came to live near Indianapolis, staying for a while with Greg Staab on a flat street in Speedway. They race dirt sprint cars on weekends. Staab and Jim Luebbert have been there for Dave too, old West Siders dragging him back onto the path, trying with some success to keep him away from the bad influences, finding him work. Dave cooks a few days a week at Staab's restaurant over in Brownsburg, the Pit Stop Barbeque & Grill. He makes a tilapia almondine that has customers coming back for more.

Dave had brought his bat and glove with him to Vietnam, part of the luggage he processed in and out at Fort Dix, and once in a while he and a few of the other soldiers threw around a baseball or played pepper. There was a television set at the base and on the day after the 1970 All-Star Game Dave got summoned over so that he could watch highlights of the game and of the final play at home plate. Just as this was the year that would reorder Dave's life, in event after event, so too would Pete be changed. He would be changed most deeply by the death of Harry, of course, yet he would also be changed—or rather the understanding of Pete Rose, his aura and reach, would change and grow and sharpen—with a single episode in that All-Star Game. The play attached itself to him then, almost perfectly scripted for the man, a glimpse of Pete Rose that seared him into the minds of many millions of Americans, never to be wiped away.

HE IS looking in off the second base bag, feinting forward and back, checking to make sure that the Angels' Sandy Alomar, playing second base for the American League All-Stars, doesn't slide over to try to pick him off. The crowd rocks loud, swirling with energy—Harry Rose, Richard Nixon and 50,000 others lean forward in their seats. Two outs in the inning and Pete Rose is fixing to get a good jump.

He was midway through that year of years, back-to-back batting titles just behind him and his average up over .320 again, piling up base hits as the roaring catalyst for a team 10 games clear into first place. Those 1970 Reds had plenty of hitters: Bench, Perez, Lee May, Bernie Carbo, Bobby Tolan. First thing Sparky Anderson had done when he'd taken over as manager before the season was to name Pete Rose captain—why not make it official, give Rose the credit he deserves, Sparky figured. Pete ran the game on the field anyway. And it was Rose who, the same day Sparky had gotten the job, had called and asked, "What can I do to help? What can I do to help us win?" Anderson gave Rose the assignment of bringing out the lineup card to the umpires before every game, wanting Charlie Hustle to represent the Reds.

Rose and Bench were in on some things together: part owners of a Lincoln–Mercury dealer up near Dayton and of a 40-lane bowling alley in Fairfield, Ohio. There were endorsements too, so Rose had money coming in even apart from his $105,000 salary, a little extra to spend on his cars and a bigger wad to gamble. Everybody knew about Pete and the ponies of course—his voracious visits to the track, not just in Cincinnati but also when the Reds were on the road, were not something Pete was inclined to hide—and many people around him knew that he'd been betting with bookies for years. It was the trail of bad paper that got baseball interested. The major leagues' new security director Henry Fitzgibbon said he was getting info on Pete from around Cincinnati, often about bookies being rankled when Rose didn't pay up fast enough or even at all. ("He thought because he was Pete Rose it was O.K. that he didn't pay," former Reds pitcher Jim O'Toole says.) The one thing you do not want if you are a baseball security boss is one of your players owing bookmakers even a cent.

Fitzgibbon met with Rose again and again through the early '70s. He would warn Pete about hanging around with the wrong type of guys, remind him what had happened to Tigers pitcher Denny McLain when he started messing with real money and got too close to bookmakers, so close that they had a stake in him. McLain had been suspended the first half of the 1970 season and Fitzgibbon had handled the case.

But Fitz never found enough to go on when it came to Rose, and Pete was all friendly and effusive in his denials. "No big deal," he'd say. "Just going to the track." And Pete's gambling certainly never bothered folks from the West Side much—who doesn't like a little action after all?

Rose had come out with an autobiography by then, had already had enough of a life at age 28 in Ohio that the benign and hero-building book, *The Pete Rose Story*, made sense to a Manhattan publishing house that printed in Cleveland. Rose dedicated his book in part to his father and also to the media and the fans. "What I'd really like to do, other than please you with this book, is hit .300 for ten straight years," he wrote in Chapter One (the text credits "editors in New York" for assembling Rose's notes and thoughts into coherency). "If you hit .300 for 10 straight years you get a chance at the Baseball Hall of Fame. I'd sure like that. . . . Any player out there today who doesn't want to end up in the Baseball Hall of Fame should turn in his uniform and quit."

The All-Star Game was on televisions in some 16.7 million households, watched by 56 million fans (better than 25% of the country), and by the 12th inning it had been a hell of a game already. If anyone thought the players didn't want to win it, that notion disappeared while watching the bottom of the ninth inning when the National Leaguers, down 4–1, could have packed it in—freed themselves to get home early or go out for a bite downtown. Instead there was a sharp intensity in the dugout as that inning began. The NL had its winning streak on the line, "and we were not about to let that go," says Bench. The Giants' Dick Dietz hit a home run off Catfish Hunter to start the comeback, and there was no quit after that. Six batters into the inning Roberto Clemente's sacrifice fly sent home Joe Morgan with the run that tied the game at 4–4. Extra innings. "I remember scoring that run like it was yesterday," says Morgan, who was an Astro then. "The place was whooping it up."

"That whole game felt like the World Series," says Billy Grabarkewitz, a Dodger who came into the game at third base. "We played hard—there was a real rivalry between leagues. That was the biggest game I'd ever played in and a lot of the young guys felt the same way." Tom Seaver, ace of the reigning champion Mets, had talked to the media before the game about what performing well in an All-Star Game could do for a player, how it could lift his confidence and build his ego.

Not that Rose needed a reminder of any of that. The day before the game, after he and Bench and the other Reds had put on suits and ties and met the press, Pete and Karolyn had played host again, this time to a couple of players from the Cleveland Indians, the veteran pitcher Sam McDowell and the 23-year-old catcher Ray Fosse. They had all gotten to talking at the Monday workout where Rose was bounding around on his new home field. ("Hey Harp, what took ya so long?" he shouted out when he saw Tommy Harper, then with Milwaukee and making his first trip to the All-Star Game.)

That night Rose, McDowell, Fosse and their wives went out for steak downtown and afterward drove back to the Roses'. It must have been around 11 o'clock when they got to the house. Pete welcomed everyone in but then, barely through the front door, announced that he was going up to get to bed on time like he always did. Greenies or not—and certainly, as his teammates recall, Rose was among the many players who sometimes swallowed those clubhouse amphetamines for a boost—he cherished and honored his sleep. It was the key, he felt, to good health and maximum effort. "Got a big ball game tomorrow," he said to Fosse and McDowell, coming over to shake their hands. "But stay as long as you like and make yourself at home. Karolyn will fix you a drink or anything you want." And like that Rose went upstairs for the night.

Fosse and McDowell had of course hoped to stay and talk baseball for awhile—young Fosse might have had a few more questions to ask Pete about Bench, the catcher to whom Fosse was often compared—but instead they traded glances with one another and with their wives, the whole setup suddenly awkward now, and one of the players piped up, "Um, Karolyn maybe we'd better get going too."

Now it was the next night at Riverfront and there were two outs in the 12th inning and the game appeared destined to stretch longer still, into the morning hours. Clyde Wright, in his second inning on the mound, had set down five straight batters, four on ground balls. "Here's what's going to happen," Rose told Grabarkewitz just before going up to bat. "I'm going to hit a double and you're going to knock me in."

"For chrissakes, can I get somethin' good to hit this time?" he joked to Fosse behind the plate as he stepped in. Rose did not double, but on a 2–0 count delivered a single to centerfield. Then Grabarkewitz pulled a single to left—he said he hit a slider, Wright swore it was the heat—and Rose advanced to second. That set things up for Hickman, the Cubs outfielder having the season of his life. "I had never been so nervous before a game," he would say later.

Wright threw a pitch belt high, outer half of the plate, and Hickman lashed it on a hard line drive into the outfield. The ball skipped on the new artificial turf toward Amos Otis in center. Now Rose was churning hard, approaching third base and then turning for home, sprinting down the line. He began to pitch forward, about to dive headfirst into home plate, a play few other players, fearing injury, would dare, but which for Rose was part of his job, a signature play. Except there was not any place for Rose to slide. Fosse stood straddling the base path, blocking off home plate, waiting for the throw from Otis. The ball had been hit so hard that they had a decent chance, Fosse figured, to get Rose out.

There is a story bright in the annals of Harry Rose that during his years as a semipro football star he was invited onto a local TV station to be interviewed and to demonstrate the art of tackling. A wooden chair had been set up in the studio and the thought was that Harry, who showed up to the interview in full uniform and gear, would approach the chair from this angle and that, reveal some technique and explain certain nuances, like when it is better to hit a man high or low, perhaps. Instead, when his cue came Harry took a running start and hit the chair as if it were trying to score, shattering it completely. Wood pieces everywhere. The staff at the station agog.

Now much of the crowd at Riverfront was standing as Rose hurtled toward home. Harry leaned forward. Karolyn whistled and stomped at her seat and in both dugouts players were rapt. Rose was all mission coming down the line. Five feet, 11 inches, 194 pounds, muscular through the shoulders and chest, thick through the hips and thighs: He had a body capable of enormous leverage, a cruel body. Fosse, at 6' 2", was crouched only slightly and looking toward the outfield for the throw from Otis, about to arrive. "There was never any doubt that there would be a collision," says Claude Osteen, the National League pitcher who watched from the dugout. "That was the play in front of us. We all saw it."

Rose, his head down—he had stumbled slightly after realizing a slide wouldn't work—drove straight into Fosse, left shoulder to left shoulder, left knee to left knee, just before the baseball came in. Fosse never got his mitt on it, being hit so hard that he tumbled, literally, head over heels. Rose, as he tumbled himself, reached out and touched home plate with his right hand as he landed. The winning run was in. He stood quickly, scooping up his helmet, and leaned down immediately to ask Fosse whether he was O.K. The catcher was on his knees, badly dazed. Dietz, who had been beyond the plate waving Rose in, embraced Pete, helped him limp away, and then others came to congratulate him—Clemente and Willie McCovey. Leo Durocher, the Cubs' manager who was coaching third base, had been clapping and whooping nonstop, ecstatic like the rest.

In the National League locker room the celebration continued with everyone especially lauding Pete. ("There were so many great players in there," Grabarkewitz recalls. "It just felt like a really special team and a really big win.") Pete was thrilled with how the game had gone and although he said, "I didn't want to hurt Fosse," he was unapologetic about the collision, as were all of those around him. "If anyone had expected Rose to come into the plate any other way than he did they've never seen him play," said Mets and National League coach Joe Pignatano.

"Well, that's football," said Fosse over on the American League side, his left shoulder stiff and throbbing. "Some guys on the bench thought he could have gone around me. I don't know. It's the way he runs. He's got to score it anyway he can, I guess."

Fosse was hurt—a fractured shoulder as it turned out—although he was being widely hailed for the play. The way Fosse had blocked the plate and had "done all he could," as some accounts read, to prevent the winning run, had won the Cleveland catcher immediate and considerable renown. "Now," wrote *Sports Illustrated* of Fosse a couple of weeks after the collision, "his constituency [is] nationwide."

Three decades after that play at the plate, the most iconic single play in the history of the Major League All-Star Game, you still find people—American League fans invariably, fans from Boston and Cleveland especially—who say they haven't forgiven Rose for what he did to Fosse, their memories perhaps worn or their view selective or their willingness to be guided by logic and reason overcome by certain feelings in their gut. These are invariably people who also hold other views on Rose. [3]

The case that Rose should not have crashed into Fosse usually devolves into two specious points: first, that because of the shoulder injury Fosse was never the same player. And although he batted .297 the rest of that year, and made the All-Star Game again the next season and appeared in an average of more than 135 games a year from 1971 through '73, it may well be true that the collision, along with what Fosse relates as a lack of proper medical attention afterward, helped derail a potentially excellent career. Fosse continued playing despite being hurt (he also suffered several other significant injuries over the years) and his production fell markedly after '70. He was part of two World Series championships with the A's and appeared in his last big league games in '79, with the Brewers. Since '86 Fosse has worked as a commentator on A's radio and television broadcasts. "My career completely changed once I was hit [by Rose]," he said recently.

More common is the argument, and this one could be categorized as inane, that Rose should have approached the play differently because this was an "exhibition game," that is, a game that did not count for his

---

[3] John Dowd, who would so ably lead the investigation and prosecution of Rose's gambling case, and who grew up a baseball fan in Boston, says of the rumble into Fosse: "I didn't like it, Rose didn't have to do that." When it was suggested that Fosse was blocking the plate, leaving scant alternative to a man hoping to score the winning run, Dowd bristled, "I just didn't like it."

team's position in the standings. It's a narrow way to define a game. The Reds won the National League West by 14½ games in 1970. The Indians finished 32 games out of first place in the American League East. For neither team that season was any single regular season game "more important" than the All-Star Game.

In fact that All-Star Game was for some players (and both Rose and Fosse then fell into this category) the most exciting and meaningful game of their careers at that point. There were long, stand-alone special sections in newspapers across the country dedicated to the game. More people watched it than any game that year. You might well argue that the game-winning single was the biggest hit that Jim Hickman got in his 13 years as a major leaguer. "It didn't feel like any exhibition game that I've ever played in," says Joe Morgan.

In terms of money spent and money earned and in terms of attention paid and most relevantly in terms of its value to the participants themselves, that All-Star Game was extremely more "important" than, say, the regular-season Dodgers-Reds game three weeks earlier at Crosley Field. In that one Maury Wills bowled over Bench at the plate to score. That was the way baseball was (and still often is) played, and certainly the way Pete Rose played it. In an actual exhibition game earlier in 1970, against the Mets in Tampa, he had slid home headfirst to score the winning run. Had Fosse not been blocking the plate in the All-Star Game—his doing so without having the ball in his possession, incidentally, may have been illegal[4]—Rose would have slid in headfirst then too. No collision, no real injury risk to anyone but himself.

---

[4] A note under the rule book's section 7.06 (b) reads: "The catcher, without the ball in his possession, has no right to block the pathway of the runner attempting to score. The base line belongs to the runner and the catcher should be there only when he is fielding a ball or when he already has the ball in his hand." By that rule, Fosse, as many catchers before and since, was clearly in an illegal position. Elsewhere in the rule book, however, a definition of obstruction allows that a fielder awaiting a thrown ball "may be considered 'in the act of fielding' " and so allowed to be in a runner's path—that determination falls to the umpire's judgment. Had Fosse, without the ball all the way, prevented Rose from scoring, he may or may not have been called for obstruction.

Fosse's stature was lifted by the collision and it remains the incident that he is most closely associated with, far more so than any of his accomplishments as a player. Decades later during autograph sessions in Cooperstown or Las Vegas, Rose would comment on this, saying, "All I did was make Ray Fosse famous." And although Rose is rightly mystified by criticism of the play, there is a certain smugness in saying a thing like that, an unseemliness given the way that Fosse's career slipped. "No one would have hardly heard of him if it wasn't for me," Rose adds. Whatever measure of truth that statement contains, it seems a thoughtless thing to say.

The collision elevated Pete as well. The stories that so many casual fans across the nation had heard about the hunger with which Cincinnati's Charlie Hustle played the game were true! He really was all that, really was about laying himself on the line and trying to win at any cost. He showed it. "When we got back to Los Angeles, all anyone wanted to talk about was Pete," said Osteen. Rose was given an ovation by his teammates when the Reds reassembled two days after the game. He wound up missing a few days with a badly bruised left knee, his kneecap full of blood and grotesquely swollen by that winning play.

———————

THE STORY of how Bold Face Park, the field down by the Anderson Ferry where Rose often played baseball as a boy, got its name, is as follows: For many years the area was controlled by a Mohawk Indian tribe led by a chief named Bold Face. In the autumn of 1790 a white settler named Jacob Wetzel came to this park, which was then a clearing in the woods, and sat resting upon a log. It was hunting season, which meant that Wetzel was armed and also that the Mohawks were especially protective of their land, upon which wild turkeys roamed.

As Wetzel sat, Chief Bold Face emerged from the trees and a confrontation ensued. The two traded missed rifle shots and then engaged in a fierce hand-to-hand battle. Each man drew a long hunting knife. Chief Bold Face began to get the better of the struggle, and he landed on top of Wetzel as they rolled to the ground—poised for the kill until Wetzel's dog suddenly flew into the fray, closing its teeth on Chief Bold Face's neck. With the reprieve, Wetzel plunged his knife into Chief Bold Face, wounding him fatally. Before any tribe members could descend upon him, Wetzel fled, escaping in a canoe down a creek and into a protected cove. He would hear the mournful wails of the Mohawks as they stood over their fallen leader. And he would live to tell the tale. It's the kind of legend that sticks.

For 180 years, more or less, that area—later cleared and groomed and later still outfitted with picnic tables and ball fields and playground equipment—was known and labeled as Bold Face Park. Late in that August of 1970, about six weeks after Rose had won the All-Star Game for the National League in Cincinnati, the city's recreation commission held a ceremony announcing the renaming of the park: It would be called Pete Rose Field, the earth there now being assigned to a new American legend, himself a native. Tourists coming to Cincinnati sometimes drove down to have a look.

Rose would captain the Reds to the World Series in 1970, the first of the Big Red Machine era. He led the National League with 205 hits, 15 of them home runs. In Cincinnati, Rose was a uniting figure in fractious times. Hippies would gather in those days at Fountain Square downtown, the anti-Vietnam feelings and the anti-establishment feelings rife and explicit. They gathered in tasseled vests and old jeans, and let their hair hang down and smoked pot and kissed one another.

Baseball may have been the establishment game, but Cincinnati was a baseball town no matter how long you wore your hair. At the fountain one could hear the hippies talking about the Reds in the pennant race and talking as well in the most glowing and appreciative terms about Pete Rose. It did not matter that Rose had what Reds manager Sparky Anderson called the last crew cut in America, nor that he played with an aggressiveness no peacenik could truly countenance. He was real and authentic and he stood for something. A reporter in from San Francisco late that season heard one shaggy kid suggest that Rose had made a societal impact on a level with one of their counter-culture goddesses, Janis Joplin. The way that Pete Rose played baseball could blow a hippie's mind.

On the eve of the postseason—Cincinnati would sweep the Pirates in the National League Championship Series, then lose the World Series to the Orioles in five—an article written by that same reporter, Wells Twombly, appeared in *The Sporting News* under the headline IS THERE REALLY A PETE ROSE? Twombly wondered whether Pete was really just "a mass of wires and transistors underneath that life-like skin, just like Abraham Lincoln at the New York World's Fair." Who else but a robot after all could go, go, go all the time the way Pete did, never slowing and all the time producing 200 hits a season, a figure who would "run right through catchers [and] never say a bad word about the sport."

"A player like Rose comes along only once in a lifetime," is the way Anderson framed it. Maybe, Twombly's joke continued, Anderson was being literal when he said that Rose, with his attitude, was "absolutely unreal."

Rose was then a little more than 1,500 hits into his career. He had put together just six of his eventual 15 seasons of batting better than .300. He had not yet won an MVP award, or a World Series. He would still play in 12 more All-Star Games. Yet there was already an acknowledgment, inside of the game and outside of it, that Rose was a player for the ages.

"Tests ought to be made," Twombly wrote approaching the conclusion of his droll piece. "If he's human, he ought to be shipped right to Cooperstown."

Chapter 7

Cooperstown, 2012

THE LOOKS that Rose drew as he moved about Cooperstown on that 2012 induction weekend were not directed solely at him but also at his companion Kiana Kim. The keen, almost rubbernecking, interest stemmed partly from the implausible May-December romance and partly from the fact that for much of the time in Cooperstown Kim wore tight, skimpy jeans shorts, high heels and a strapless blouse. Even with a Reds cap on she did not quite blend in with the crowd. Kim is tall, fit and leggy and has modeled in all manner of poses and states of undress. Her explanation for why people sometimes stopped on the street and asked to take pictures with her is that folks in Cooperstown were not used to seeing "a girl from L.A."

Kim's enormous breasts were a popular topic of conversation throughout the weekend, and their uncertain fate was to form a plotline in the upcoming reality show on TLC. Some years ago Kim had a breast enlargement in hopes of aiding her modeling career. "I figured bigger is better," she says. Now, older and wiser, she wanted to have her breasts scaled back down. "A tit reduction," Pete called it off camera. He was solidly opposed.

One night in Cooperstown Pete, Kiana and her children Cassie and Ashton went for dinner with a couple of television producers who were exploring the possibility of doing a documentary on Rose for HBO, a project unrelated to the reality show. (During his Friday autograph session at Safe At Home, Rose was fitted with microphones under his shirt. "That's HBO on this mike, TLC on this mike," he said tugging at each shoulder. "I feel like I'm going to get electrocuted.") Over dinner Pete and Kiana sounded out the group on some potential titles for the TLC show, playing directly on Kim's ample chest and Pete's tough past—including the five months he served in prison for filing false tax returns: "We could call it *The Jugs and the Thug*," Kim offered with a laugh. "Or, *The Melons and the Felon*." Pete said he kind of liked *The Playmate and the Cellmate* but that his top choice would be *Tits and Hits*. He understood that having the breast reduction would be entirely Kiana's decision and sensing the inevitable—Kim would indeed have the procedure on the reality show, which aired in early 2013—he grumbled, "And what about me? I'm the one who tucks these babies in every night." The grown-ups snickered but Kiana's children looked away. Then young Cassie said suddenly, "You know Pete is the same age as my grandma."

So, briefly (sigh): *Pete Rose: Hits & Mrs.*, is what the show was finally called. The six-part series centered around Pete and Kim's relationship and a domestic life challenged by the fact that Rose spent as many as five days a week living and signing autographs in Las Vegas, and sometimes as little as a few days a month at Kim's place in Valencia, Calif. They had met in 2007 at a Mercedes dealer at which Kim was buying a car. Pete, there to visit with the dealership owner, a pal, asked Kiana if she would like a signed baseball from him. "Why?" she asked. Kim didn't know who Rose was—for a little while after they were introduced she thought he had played for the Redskins, not the Reds—but he wooed her by offering to set up her and a friend in a hotel room if they ever came to Vegas. Rose at that point had been married for more than 20 years to his second wife, Carol, but this in no way dampened the enthusiasm of his pursuit. Kim did indeed come to Las Vegas for a visit and Rose later made an appearance at a hair salon Kim owned in Valencia, creating some buzz. Not long after that he brought her with him onto the *Howard Stern Show*, an appearance that according to Kim's website briefly made her "the #1 searched person on Google."

Kim is quick and savvy in conversation and she saw *Hits & Mrs.*, her business successes and her arrival as the acknowledged fiancée of the Hit King as "an inspiration to other Korean women that yes you can make it in America." Her parents emigrated from South Korea to California to open a liquor store when she was five, and she has been inspired by their determination and their hard work. Her father's a baseball fan (he "flipped, in a good way, when he found out about me and Pete," Kim says) although his English remains only fair. During a getting-to-know-you lunch that aired on the reality show, Rose pulled out a mobile device and showed her parents—who were allegedly unaware of just how saucy their daughter can get on camera—a photo of Kim posing just about naked. A lot of visible backside and a come-hither look. Her mother's eyes widened and she pointed at Kiana "That's you?" Her father straightened his jacket and cut his eyes but didn't say a word.

Not everyone close to Rose has been thrilled about the love that Pete and Kiana share. When, for an episode of *Hits & Mrs.*, the couple put together an engagement dinner near Kim's home, none of the children from Rose's previous marriages—not Fawn or Pete Jr., his kids with Karolyn, nor Cara and Tyler, his kids with Carol—showed up. (Neither was anyone on hand from Rose's life as a ballplayer. The event felt somewhat depressing on camera although Pete did not seem troubled. "I don't think about who wasn't there," he said.)

"Whatever he wants to do, well that's fine," Pete Jr. had said a few weeks earlier about the Kiana relationship.

In a later episode of *Hits & Mrs.*, Fawn and Cara met Kiana and explained that they hadn't been able to get to the engagement party because Cara had been working late. "If he's not happy we'll kill ya," Fawn joked to Kiana about her father. Afterward Cara took Pete to a tattoo parlor where he got a rendering of the Reds mascot, Mr. Redlegs, on his left shoulder. Cara says she has 16 tattoos herself.

Rose performs some fatherly tasks for Kiana's kids during the show, including chaperoning a coed pool party, warning Cassie to guard against libidinous high school boys and trying to get Ashton to stop playing kill-'em-all video games and take a little BP. (The kid really does not go much for baseball.)

Hits & Mrs.—panned by critics and bumped from its time slot after four episodes—was not nearly so tawdry as the Kardashian shows or *The Real Housewives* series, nor did it have the stealth wholesomeness of its pioneering forefather *The Osbournes*. There were some excruciatingly crude passages in the show, including one in which Pete recaps a sequence of scatological misadventures in such awful detail (he goes so far as to call himself the Shit King) that it engendered a certain wonder: if that is what the show's editors saw fit to include, one could only imagine what horrors were left on the cutting room floor.

Still if you had even a slight interest in Rose, the short-lived *Hits & Mrs.* proved fairly watchable. Pete was engaging, frank and never grim. And of course there was a rich subplot, the theme that has come to define Rose's life: his ban from baseball and exclusion from the Hall of Fame. During the 2012 induction weekend, cameras followed Pete as he took Kiana and the kids to the steps of the Hall of Fame then said he'd wait outside and, with an odd expression apparently meant to approximate wistfulness, watched them walk in. Hokey as a two-dollar bill.

Rose can walk into the Hall of Fame any time he wants, of course, and he is far more knowledgeable than most people as to the content of the exhibits and the roster of inductees. He is often asked his views on potential or recently elected Hall of Famers and he almost always provides a well-reasoned response. Rose was highly supportive of Ron Santo, for example, long before Santo was inducted in 2012. "He has more home runs and a much higher on-base percentage than Brooks Robinson, and Brooks is in," Rose would say, comparing the third-base peers. Rose understands that Hall of Fame voting can be fickle and inexact, and also that it is definitive and singular in its authority—that whatever flaws the process might have, election by vote is the only way for a player to get in.

THE PROCEDURE for election to the Hall of Fame has been clear from the start and the rules remain largely unchanged. The founders' vision was that players chosen for induction "should reflect the feelings of baseball fans in general," as James A. Vlasich writes in his 1990 book *A Legend for the Legendary*. Vlasich drew from the papers of Alexander Cleland, the man who in the '30s conceived of the creation of a museum in Cooperstown to honor baseball's history, and from the writings of Ford Frick, who as president of the National League was enthusiastically involved in shaping the Hall of Fame's purpose. Cleland, Frick and others felt that "the ultimate decision for enshrinement should rest with the Baseball Writers," Vlasich continues. Such a method, they felt, would "allow the average fan some voice in the selection process."

The Baseball Writers' Association of America selected the first class of Ty Cobb, Walter Johnson, Christy Mathewson, Babe Ruth and Honus Wagner in 1936 (three years before the building itself officially opened) and its members have selected every class since. To vote, a writer must have belonged to the BBWAA for 10 years or more. He or she may continue to vote indefinitely, even long after having actively covered the sport, which means that the number of voters has grown over time. For the class of '36, for example, 226 ballots were submitted. These days about 570 ballots come in each year. Each ballot contains space for the names of 10 players, although most voters don't put down that many. In 2013 the average ballot listed 6.6 names.

To merit a place on the ballot a player must have appeared in at least 10 major league seasons and be five years removed from the season in which he played his final game (the wait period was waived only once, and worthily, for Roberto Clemente in 1973 after his death in an airplane crash).[1] A player can stay on the ballot for as many as 15

---

[1] The five-year wait period first went into effect in 1954. At the time that the Yankees' Lou Gehrig was inducted by special election in '39, the same year in which he stopped playing due to the ravages of ALS, all players who were no longer active were eligible for the Hall.

years, provided that he continues to be named by at least 5% of voters.

While some in the game suggest that the pool of voters might either be expanded or refined—it could include television and radio broadcasters, perhaps, or some among the growing breed of researchers who use advanced statistical metrics to dispassionately evaluate player performance—the voting process in fact works quite well. It's very democratic. Because a candidate must be named on 75% of ballots to achieve induction and because the writers, over the whole anyway, know their stuff and because the sample size is large, the voting usually gets it right. Who is and is not enshrined still tends to reflect the feeling of the baseball fan in general.

That does not mean there hasn't been a lot of water-cooler debate. Another reason Cleland and Frick chose this method of induction was their belief that, as Vlasich conveys, it would "start a national controversy over who should be chosen" and thus generate publicity. And each year the clamoring begins anew. Writers, analysts, talk-show hosts and fans avidly parse and parry to determine which players, based on statistics and sometimes other less measurable factors "should" or "should not" be enshrined in Cooperstown. It leads to a lot of huffing and puffing.[2]

One common instigator of complaints by Hall of Fame purists has been the Veterans Committee, an auxiliary voting body charged with inducting umpires, managers and front-office executives, as well as long-retired players who for one reason or another were bypassed by the BBWAA. Since the mid-1940s when the committee[3] elected a raft of old-time players, some

---

[2] I can be guilty of huffing and puffing myself, and continue, for example, to be baffled at the lack of voter support that was given to former Cardinals and Mets first baseman Keith Hernandez, an 11-time Gold Glove winner and the only first baseman of his time or since who could transform a game defensively. (Teams would not bunt against him.) He had an on-base percentage of .384 (about the same as Tony Gwynn's) and an OPS of .821 (better than Rickey Henderson's, better than Johnny Bench's) and . . . well, huff, puff, you see what I mean.

[3] In the '40s it was better known as the Old-Timers Committee, and the group has had other names and various membership structures over the years. Currently it's divided into subgroups: the Expansion Era Committee, the Golden Era Committee and the Pre-Integration Era Committee. For these purposes, Veterans Committee works as a catchall.

with less than immediately obvious credentials, the group has been called to task for "watering down" the cream-of-the-crop standards of the Hall.

In 1946 the Veterans Committee elected Cubs' infielder Joe Tinker, a .262 career hitter with high error totals who achieved his fame by way of his surname's sonic and rhythmic value to the enduring 1910 poem, *Baseball's Sad Lexicon*—"These are the saddest of possible words/'Tinker to Evers to Chance'"—by Franklin Pierce Adams. ("I mean, Tinker didn't even *write* the poem," Bill Francis, the Hall of Fame researcher, says with a smile.) Fifty-five years later, in 2001, the committee elected the Pirates' fine-fielding second baseman Bill Mazeroski, who had a career *on-base percentage* of just .299 (that is stunningly weak; no other Hall of Famer's is so low) and never received even 43% of the BBWAA vote during his time on the regular ballot. There were other controversial choices in between, notably in the 1970s when Frankie Frisch sat on the Veterans Committee and used his influence to push through a handful of his former Cardinals and Giants teammates including underwhelming pitcher Jesse Haines and first baseman George Kelly. Frisch's cronyism led to the committee's powers being reevaluated and since then it has been repeatedly modified and monitored by the Hall's board of directors.

It may be ever so slightly diluted, perhaps, but the plaque gallery in Cooperstown remains extraordinarily exclusive, home to only about 1% of players who have appeared in the major leagues. (In a given season there are about eight future Hall of Famers sprinkled among all 30 big league teams.) A far higher percentage than that receives consideration of course and each ballot includes around 30 names for voters to choose from, often more. That explains why players such as shortstop Royce Clayton (.258 batting average, one All-Star Game in 17 seasons) and righthander Woody Williams (4.19 ERA, one All-Star Game in 15 seasons) appeared on the 2013 ballot. (Neither got a vote.) Such inclusiveness obviates the need for write-in votes which are rarely entered and which, since 1945, have not been officially counted. In fact over the last six decades of Hall of Fame voting no player is known to have ever gotten more than two or three write-in votes in any election. No player, that is, except Pete Rose.

ON THE eve of the induction ceremony each year, Saturday night in Cooperstown, N.Y., the former players ride as conquering heroes down a Main Street thick with onlookers on each side. They sit and wave from the beds of slow-rolling pickups, on each truck a single Hall of Famer dressed in a jacket and tie. Fans jostle gently along the sidewalk and shopkeepers come and stand in their doorways to watch. Ice cream gets sold from outdoor stands and small children perch on their fathers' shoulders. The Parade of Legends, the Hall of Fame calls it, and the pickup trucks, as any of the event's organizers can tell you, are provided by Ford.

The parade runs maybe two-tenths of a mile heading east from near Doubleday Field to the doors of the Hall of Fame itself. Jane Forbes Clark, the chairman of the Hall's board—as well as the most powerful person in Cooperstown—and Jeff Idelson, the Hall's president, ride in the lead truck. They were followed in 2012 by a pickup carrying Tim McCarver and Bob Elliott, media members who shortly before had been honored with lifetime achievement awards. Then came the players themselves, traveling in the order in which they were inducted. It was about 6:30 in the evening and the bronze sun cast its light on each player's face. Here was Whitey Ford, age 83, and Ozzie Smith who'd turned 57, and Robbie Alomar at 44. Some players had their wives beside them.

"Hey Eck, we got to ya in 1990!" a man in a Reds cap bellowed to Dennis Eckersley, whose Oakland A's were beaten by Cincinnati in that World Series. Eckersley smiled, nodded and saluted. "Hang in there, Tony," a woman called to Tony Gwynn, the revered Padre who has battled cancer of the mouth. "We're with you." There were 43 pickups in the procession, the last two of which carried the Santos and then the Larkins, the newest inductees, who throughout the route were engulfed in cheers.

At the parade's end a reception followed inside the Hall of Fame, held for the players and their families and friends, as well as for people connected with the Hall of Fame or with Major League Baseball, along with other guests who had some kind of in. Waiters held trays of champagne and bubbly water, and there was a bar set up at the far end of the plaque gallery. Everyone was very well-dressed. Plates of hors d'oeuvres soon started coming around.

Space was tight—it was awfully crowded—and some of the players looked for ways to find a bit of room. They mingled in the gift shop, they mingled upon the stairs. Bob Gibson and Phil Niekro exchanged greetings on a rampway. Red Schoendienst stood in a corner beside Lou Brock. Nearby someone chatted with the umpire Doug Harvey, whose hair appeared as thick and paper-white as it had been during his final seasons of ordaining pitches as balls or strikes. All the ballplayers still call Harvey God.

An area of the Hall of Fame had been set aside for Larkin and the Santos, so that they could sit and could be easily found by well-wishers hoping to share a few words. Later that night there would be another, separate gathering in Larkin's honor, a private party on Pioneer Street hosted by the Reds.

"You should come," Bob Castellini Jr., a son of Reds CEO Bob Castellini, had said to Pete Rose that afternoon. But Rose declined. "That's a circus we don't need, me being there," he said. "It'll take away from Barry." Anyway, Rose added, he had gotten up early that morning and flown up to Buffalo to sign autographs at a sports card and merchandise store—his appearance there had sold out—then come back to do the afternoon session at Safe At Home. (As long as there is money to be made Rose would work every day if he could.) His all-important bedtime was beckoning. "I might just be goin' upstairs after this," Rose said. Castellini nodded. "O.K., yes. Thanks, Pete."

So Rose didn't go to any of the parties that weekend, but several players he knew well did. That included three men who for many years in the prime of their respective lives spent every day of the baseball season together, and with Rose, making history. Being in Cooperstown provided a chance for another reunion of sorts for Johnny Bench, Joe Morgan and Tony Perez, each a Hall of Famer and each a member of Cincinnati's Big Red Machine.

Chapter 8

Rose in the Machine

T HE TRUE Reds historians, the connoisseurs, say that of all the memorable plays and dramatic sequences that elevated the Big Red Machine, that incomparable team of the 1970s, the single most important play originated not in the batter's box but on the base paths and resulted not in a run being scored but rather in the Reds making an out. For all the crucial playoff home runs hit by Johnny Bench (the ninth-inning clouts against the Pirates, the Mets, the Phillies and the Yanks) and for all the outlandish production provided by Joe Morgan, who over the course of back-to-back MVP seasons reached base an astonishing 45.6% of the time, scored 220 runs, drove in 205, stole 127 bases and, for good measure, won two Gold Gloves at second base—for all of that the play that defined the Reds in the way those ballplayers, and certainly their fans, liked being defined was an aggressive, fundamentally sound, game-turning, straight-on hustling slide into second base in the sixth inning of the deciding game of the 1975 World Series.

"A lot of people agree that Tony Perez's home run in that game was the most important home run in Reds history," says Chris Eckes, the chief curator of the Cincinnati Reds Hall of Fame and Museum. "And Perez would never have gotten the chance to hit that home run if not for Pete Rose breaking up a double play."

It was Oct. 22, 1975, Game 7 against the Red Sox at Fenway Park and one day after Game 6, the classic 12-inning game about which paeans have been sung and books written, as famous a World Series game as any ever played, a game that was tied for Boston by Bernie Carbo's three-run homer with two outs in the eighth inning, then won for Boston by Carlton Fisk's home run in the 12th, a ball that soared toward Fenway's leftfield foul pole—high enough, far enough ... and waved finally and forever fair by Fisk's gyrating body 310 feet away. The inning before, game tied 6–6, Rose had been hit by a pitch and upon arriving at first base said to the Red Sox's Carl Yastrzemski, "This is the greatest game I ever played in!"

Rose said that same thing again and again during Game 6, to whoever on either team would hear it, and even in the postgame clubhouse, where his joy at being involved in those spellbinding 12 innings proved undiminished by the loss. The Reds would simply win the next day, Rose was sure, and wasn't it wonderful that the 1975 season would now provide a Game 7 and one more day to play the sport he loved. "You'd want the World Series to go on for 30 games if it could," he said.

Cincinnati manager Sparky Anderson was somewhat less exuberant in the aftermath of Game Six, and thus unsettled by Rose's glee. "Big Red Machine my ass!" Sparky used to snarl after a loss, glowering at his stable of stars. "We ain't done nothing yet." As far as Sparky was concerned the Reds had let Game 6 and surely the Series slip away. There was nothing "great" about it. In Game 7, when Boston took a 3–0 lead in the third inning and held that lead into the sixth, Sparky kept shuffling uneasily around the dugout, his hands jammed into the pockets of his warmup jacket. He grimaced and looked down and exhaled through puffed cheeks. He took off his cap and ran his fingers through his hair. The Reds could easily lose this deciding game, and then what? Would all of the success, all the fanfare around his team be for naught?

Lose this one and suddenly Sparky's résumé might look, well, a little empty at the top. Four winning seasons in the minors had brought him to the Reds in 1970 at age 36, the youngest manager in the big leagues. Now he was 41, his hair white as foul-line chalk. He presided over one of the great offensive teams in history, a team laden with high-priced players and, through 1975, a team that had won more than 60% of its regular-season games under him. Yet these Reds were still title-less. Cincinnati lost in the World Series in '70 and again in '72, got beaten in the first round by the underdog Mets in '73 and missed the playoffs altogether in '74. Now it was '75 and after going 108–54 in the regular season and sweeping the Pirates in the National League playoffs, the measure of this team had come down to this single Game 7. Lose it and maybe Bob Howsam, the powerful team president newly staked to a contract extension, would see fit to make changes. Maybe Sparky gets let go. Maybe the legacy of the Big Red Machine becomes something different entirely. Five innings complete and the Reds had yet to score a run in the game, and Bill Lee was still sharp on the hill for the Sox. Rose led off the sixth inning with a hard ground ball single through the right side.

YOU COULD say, and you would be right, that Rose wasn't even the best player on the best of those Cincinnati teams. The Greatest Red of All Time—sure, by the mid 1970s Rose had that nailed—but in the peak years Morgan was more dynamic and Bench more powerful and both were far more conspicuous in their athleticism. Truth is, Rose could look kind of dumpy out there.

There was no question however that Rose, Captain Pete, winner of the 1973 National League MVP award, was the team's most indispensable player. Not just for his exceptional consistency—the 200-plus hits, the 110 runs scored, the on-base percentage around .400 year after year af-ter year—but also for his boundlessness, his commitment, his yea-saying way. He goaded and prodded, he heeded every nuance of the game. "He rubs off on you," said Morgan, a borderline All-Star over six full seasons with Houston who became a Hall of Fame player after joining the Reds in '72. Years later Morgan would add this: "Every day I got to have my locker next to Pete Rose and that meant that every day was a good day.

You could not help but feed off the excitement he had, and off the way he approached, or really attacked, every game. He made me better. He made me a much, much better baseball player. If I hit .320 he would be so happy for me. Of course if I hit .320 he wanted to hit .330."

Reds of every age and skill level sought to follow Rose's lead, tried to abide by his work ethic as best they could. (Nobody could truly keep up.) Rose won their loyalty with the way he played and with the things he said. His self-referential chatter to the press, his blurting out that he was hitting .450 for the month so far, or his reminder to everyone that he had yet another 17-game hitting streak going, rarely passed without his also saying something complimentary about a teammate. Something generous and smart. Rose talked about ballplayers in a manner that made others appreciate them: There were not 10 guys in baseball history he would rather have up to bat with the game on the line than Tony Perez, Rose said. And he was happy to drop down in the batting order to make room for a young man who could run as well as Ken Griffey. He praised pitchers Clay Carroll and Don Gullett for their moxie when behind in the count. He lauded utility infielder Denis Menke for his steady glove. One thing he really appreciated about that Oklahoma farm boy Johnny Bench, Rose announced, was that "he moved to Cincinnati year-round, right away." Rose knew Cincinnatians would like that about Bench too, of course, and that they would like that Rose had pointed it out. Most of all, though, what the citizenry liked best about those marvelous Reds teams was Pete Rose's bustling blue-collar style. This was in the mid-1970s and some Cincinnatians were given to boast of the city's heritage as, "the machine tool capital of the world."

If Rose seemed to be in perpetual motion at the ballpark there was, at least, one situation in which he would invariably pause: When a new pitcher came into the game for the opposing team. Rose quieted himself and from the top of the dugout or with one knee on the grass, he watched the pitcher warm up, watched each pitch he threw and all the movements in between. Rose would keep watching intently—absorbing, digesting, plotting—as the pitcher faced his first Reds batter. He stared at the pitcher like Kant at his church steeple, you might say, assuming, that is, that Kant was staring so as to note every chip or toehold and, rather than ruminating upon the vagaries of life, was more pointedly assessing how best to climb the damn thing.

The 1975 World Series came at the end of a season that began like all the others for Rose: swinging the bat. When the Reds batting practice pitchers in spring training begged off after a while, fatigued, Rose would go hit in the cage. After a time his blistered hands would begin to bleed and then, as pitcher Ross Grimsley, a Red from '71 to '73, later remembered, "he would go inside, wrap them up with some tape, and go back out and hit some more. I never saw anyone else do it quite like that."

HE COULD be a son of a bitch to play against, though. Unrelenting. "When you were playing in a game against Pete Rose you knew that you were playing in a game against Pete Rose," is how the former Dodgers first baseman Steve Garvey describes it. Says former Padre Kurt Bevacqua, "Frankly, it could be a pain in the ass."

Rose would take an extra base on you if you ever let up. He'd kick the baseball from your glove if he got the chance. He would yell at pitchers from the batter's box (to the feather-tossing Randy Jones: "Whyn't you go warm up and then come back and throw a real pitch") and after making an out he would cross in front of the mound screaming: "You've got nothin'! Nothin'!" Could have been a rookie out there pitching or Tom Seaver or Moses himself. "You got nothin'!" Rose would scream. He had nine uniforms at the start of the season and by June they'd all been stitched.

To his edge Pete brought a grin rather than a snarl. Thing was, if you were a baseball player, no matter who you played for, you were pretty much O.K. by him. He took an interest in you, knew not just your batting average but also how many doubles you had, and whether things were going well lately, hitting-wise. He'd tell you to keep your head up if you were slumping and if he had ever met your kid at the ballpark, he would ask about him later. He watched young players and gave them advice. Just as he did with Bud Harrelson when the shortstop stuck with the Mets in '67. Pete came over and introduced himself, said he knew

Harrelson could really pick it out there, but that maybe he should think about working with a slightly smaller glove, that it would help him get rid of the ball quicker. There was an intimacy to the suggestion, and it made sense, and Harrelson never forgot it.

The unshakable part of Rose was that he would angle to win in any way he could, even if the Reds were losing 9–2. That was the score in the third game of the National League playoffs against the Mets, Shea Stadium, 1973. Cincinnati had taken the opener at home when Rose's home run off Seaver in the eighth tied the game 1–1, and Bench then hit one to win it in the ninth. The next day New York's Jon Matlack shut the Reds down 5–0, and afterward Harrelson—a guy who hit about .235 most years—cracked to reporters that against Matlack the mighty Reds had "looked like *me* hitting."

"Pete didn't like that," Morgan said to Harrelson on the field before Game 3 at Shea. "He's going to use it to fire up the team."

Fifth inning, Game 3, and the Reds were down by that 9–2 score to lefthander Jerry Koosman. For the Mets, Rusty Staub had hit one home run and then another and when he came up the third time Dave Tomlin, the Reds lefty, threw inside at him, just missed. "Then I flew out," Staub recalls, "and afterward I went straight to Koosman and said, 'Don't hit anybody, don't do it. We're up big in this game. Don't wake them up.' But Koozy is Koozy, so the next inning he went after Pete. Didn't hit him, just sent back a message with a close pitch."

Rose did not much like being thrown at—"He doesn't walk a guy all night but he's in tight on me?" he groused—so he glared at Koosman and singled to centerfield. Now he was on first base with one out in the fifth, hating the score of the game, when Morgan hit a ground ball to John Milner at first base. Milner threw to Harrelson for one out and Harrelson threw back to Milner for another, and while the ball was in the air Rose came hard into second base, clipping Harrelson's right leg and bowling him over. When Rose popped up he got his elbow higher than he needed to and into Harrelson's cheek. Though the momentum from the play drove the two players several feet apart, Harrelson turned and cursed at Rose and Rose, the heavier of the two by more than 40 pounds, came back at him with an angry push, neck high. Harrelson grappled back and then, says Harrelson, "he just kind of lifted me up and laid me down to sleep."

Suddenly they were down on the infield dirt rolling around "in this crazy cloud of dust" as Staub says. Players from both teams rushed out and joined the brawl. Everyone was out there, flailing and grabbing and yelling, the scene teetering on madness or perhaps already there. This was the event during which the Reds' screw-loose pitcher Pedro Borbon took a bite—an actual, visible bite—out of the Mets cap belonging to Buzz Capra.

Mets fans, even with their team up handily on the favored Reds, were now in a heightened and ugly mood, and when the brawl had sub-sided and the Reds players came out to their positions, those fans threw things at Rose out in leftfield—eggs, apples, rubber balls, a lightbulb. Why the people had some of these items at the ballpark anyway was a puzzle. Then a full beer can sailed onto the field and a whiskey bottle landed too close. Pete started jogging in toward the dugout and Sparky stepped forward and waved his whole nine off the field. "You know," Sparky said later, "Rose has given too much to the game for him to die in leftfield at Shea Stadium."

To get the game started again the Mets had to send out a committee led by baseball royalty—Willie Mays, Yogi Berra and Seaver, with Staub and outfielder Cleon Jones as well—to tell the fans out there: "Look at the scoreboard will you? Keep this up and we'll have to forfeit."

Later on after the game (the 9–2 score held up) the players talked about why and how the fight happened. Harrelson started off saying, "I like the way Rose plays, just not the way he came into second base." Then he suggested that he himself may have overreacted a bit. Harrelson allowed that had been a little spooked out there to begin with in light of the collisions he'd had already that season—one, with Cincinnati's Bill Plummer, broke a bone in Harrelson's hand; another, with Pittsburgh's Rennie Stennett, fractured Harrelson's breastbone. "I've had trouble at second base, and that added to the situation," he said.

Rose, though, maintained defiantly that he had done nothing wrong, that he had not been targeting Harrelson nor trying to rouse his struggling team for the rest of the series. He had not come in late, he insisted, and he had just bounced up from his slide as usual and, what's more, he had not appreciated being cursed at. "I'm not a dirty player," Rose said. "If I were dirty I would have leveled him."

At the next game, after Harrelson had arrived at Shea Stadium wearing a Superman shirt with the "S" insignia x-ed out, and players on both teams had laughed off the suggestion by M. Donald Grant, a minority owner of the Mets, that Rose and Harrelson shake hands in a public truce at home plate, the bleachers were full of signs: ROSES DIE, BUDS BLOOM, along with less poetic messages. Boos and rancor followed Rose each time he came to the plate in the tense Game 4, a game knotted at 1–1 into the 12th inning when Rose stepped in with one out and no one on base. He fouled a few off and let a couple of balls go by and then, on the sixth pitch from the righthander Harry Parker, Rose pulled one into a soaring arc over the rightfield fence. Home run.

He circled the bases pumping his fist high, and now the boos were mixed with moans, a strange elephantine sound coming from the stands at Shea. The Reds won by that 2–1 score. After a regular season in which he hit all of five home runs, Rose now had two in four playoff games, each one keeping the Reds alive. Not that that was enough. "I would have given a week's salary to go 4 for 4 in the game today," Rose said, meaning as a way to fire back at the New York crowd.

The battle with Harrelson was to many an almost vaudevillian blip. Rose and Harrelson cracked jokes about it in the off-season. Playing a tennis exhibition against Bobby Riggs in Dayton a few months after the game, Rose was chased around the court by a woman in a raincoat (actually Riggs himself) wielding an umbrella and introduced as "Bud Harrelson's mama." Years later in retirement, during one of the card shows they did together, Rose signed a photo of the fight to Harrelson, "Bud, Thanks for making me famous, Pete Rose #4256."

Neither did the New York baseball writers hold a grudge on their home team's behalf. In early 1974 the writers brought in Rose for a dinner and bestowed upon him their annual "Good Guy Award," not in irony but in recognition of how accommodating he could be to them (whatever the score of the game) and handing him as a gift a gold Swiss-made clock with his name engraved on the front. The clock would sit upon Rose's mantle back home.

The Harrelson rhubarb heightened the perception of Rose yet another level—adored or despised but never ignored. Many opposing fans viewed the brawl as further proof of Rose's excessiveness. They threw things at him again in 1974: golf balls in San Francisco, vegetables in L.A. The Giants' fans said they were just having harmless fun (and had missed him on purpose). They loved Rose really, they said. The Dodgers' fans claimed they were peeved because Rose had flipped them off from the outfield. Pete, all guiltlessness once again, said that no, he was just reminding George Foster in centerfield that there was one out in the inning and that raising his middle finger "is how I always do it." (Pete loved to flip the bird, casually or with a little emphasis—a half grin, teeth out on his a lower lip: "Screw you and up yours" at once, delivered, invariably, with a liveliness in his eyes.)

For the team from Cincinnati, the fact that people would throw things onto the baseball field like that just didn't make sense. "It makes me ashamed that I belong to this country," Sparky had said starchily in the aftermath of the Mets' fans' deluge. "[I can't] imagine a thing like this happening in the United States of America." The Reds were all clean-shaven and wore their socks the same height. If a player slouched too much in the dugout there was a chance the phone would ring and it would be Bob Howsam, or someone calling on Howsam's behalf, telling the player to show some respect and sit up straight.

There were those in that summer of 1974 who wondered whether maybe this kind of unrest at baseball stadiums wasn't so strange after all. How maybe with the way things had been going lately in America, the Vietnam riots still near to mind and the kidnapped heiress Patty Hearst wielding a carbine on behalf of the raging, down-with-capitalism Symbionese Liberation Army, and the way the Presidency itself was falling apart in the grip of Watergate, and the rise too of pornographic films into the mainstream, maybe all this explained why there was something like a loss of civility and why baseball fans in San Francisco or Los

Angeles thought it was O.K. (partly in jest, partly in genuine distaste) to call out loud enough that not only the player himself but also the children in the stands could hear, "Rose, Rose, fuck Rose."

Not that any of it changed the way that he played. Riling the opposition was part of the self-imposed assignment. A man had a constitutional right to boo all he wants at a ball game, and Rose would be the first to say that. Anyway, said Bench, "As we see it Pete has never been booed. For a player, you haven't been booed unless you've been booed at home. And that was just not happening to Pete Rose."

AND SO: 1975, World Series Game 7, Red Sox with that 3–0 lead, sixth inning and one out now, Rose still on first base. Bench up against Bill Lee. Eleven more Reds outs and Boston wins it all.

Just don't hit a ground ball Johnny, Rose thought, taking his lead. *Not a ground ball.*

Rose knew the possibility was high; Lee induced ground balls for a living and a strong righthanded pull hitter like Bench could be especially vulnerable. Lee's fastball had a natural sink to it, tailing to the left, and Boston had already turned two double plays in the game. *Not this time though*, Rose thought. *Not now.* "There are some things that you just can't allow to happen," Rose would later say, "and a double play at that point was one of them."

If you were to draw a textbook diagram of a double play, or to set it up on an instructional field to teach young men the basics of how to turn it—make sure that they get down the classic, sure-thing 6-4-3 double play first—it would look like this: A ground ball hit hard but not too hard, arriving on a big, true hop to the shortstop's glove side, just the way the ground ball that Bench did in fact hit off Lee reached Boston's Rick Burleson. He fielded the ball at about shoulder height, maybe eight feet from the second base bag. Then Burleson tossed it underhand ("a nice easy flip" as the TV broadcaster described it) to Denny Doyle at second. Doyle was then in his sixth season as a highly dependable infielder known for this very thing—for being a reliable and fluid middle-man on the double play. Doyle caught the ball chest high, put his left foot on the bag and turned to make his throw to first base, knowing there was no need to rush. A good throw to Yastrzemski at first base gets Bench by four strides and the Red Sox go into the dugout with a 3–0 lead and three innings to play. Denny Doyle turns this play 19 times in 20, maybe more.

Only here at this moment came Rose, thicker still than he'd been when he collided with Fosse or Harrelson, charging into second base and already much nearer the bag than Doyle (or anyone) would have expected. Rose went into a hard slide, feetfirst, disrupting Doyle who hopped up to safety just as he let the ball go. The throw sailed high over Yastrzemski's head and into the Boston dugout. The inning was still alive and Bench went to second base. Then Perez stepped in and hit Lee's second pitch, a blooperball, half the way to Kathmandu.

The Boston lead was just 3–2 now and the Reds, roused in the following innings by Rose's exhortations from third base or in the dugout, would win the game 4–3 and with it the World Series. Rose singled in the tying run in the seventh and walked ahead of Morgan's game-winning hit in the ninth and wound up hitting .370 over the seven games—yet those Reds cognoscenti will never forget that it was a first-to-second base hustle-and-slide on a routine ground ball, a simple effort play that anyone could push to make but few do, which made the difference. Rose was named MVP of the Reds first Series win in 35 years. "This is the happiest moment of my life," he said amid the locker room spray. His voice was hoarse from all the yelling he'd done on the field.

Rose's slide into Doyle was cited when Rose was named *Sports Illustrated*'s 1975 Sportsman of the Year, as was the central event of the Reds '75 season: Rose's immediate willingness in early May to switch positions from leftfield, where he had been a two-time All-Star and an MVP, to third base in order to get the power-hitting outfielder George Foster into the lineup. Sparky asked Rose to do it and Rose, who had not played the infield for nine years and had hardly played third base ever at all, said, "When do you want me to start?" In the very next game there he was, having paused only to slip on a protective cup: Pete Rose, third baseman. The move seemed so implausible (Bob Howsam, away from the team, thought the out-of-town box score in his morning paper was a mistake) that it did not easily sink in around the league. "What are you doing over here?" the Phillies' Greg Luzinski asked Rose in surprise when the Reds played in Philadelphia 10 days later.

The way that Rose embraced the switch—coming out early each day to practice at his new position, not complaining, not letting the move affect him at the plate—was a fine example, baseball men agreed, of how a good teammate should be. The Reds were at .500 when Rose made the move; after that they won 96 games and lost only 42, with Foster knocking in 78 runs in 134 games. The next spring Rose received the Roberto Clemente Award given annually to the player who, in part, best exemplifies the spirit of sportsmanship.

Rose was still at third base in 1976 when Cincinnati reached the World Series again—this time against the Yankees. The Yanks offense started at the top with their most consistent hitter and fastest runner, Mickey Rivers. Anderson reminded Rose before the Series of the obvious, that he needed to play in close when Rivers came up, discourage the bunt, but Rose was way ahead of him. In the first Yankee at bat of Game 1, Rose stood so near to Rivers, a lefthanded batter who might have slashed a hard line drive down the third base line, that some Reds in the dugout couldn't bear to watch for fear that Rose might get maimed on the spot. ("He could have shaken Rivers's hand out there!" said Sparky.) Rose looked daggers in at Rivers and called out to him as he stepped into the box and Rivers did not like what Rose was doing. He did not bunt in that first at bat and he did not hit. He struck out. Normally a serene and easygoing player,[1] Rivers did not appear at all at ease against the Reds. He went 0 for 4 in the first game and over the course of the Reds' four-game sweep—Pete bearing in on him all the while—Rivers hit .167. "You can thank Rose for that," said Sparky.

---

[1] Rivers's life philosophy is perhaps the most valuable ever suggested by a major leaguer. "I don't worry about things that I have no control over because I have no control over them," Rivers has said. "And I don't worry about things that I have control over because I have control over them."

IN THE off-season, Rose gave rousing speeches to groups across Ohio, bringing in $2,000 a pop. He was the very model of a modern Cincinnatian—beaming, bustling, bareknuckled—and his work ethic resonated far from the diamond. That's why he was so coveted as a speaker. "Whatever business you were in you could point to Pete and tell your people, 'That is the way to do it. That is the kind of effort to give,' " says Bob Crotty, who was a vice president at the very successful uniform rental company Van Dyne Crotty. "Pete translated to any kind of business." The Cincinnati mayors—Sterne, Luken, Springer—all at one time or another said similar things about Pete and the model he served and how inspiring he could be.

Rose prospered and knew what he liked. Through the mid 1970s he and Karolyn drove fancy cars: a new and limited ink-black version of a 1934 Model A Ford with the license plate 14-PR; a Porsche; a Maserati; a Lincoln Mark IV; a Rolls-Royce with the license plate PETE. You better believe Karolyn drove that Rolls over to Kmart or McDonald's or to pick up the kids from school. You put a West Side girl in a car like that and she wants to be seen. Karolyn got herself a sports talk show on Cincinnati radio for a while and being on air did little to curb the mouth or the flair. When Muhammad Ali called in as a guest she referred to him as Cassius Clay. (He sighed and scolded—he knew Pete and Karolyn a little bit—but did not hang up.) Another day she said the local hockey team's game would start at "puck-off time." She spoke bluntly and crudely and though there was far more style than substance in what she did, Karolyn described her radio persona like this: "Howard Cosell. Woman."

Pete was all over the airwaves, too. He did ads with a perky blonde for a hair spray, Vitalis Dry Control, which made sense: a national hairdressers' association had named Rose's Prince Valiant 'do one of the 10 best heads of hair in America. He appeared in ads for Jockey underwear and Swanson pizza and in another series of spots Pete held up a blue bottle of cheap aftershave and reminded people, in song sometimes, that there was something about an Aqua Velva man. Rose was recruited by the commissioner's office to do a public service spot for baseball. "Hi, I'm

Pete Rose," he began, and over a clip of him rounding third and diving into home he talked about his love for baseball and the game's appeal as a family attraction and then the camera cut to images of Karolyn, Fawn and little Petey cheering in the stands.

Petey was a conspicuous part of the ballpark scene then, and had been as soon as he could walk. "Me and Daddy won MVP," Petey, then four years old, said parading around in his Reds jersey after Rose got the award in 1973. The kid was given to razzing batting practice pitchers for their lack of control and Rose, in his clubhouse locker, kept in a peach basket Petey's miniature spikes and tiny shower shoes.

Fawn tended more toward another of her dad's passions—horses (she didn't bet them, she rode them), and she wished her father could watch her ride more often. "Why can't my dad have a summer vacation like other dads do?" she asked Sparky Anderson. "Because I need him," the manager replied. Sometimes the kids went to Pete Rose's Restaurant over on Westbourne Drive. The place was always busy. You could get a nice stack of pancakes for a decent price and the waitresses wore jerseys with the number 14 on the back.

Reds games were an event in those years—in '75 the team won 64 and lost just 17 at home. That's 64 and 17. Before, during and after games fans packed into Sleep Out Louie's on West Second Street, the hottest singles bar in town. Huge. Brick walls, cement floor. Live music most nights. Cowboy hats. A bartender might serve 5,000 drinks a night in that place, and the jocks were always showing up, some of the Reds and hockey players from the new WHA team, the Stingers. You could get in through the side entrance if you had a special pass or else you waited out front in a long line. "We get a lot of secretaries and attractive women here and they draw the men," the manager explained.

Because this was Pete Rose's town most everyone at a place like Sleep Out Louie's knew who Dave Rose was, too. He never minded stopping in for a few. One night a couple of those pro hockey players started baiting Dave, saying stuff about how he didn't measure up to his big brother Pete. That was the wrong thing to do. "I was coming down Second Street," says Jim Luebbert, the old West Side friend of the Roses, "and saw this big crowd standing in front of the place and cops coming up—a real commotion. I said to myself, 'Shit, I hope Dave hasn't gotten into anything.' " Turns out he had. Dave's response to the baiting was to beat the living hell out of those guys. Both of them. No hockey players ever had any tough talk for Dave after that.

Pete went to Sleep Out Louie's more as a day shift guy, to get a bowl of chili with someone from an ad agency, maybe. Then he started coming by for orange juice early, 10:45 a.m., in order to inspect the rounded bottom (it had been highly recommended to him) of a certain new waitress, Carol Woliung. It never seemed to bother him that he might have been home with Karolyn and the kids at 10:45 in the morning rather than in a beer-slick barroom setting his sights on a woman a little better than half his age. (Rose at least proved committed in his efforts, given that years later Carol would become the second Mrs. Rose.)

There was plenty of money in those years and Pete still loved to gamble of course: off days at the local track—horses, dogs, either way—big bets on the Derby.[2] And football, too. Pete may have been the only ballplayer who was actually pleased that Game 2 of the 1976 World Series got scheduled for Sunday night rather than as a day game. A little autumn cold he didn't mind—"I'd play in the snow," he said—and the nighttime start, he reasoned, gave him more time to monitor the NFL games being played during the afternoon.

Rose had led the Reds to two of the four championships in their history, or you might say two of the three, as one of the World Series wins had been a gift from the favored White Sox who lay down in the game-fixing scandal of 1919. With Pete and the Big Red Machine, Cincinnati was on top fair and square. After the '74 season Rose had mentioned to a reporter in passing that with 2,337 base hits after 12 seasons he was ahead of Ty Cobb's pace. But don't get any ideas, he added with his grin. Anybody ever actually reaching Cobb's total was "impossible."

---

[2] A breeder over at Keeneland in Kentucky paid homage by naming one of his thoroughbreds "Pete Rose." The two-legged Pete received a pair of horseshoes as a gift when the horse was retired to stud.

So even if there had been a little back and forth between Rose and the team about his salary over the years—Pete seeing his value rise and the Reds, with Bench and Morgan also to be paid, having limits on their spending—there did not seem much ominous about it. If there was one thing that a Cincinnati baseball fan knew in his heart, it was that Pete Rose would never leave.

Chapter 9

Raising Philadelphia

I T DOESN'T much matter to the romance or even the authenticity of the place that Cooperstown was not where baseball was first played, or that General Abner Doubleday was not the first to play it. It might just as well be true. The baseball narrative, like so many others, of our country and of ourselves, is embroidered from countless yarns, myth and embellishment weaving seamlessly with fact. In 1939 in Cooperstown, as the Hall of Fame opened on the (supposed) 100th anniversary of when young Abner (allegedly) first noodled out the parameters of the game, 44-year-old Babe Ruth, fresh from a local barber's shave, really did step into the batter's box at Doubleday Field, where a cow pasture had once been. Two years later Bob Feller, 22 years old—and with a curveball he could bend 'round a maypole, they said—pitched from the mound on the very same diamond. Ted Williams swung here and Stan Musial and Willie Mays. And each year new Hall of Fame inductees come and tread on the infield and see the trees encroaching upon the grandstands and the narrow church spire rising up past the leftfield line. So Cooperstown serves as a worthy mecca where grown men wear baseball uniforms in the street, even if the game was not, in fact, first played on these meadows, even though the rules were most assuredly not devised by a local little Abner who had grown up to be a West Point man.

Maybe—and sure, yes, why not?—Myles Standish put his knee-high boot on Plymouth Rock, and young George Washington threw a silver dollar from one bank of the Potomac to another, and old John Henry died with a hammer in his hands, and Davy Crockett wrestled a bear. Maybe—why not?—Ruth raised his right arm and pointed out to center-field during a World Series game in Chicago, then hit a home run right to where he called it. And, sure, Cool Papa Bell was so fast he could flip the light switch by the bedroom door and be beneath the sheets before the room went dark. And, yes, Mickey Mantle once hit the ball 565 feet.

The stories stir and please us and speak to admirable virtues— perseverance, strength, daring, skill—and so we want them to be true, or true enough. When it comes to Pete Rose, a player about whom tales have been told, a player given to self-aggrandizement to be sure, a player who himself represented an ethic that a citizen might admire, one might expect the famous baseball stories of his life to be embroidered thick with myth as well. Except that in the case of this particular ballplayer in this docu-mented time, the legends, the best and the worst of them, are true. You can ask the people who were there when they happened. You can look them up.

The Phillies had not won a championship in the 76 years of the World Series and now here it was October of 1980, not quite 20 months since Rose had pulled on a Philadelphia uniform for the first time, and the team was playing Game 6 against the Royals. The Phillies, ahead three games to two, had a 4–1 lead with one out in the top of the ninth inning, right on the verge of winning it all. But the bases were loaded for Kansas City, and Frank White, a pesky little hitter, was at the plate. Philadel-phia closer Tug McGraw had walked one guy and given up two singles in the inning and stomachs were now as pretzels in the Veterans Stadium stands. Every Phillies fan knew well that seeming success could in a single moment unravel. Rose was 39 years old and playing first base.

The pop-up that White hit on the first pitch from McGraw shot high and foul toward the first base dugout. Phillies catcher Bob Boone, already a two-time Gold Glove winner and on his way to five more, ran toward the ball's landing spot, as did Rose. Boone arrived first. The crowd was very loud and the ball was descending from a great height. Boone had his glove turned slightly the wrong way and he reached a bit when he went for the ball, fearing, he later said, that he might collide with Rose. And though the baseball landed smack in the pocket of Boone's glove, it popped out, that crucial out surely and portentously lost if not for the fact that Rose was right there glued to the play. When the ball came free Rose lunged and gloved it in midair—out!—then turned and charged toward the diamond, to keep the runners where they were. Then Rose spiked the ball into the turf, gleeful, caught it on the hop, tossed it underhand to McGraw, flashed the two-out sign, clapped his hand and glove together, and ran over to pick up his fallen cap.

"After that play," says Phillies pitcher Larry Christenson, "we knew we had it." McGraw struck out the next batter, Willie Wilson, and Philadelphia won its first World Series.

"Who does that?" Phillies third basemen Mike Schmidt would say of Rose's catch, three decades later. "I mean who does that? You can say that that is where a first baseman is supposed to be on that play, that's what he's supposed to do, that you're supposed to keep alert to the baseball and not turn away. But that ball was caught, in the catcher's glove, and then it wasn't. Really who does that? I played 20 years of professional baseball. I played with a lot of first baseman, and some very good first basemen and Pete is the only one of them who makes that play."

HE HAD come to the Phillies after starring in a free-agent circus unlike any ever seen. Rose was leaving the Reds. Tony Perez had been traded in '76 and after back-to-back second-place finishes behind the rival Dodgers the Reds general manager Dick Wagner had also let Sparky Anderson go. The Big Red Machine was being dismantled and there was, naturally, an enormous amount of public hand-wringing over Rose's fate.[1] But the way Wagner figured it, Reds attendance would hold steady even without Rose

---

[1] After the Reds allowed Rose to get away bumper stickers appeared around Cincinnati: "For Pete's Sake Boycott Opening Day."

so long as the Reds fielded a winner. The way Pete figured it, he could make some serious cake out there in the open market. Before becoming a free agent Rose had said that Cincinnati only had to offer him $450,000 a year for four years for him to stay, but that was before he got a whiff of what was really in the offing and by the time the Reds offered $475,000 it was too late. Rose was in line to make much, much more than that and also to show that his brand of baseball traveled beyond his home city, that he could be a winner somewhere else.

Rose may have been at an age when many players go year-to-year (if they're still going at all), but instead he seemed to be comfortably atop his crest. As his free agency began, he was coming off a 1978 season in which he'd led the league in plate appearances for the third straight year, smacked a league-best 51 doubles, hit above .300 for the 13th time in 14 seasons and reeled off a nation-stirring hit streak of 44 consecutive games. The streak was an improbable feat for any player—no one had even gotten to 38 straight since Joe DiMaggio's 56 in 1941—but almost unfathomable for a 37-year-old. He bolted around the base paths all streak long and grinned to the cameras and quipped pricelessly and got himself a hit every single day, embracing the feat and embracing the game just as the game and the crowds embraced him.[2] Rose was showing the first strands of gray at his temples but each day he played like the youngest and most driven player on either team. Still, now, same as he ever was. He often reminded people that his father kept on playing semi-pro football past the age of 42.[3]

---

[2] The time and tenor of Rose's streak is covered in detail in the chapter on Rose in the book, *56: Joe DiMaggio and the Last Magic Number in Sports* by Kostya Kennedy.

[3] Rose had also in 1978 stroked his 3,000th career hit, a single against Montreal on May 5. As he stood at first base, his name went on the scoreboard as the latest member of the 3,000 hit club, joining a group of baseball saints, and sinners. The names of unstained icons glittered on the scoreboard—Hank Aaron, Stan Musial, Roberto Clemente—and there were also Ty Cobb and Tris Speaker (both implicated, though cleared, for betting on baseball), and Willie Mays (banned from baseball in the 1970s for working for a casino), as well as Cap Anson (who played in the late 1800s as a chest-beating racist, intolerant and vicious even by the often ignoble standards of his time). All told, that 3,000-hit club—now, with Rose, 13 players deep—represented an odd kind of baseball melting pot.

"I know my face looks old," he said, tossing the line out to potential suitors as the bidding began. "But if you'd slid headfirst for 16 years you'd be ugly too."

Ted Turner, the Braves owner, offered to sign Pete for a million dollars a year for "three years, four years, five years, whatever you want." Turner had seen 45,000 fans come out to Atlanta-Fulton County Stadium the night that Rose ran his hitting streak to 44; and he had heard the crowd chanting "Pete, Pete, Pete," the next night when the streak was stopped; and he had seen Rose go 4 for 5 with a home run in the same stadium on the night after that. Turner was ready to guarantee a scout's job for Pete's brother Dave as well.

In Kansas City, Royals owner Ewing Kauffman offered Rose (as lagniappe to a fat multiyear contract) a stake in a pharmaceutical company. The Cardinals' presentation included the rights to a beer distributorship. Pirates owner John Galbreath was a thoroughbred guy (he'd had two horses win the Derby) and as part of a Pittsburgh package he said he would throw in a couple of broodmares—and schedule some stud sessions with his top stallions—so that Rose could get into the racing game. ("Very interesting," said Rose of Galbreath's suggestion. "I thought you had to be King Farouk or somebody to get into the breeding part of it.") The Mets made a respectable offer too.

Rose flew with his agent on a Lear jet going from city to city, and everywhere the TV stations and the news stories followed each visit and every twist along what was fast becoming a grand and beguiling tour.

Bill Giles, the Phillies' executive vice president then, saw all of this and judged the stakes. He knew that he wanted to get Rose to Philadelphia more than he wanted anything else in baseball. "When we played them in the 1976 playoffs, Rose just intimidated us from the start," says Giles. "There was a sense that the guy on the other team wanted it more than we did and I didn't like that. When you see a guy hit a clean single and turn it into a double that can be intimidating to a team. It had that effect on us."

Rose batted .429 in the Reds' three-game playoff sweep of Philadelphia in '76 but he had gotten into the Phillies craw even earlier, during a late-August series at Riverfront. In one game Rose did indeed single to center and, noticing centerfielder Garry Maddox taking too wide an angle on the ball, continued hard into second base, safe on a headfirst slide. Two nights later, with the Reds trailing 4–3 in the ninth, Rose lit out on a passed ball and scored the tying run—from second base. Four innings later he beat out the back end of a double play to help secure the extra-inning win. "I felt if we could get Rose it would change everything on this club," said Giles. "I believed in him in a way I have not believed in any other player. Some of that, I know, came from my dad."

When Warren Giles, Bill's father, was National League president through the 1950s and '60s, he'd lived in Cincinnati (he'd been G.M. of the Reds before taking over at the league) and he came out often to see the home team. Warren knew about the gambling stories, the talk about Rose and the bookmakers, but it did not diminish his appreciation for the way that Rose went about things on the ballfield. He impressed this point on Bill. Once near the late stages of Warren's life—he would die of cancer in February of 1979, three months after Bill made Rose a Phillie—Bill asked his father, for posterity really, who was the greatest player he had ever seen. "I expected him to say Willie Mays or Stan Musial or Joe DiMaggio," says Bill. "But he just looked at me, he was kind of weaker then, and said, 'Pete Rose—for his determination.'"

Still, when Pete came into Philadelphia at the height of the free-agent chase, Giles could not get Phillies owner Ruly Carpenter to move above $600,000 a year. Against the other offers out there that was not going to do it. Rose's visit to Philadelphia was done. He was going home. "They asked us to pay for the chartered jet back but we thought that was too much," says Giles. "So I drove him and his agent, Reuven Katz, to the airport. I was wooing him like you would woo a woman. I gave him flowers for his wife and Phillie Phanatic dolls for his kids. I took out the National League record book and reminded Pete how close he was to all these league records, as a way to try to knock Kansas City out of there. I said, 'And in Kansas City they might use you at DH.' I knew he would never have wanted that. Then I asked Reuven Katz if I could have just a little more time, and that night I had the idea."

Giles went to executives at the TV station that aired the Phillies games,

WPHL, and asked them to help with the contract. This was an entirely novel suggestion; Giles was asking for an extra $200,000 a year to be added to the rights fee. The station manager asked around of the clients and found that sure enough WPHL would be able to charge advertisers more—a lot more—with Rose in the fold. This was partly because of the understanding that a Philadelphia team with Rose on it would attract more viewers than a team without him. But it was also about companies wanting to be part of something, that is, part of bringing Rose to Philadelphia. "Some things transcend numbers," WPHL's general manager, Gene McCurdy, explained. "And the value of Pete Rose to certain local advertisers is something more significant than numbers."

So the station pledged the extra money and the Phillies offered a contract that would come to more than $3.2 million over four years. It still was not Ted Turner's offer but Rose thought about it some: He had a ball-park friendship with some of the guys on the team—Schmidt, Larry Bowa, Maddox, Luzinski—and he liked the team colors, red and white. The Phillies, a one-round-and-out playoff team three years running, had a chance to win it all, Rose thought, if someone could show their stars how to loosen up and play harder at the same time. When he signed that contract with the Phillies, Rose became the highest paid athlete in team sports.

———————

PHILLIES TICKET sales spiked after the Rose signing in early December, close to $2.5 million in added revenue by mid-January and still more after that. Rose had practically paid for his entire four-year contract before he swung a bat in spring training. Financially this may have been the best player acquisition the Phillies have ever made. Rose showed up to his first workout in Florida having flown in on the redeye from Las Vegas—he'd been booked for a speaking engagement there (his fee was up to $7,000) and Vegas was never a place he minded visiting. Hundreds of fans turned out to greet him in Clearwater, hollering and calling his name as he burst onto the field. Manager Danny Ozark was left a little slack-jawed, "Where'd they all come from?" he asked. The fans followed Rose all spring, watched him taking all that batting practice, saw him out early pushing gamely and finally smoothly through his first base drills (yes, the old dog was learning yet another new position, his fifth). They strung banners on the chain link fences around the spring training fields. When the Phillies drove over to play in another Florida town, a caravan followed. By this point, as more than one observer put it then, Rose had become, "an American folk hero."

There had been another reason that Wagner and the Reds had drawn a hard line in the Rose negotiations, a reason beyond the club's thought that $475,000 was a hell of a lot of money. There was a feeling among some in the front office that Rose's unsavory side might not sit so well with fans in the heartland. Wagner, suspicious about Rose's gambling habit, reportedly groused to other Reds executives that Rose's "legs may get broken" if the betting got out of hand—but that wasn't the real worry. One of Rose's extramarital affairs had gone too far and he was facing a potential paternity suit, one that would be officially brought forward in February of 1979 by a Florida woman named Terry Rubio. Her daughter had been born in '78 and named, in what rang as an odd homage to Pete's sidekick in the Cincinnati infield, Morgan. Pete had gone around with Rubio for quite a while, including during her pregnancy. He had given her a car. The paternity suit was fodder, briefly, for national TV; eventually, Rose and Rubio settled out of court.[4]

Pete's marriage to Karolyn was nearing its end. She and the kids began their 1979 season living in Philadelphia—Karolyn was hollering in the stands at the home opener as Pete got three hits in a Phillies win—but were back living in Cincinnati by the end of it. The main reason was that Pete continued to see Carol Woliung, who was soon to find work as a Liberty Belle cheerleader with the Eagles. As the relationship with Pete unraveled, Karolyn made it publicly clear (leavening her story with what-the-heck humor) that Rose had been stepping out on the marriage for years, a fact that those around the game well knew. Pete was brazen. At Riverfront Stadium he had reserved seats not just for Karolyn and the

---

[4] Close to two decades later, in 1996, Morgan Rubio filed her own suit against Rose, seeking that he officially acknowledge her as his daughter, which he did.

kids (and for his sisters Caryl and Jackie, and for Dave when he was in town) but also had a single seat along the third base line set aside each night for his girlfriend. Old West Side buddies of Pete's used to tweak him by getting to the Reds game early, sitting in the girlfriend seat, and, for the longest time, refusing to move.

1979 was also the year of the Pete Rose *Playboy* interview, a long and wide-ranging exploration published in late summer, that became a noisemaker around baseball and an instant classic of its form. If the magazine's pair of interviewers (Maury Z. Levy and Samantha Stevenson) were at times smug in their questioning—haughty, even, when set against Pete's defiance and straight-shooting cockiness—they were also challenging and persistent. The interview took place in several locations over several weeks and ran, with its introduction, at close to 14,000 words. "I don't talk good but you understand everything I'm saying," Rose observed about halfway through. This was and remains a marvelously entertaining thing to read.

Pete rambled, and just kept being Pete. He nipped at Dick Wagner and the Reds for the failed contract negotiations, saying that maybe the G.M. didn't like "the flamboyant style I have off the field." He talked about his $8,000 wristwatch and his Rolls-Royce, and all the money that he made. "I don't give a shit what people think," he replied when *Playboy* suggested his big salary rankled some fans. He pointed out that he got just as dirty on the ball field earning $800,000 a year as he did when he was nine years old. He revealed some intimate details, for example that he liked women with pretty mouths but that during lovemaking he did not like his nipples "to be kissed. I don't know. I can't stand it."

Pete suggested in the *Playboy* interview that baseball eliminate all off days (he certainly didn't need them). "Winning and losing is everything," he said and asserted that he hoped to be remembered as the guy who worked "the hardest and the longest to become a switch-hitter, the best that ever lived." He suggested that his being white—or better put, not black—at this point in American history might help him when it came to his advertising opportunities. "Look if you owned Swanson's Pizza would you want a black guy to do the commercial on TV for you? Would you like the black guy to pick up the pizza and bite into it? . . . I mean would you want Dave Parker [a black superstar then with Pittsburgh] selling your pizza to America for you? Or would you want Pete Rose?"

Pete wasn't saying this was right or this was wrong. He was just saying. Swanson responded that it had done ads with black athletes, football players, in the past.

Pete described Karolyn to *Playboy* as a "perfect baseball player's wife" (this was before the impending divorce was known) and added, "She knows what I like for her to say and not to say." With her warm and outgoing way, Pete asserted, Karolyn was, "like a Jewish person. You know, all they do is kiss and shake hands."

"Is that right?" *Playboy* responded. And Pete said: "Yeah, you know it's true."

He engaged as well in a discussion of amphetamines in baseball, calling them greenies, uppers and diet pills interchangeably, and during a quixotic foray divulging that "a lot of guys" took them. Rose implied that he might take greenies too, so *Playboy* asked: "You keep saying you might take a greenie. Would you? Have you?

Said Rose: "Yeah, I'd do it. I've done it."

A few months later a Pennsylvania state investigation began into whether the Phillies had received illegally prescribed amphetamines. Players were questioned, along with some of their wives. There were denials, and hedging comments, and ultimately the investigation went away.

Near the end of the *Playboy* interview, Rose articulated a disarmingly cogent description of the philosophy—a kind of nihilism—that guided him (and has guided him to this day). Asked about rocky times in his marriage, Rose said, "Nothing bothers me. If I'm home in bed, I sleep. If I'm at the ballpark, I play baseball. If I'm on my way to the ballpark, I worry about how I'm going to drive. Just whatever is going on that's what I do. I don't worry about a bunch of things."

If there is one thing to understand about Pete Rose, to understand what helped him keep an almost inconceivable level of concentration on the field and also to understand the mental blinders he wore at crucial times through both his ascent and his fall, it is this: He did not worry.

THE PUBLIC sense of Rose may have begun to slip out of the Rockwellian and toward the noir (as Wagner and the Reds had feared), but for most fans, in Cincinnati, Philadelphia or anywhere else, this hardly mattered; not next to what Rose continued to represent on the field. A couple of years later, early in the 1980s, after Pete and the Phillies had won the Series and the Reds had become unglued, a Cincinnati zealot named Dennis "Wildman" Walker flew a banner above Riverfront Stadium that read PETE ROSE FOREVER, DICK WAGNER NEVER and was widely cheered. (The banner lifted Wildman's profile and his popularity, and his decades-long career as an exuberant Cincinnati radio host has been anchored by his near maniacal support of Rose.) If a baseball fan did not like Pete, and of course some did not, it was because of his brashness or because he rattled a favorite team, not because he had slept around or owned up to popping a greenie or even because he had fathered a child out of wedlock. Rose was still the river rat turned folk hero, baseball's biggest and richest star and a man approaching middle age who remained, for all to see, in perpetual boyhood. Or adolescence really. Peter Pan with a pecker. Hanging on the wall of the home Rose still owned in Cincinnati was a picture of a baby's body with his head on it.

True to his word Rose stayed baseball-focused, neither softened by the big money nor hardened by the upheaval in his life. On the September afternoon in 1979 that Karolyn officially filed for divorce, citing "gross neglect of duty," Pete received the news at Shea Stadium before a game against the Mets. That night he went 4 for 5. Though the Phillies, beset by injuries, fell out of the pennant race, Rose did not flag. He hit .331 in '79 and, on Aug. 5, with a hit to leftfield off the Pirates' Bert Blyleven, broke Honus Wagner's career record for singles. After his 44-game hitting streak in '78 and the promotion and excitement it caused—he'd appeared on scads of TV shows and visited with President Jimmy Carter at the White House—Rose had convinced Aqua Velva to establish an award for the major leaguer with the season's longest hitting streak. The Aqua Velva Cup it was called and the winner got $1,000 for each game in the streak. Big surprise that Pete himself won it in '79, reeling off 23 straight in September. He gave his prize money to Philadelphia's coaches and trainers to divide among themselves.[5]

He dressed funky sometimes: big rimmed sunglasses, supertight, pinkish polyester pants and nifty alligator shoes, that mop-top and over-sized sideburns. Disco fever was hot in the U.S.A., Donna Summer and Chic high on the charts, and a little RCA record label, Free Flight, put out a dance single by Pamela Neal, "Charlie Hustle." Techno-beat, synthesizer, lyrics about Pete Rose sliding and winning, and Neal's refrain "Dooooo the Charlie Hustle." Pete got a slice of what profits there were. "I like it," he decreed of the song. "It has the disco sound." The amphetamine probe had been a pain in the neck for the Phillies and it was true that Pete sometimes said things his teammates wished he hadn't, but there was no denying that the team was lifted wholly and completely when he came on board. "Just get us to the playoffs and I'll do the rest," he would say. He embraced everyone, flattering the stars, bringing the bench players into the fold, versing himself on the particulars of each player's game. "He'd say to me, 'How can you still hit good, playing just three days a week?'" recalls reserve outfielder Greg Gross. "He'd say something about my preparation and then he'd say, 'I could never do what you're doing.' That was ridiculous. Of course he could. It was just his way of making you feel better so that you played better."

Rose might pick up a lunch tab on the road. He'd bring in new, hot-stuff clothes for a young player who'd just joined the team. He never stopped telling Schmidt that he was baseball's best player, and that he had to be that for seven days of every week, not just four of them, and reminding Schmidt that even on a day when he did not hit the ball 400 feet he could help the team

---

[5] Rose liked giving things to coaches, including, in 1978, Jeeps to nine Reds coaches and trainers, a gift with a value of more than $50,000 that he wrote off on his tax return, saying they were fees for "services rendered." When the deduction was denied, Rose sued the IRS, claiming that the coaches were necessary to his success. He testified in court that given his approach to the game, he in particular required coaches and trainers to work long and off hours (early morning treatments, off-day batting practice etc.). He won the case mainly because the jury, as Rose's lawyer Robert Pitcairn put it, regarded Rose as a "unique athlete." Rose was delighted that the deduction was restored and made a point of saying publicly that he felt coaches and trainers were too often undervalued and underpaid.

win a game. He gushed over shortstop Larry Bowa's glove—"Hey Gnat, I'd take you over Ozzie [Smith] any day!" After a loss, Pete would sit at his locker before the horde of reporters and talk and talk in his inimitable scat, answering even the most ill-conceived questions and leaving Schmidt, Bowa, Maddox and the others to shower and dress in relative peace.

Pete Jr. worked as a Phillies' batboy sometimes when school was out in Cincinnati and Dave Rose, then making a go of things in Florida, would drive up to meet the team when it played in Atlanta, pull on a Rose Philadelphia uniform and take some BP on the field.

Rose never went out much with his teammates. That was partly because he did not drink alcohol—nothing but coffee and orange juice—and partly because he liked to go to sleep early or had something going with a girl. He hung around sometimes with a twentysomething kid named Tommy Gioiosa, a rough-edged but amiable little truckler who kept Pete company and helped get things done. Gioiosa would run an errand, or give one of Pete's girlfriends a lift home. Rose had first met him in Florida a couple years earlier and saw in him a certain spirit and a pliability. Gioiosa learned to place bets on Pete's behalf.

In the clubhouse Rose talked about wagers he had won or lost on basketball and football games. "The only reason they play *Monday Night Football* is so you can make up what you lost on Sunday," he started quipping in those years. No one thought much of it—other players and even Bill Giles went with him to the dog track—and when Pete put together betting pools for the NCAA tournament or the Kentucky Derby he had plenty of takers. Pete sometimes wrote things down with a red pen.

But away from the ballpark in Philadelphia, Rose went in his own directions, led the life that he led and did not talk much about it. He volunteered what he wanted to volunteer, told his stories with his happy verve, but did not, in gabbing with his teammates, answer many questions about his life. Nor did he make people feel comfortable about asking them. For all his effervescence there was something palpably unknown and unseen about Pete. This was the great Rose dichotomy—the paradox that a man so open, so clearly from the heart in his style, his talk, his way, had also about him the thin air of disguise. There was something concealed, unreckoned.

When he got that late-night ticket over in Newport, Ky., in 1965 there were no teammates in the car. "At certain moments a shield came over Pete and there was nowhere else to go with him," says Giles. "And then the shield would be gone." Not that the public, or even many of the people often near him, recognized this. After all, if a man flaunted his extramarital affairs and talked about pill-popping in a magazine article and strutted daily among younger, fitter teammates while as naked and unabashed and full of fresh life as Adam before the fall, then what could he be hiding?

Rose's teammates knew with certainty what they saw. They saw, for example, that when Rose took pregame batting practice, out early in the session and then back again late, he took it with purpose. He stood in the box lefthanded and hit 10 pitches to leftfield, then 10 up the middle, then pulled 10 to right. Then he stood in righthanded and did the same. Once after he had gone hitless in the last game of a road trip, and the Phillies had flown home, Rose called Giles and told him he was going to the park to hit. It was 3 a.m.

His teammates saw *The Sporting News* name Rose its player of the decade for the 1970s. They saw the way that he could foul off a pitch, any tough pitch, better than anyone in the game, his eyes forever down on the ball. And they saw this: During one Phillies home game at Veterans Stadium, Rose was being heckled sharply by a man in a seat down the third base line.[6] The man wore a Sunoco gas attendant's uniform and he kept standing up and giving it to Rose really good. "Before Pete stepped in to hit, he turned to us and winked like 'Watch this,'" recalls Phillies pitcher Larry Christenson. "Then he lined a foul ball straight at the guy, almost hit him in the head. Two pitches later Pete did it again. Foul line drive right at the guy. We looked at each other in the dugout like Pete was a god or something, like he could control things in the game the rest of us could not control.

---

[6] It is a source of high irony among professional athletes that Philadelphia translates from the Greek as "brotherly love" and that the city has adopted that phrase as its slogan. The fans are vicious and singularly so. Phillies fans rode Jackie Robinson horrifically. Eagles fans have cheered serious injuries to opposing players. Nor have fans in Philadelphia ever been afraid to eat their young. Even Rose was not immune.

"I'm telling you," Christenson continues, "playing with Pete could make you feel like a little kid. It could put that wonder into you. He was slower than he had been and he wasn't especially fit. I don't think he could have done a push-up. But he played baseball really well—hit and caught the ball, knew every situation. He made believers out of us. We had better talent in '76 and '77 but we were never a better team than when Pete was there. He was deeply part of us but even at that time he was also his own entity, and you never knew what you would see him do."

They saw Pete, in a game against the Reds in 1980, draw a walk and steal second base. Then he stole third base. Then he stole home. He was one month past his 39th birthday. They saw that by then he had become—through practice and smarts—a far-above-average fielder at first base, limited in range but aggressive, intuitive and not given to mistakes. He not only had the best fielding percentage among National League first baseman in 1980, he had more assists than anyone else at the position as well. The fifth position of his career became the fifth at which he was named an All-Star.

They saw Rose lead the league with 42 doubles that year; and though his average was down (.282), after the season he ignited the Phillies against the Astros in the National League Championship Series, reaching base 15 of the 25 times he came to the plate. They saw his fierceness in the deciding Game 5, the way he narrowed his eyes, livid, at Christenson after the righthander came back to the dugout after giving up three runs in the seventh, and how he kept exhorting the team with extravagant and unforced confidence—shades of Game 7 against the Red Sox in 1975—to stay in the game and to win it. So what if they were down 5–2 on the road against Nolan Ryan in the eighth inning; Pete worked Ryan for a seven-pitch walk in the middle of the rally that put the Phillies back in front. Nine days later, against the Royals, Philadelphia won that World Series. "I'm going to be the first unanimously elected Hall of Famer," Pete used to say in the Phillies locker room. Still, if you wanted him to sign a bat for a buddy of yours, all you had to do was ask.

His teammates did not see him on the trainer's table often (if at all) but they saw him with bruises and scrapes and the limp in his gait that came from playing the way he played at his age—and they knew that he *had* been on the trainer's table, before they'd arrived. They saw him in 1981, 40 years old now, lead the league in hits and bat .325 as the Phillies went to the playoffs again. That was the year of the two-month players strike and during that down time Rose kept sharp at a local batting cage. The machine threw a pitch every 10 seconds. Rose's uninterrupted sessions typically went an hour and 15 minutes, sometimes an hour and a half.

In the first Phillies game after the strike, Rose's teammates saw him do this: Slap a fastball from Cardinals reliever Mark Littell into leftfield for the 3,631st hit of his career, a National League record. Rose had come back to Philadelphia that same morning after traveling the 430 miles from the All-Star Game in Cleveland through the night in his Rolls-Royce. There were 60,000 flashbulb-popping fans at Veterans Stadium to see the record-breaking—the people embittered by the strike but there to see Rose nonetheless—and Stan Musial, the guy who had 3,630 National League hits, was among them. He came out onto the field after Rose's single and congratulated him with a handshake at first base—Musial, who had played his first big league game in 1941, the year Rose was born, and who got his last hit on Sept. 29, 1963, a ground ball past the rookie Rose himself at second base. (Musial had signed a baseball for young Rose before that game in '63.) With Musial now passed, Rose had only Hank Aaron and Ty Cobb on the hits list in front of him.

In the teeming postgame interview room the telephone kept ringing. It was a red phone, like a hot line, and it sat on a table next to where Rose was jabbering away into a bouquet of microphones. The word was that President Ronald Reagan wanted to extend congratulations to Rose but each time Pete picked up the receiver the operator couldn't get the call through. "Hang up and we'll try again," the operator said. After the second time Pete said to all the media (there must have been 250 people in the room): "Good thing there ain't a missile on the way."

Then, on the fourth try, a connection.

"Hello," said the President of the United States.

"Hello," said Rose.

"Pete Rose?"

"Yes, sir."

"This is Ronald Reagan."

"How ya doin?'"

Later he said to the President, referring back to the failed calls, "We were going to give you five more minutes and that was it."

The Phillies saw Pete do a commercial for Grecian Formula, a cream to get the gray out of your hair, and they saw him slip to .271 (a soft .271) as the Phillies finished in second place in 1982—though even in that year Rose played in 162 games, was named captain of the All-Star team, ran off a 21-game hitting streak and did enough that the Phillies brought him back for one more season, at $1.2 million guaranteed. That money was in part to ensure that Rose did not go play in Japan, where he was coveted and beloved and where with his all-out All-American style he had created a true sensation during the Reds four-week visit there following the 1978 season. "The name Pete Rose is right up there with Sadaharu Oh in Japan," said a major league spokesman.

Having struck equipment deals, Pete had begun using Japanese-made gloves and bats—including his custom Mizuno PR3631 as he bore down on Musial. That led to squawking and indignation: Pete Rose should stick to U.S.–made baseball gear! Would Huck Finn ride a Japanese raft? Here was another thing for fans to hurl at him. Rose pointed out that limiting his product choices or endorsement opportunities would not, in fact, be the American way. The people who were complaining, he said, "probably drove to the ballpark in their Toyotas." Besides, Rose said of the Japanese bats and gloves, "People should be happy I use them because I pay taxes on them. Does that sound un-American to you?" It was a mystifying thing to say, inexplicable, and all the more because one of his favorite things about the idea of playing in Japan (and one of the things he liked about visiting over there) was the prospect of receiving a haul of cash that could go undeclared.

The Phillies teammates saw him slump to .245 in 1983 and finally get benched, manager Pat Corrales getting up the gumption to end Rose's consecutive games streak after more than four and a half seasons. Philadelphia had also brought on Joe Morgan and Tony Perez, leading to the dubbing of the '83 team as the Wheeze Kids, a play on the Phillies' Whiz Kids team of 1950. Though the Phils reached the postseason and the World Series in '83 and though Rose batted .344 over the nine postseason games, it was clear that with his slowed speed and diminished punch at the plate, he was a husk of what he had been. He was hanging on too long in the game, it seemed, and the Phillies would not be having him back. Rose went into the off-season looking for a new team and a new contract. Though people now said the faded Rose could never get there, Cobb's record stood just 200 hits away, too close to quit. Rose stopped eating meat that off-season and began the first serious workout regimen of his career.

If you browsed back through the records and statistics of Rose's time in Philadelphia, examining a Phillies team that went to three postseasons and two World Series in five years, you would say that Pete was hardly the crucial cog. Mike Schmidt was the driving offensive force—an exceptionally powerful run producer—and Boone, Bowa and the sterling Maddox took away more runs on defense than Rose did. Even before his fall-off in 1983 Rose was by some measures, and especially by the advanced and nuanced metrics of later days, not as valuable to the offense as even players such as Bake McBride or Gary Matthews. Yet it is Rose whom those Phillies point back to, Rose who goaded the Phillies and carried them and set every example and made nearly all of them wish that they too could play baseball just a little bit more the way he did.

No one has professed a greater debt to Rose than Schmidt, who was raised in Dayton, watching the Reds and idolizing Rose. Schmidt was 13 when Pete played his first big league game. Over Schmidt's first six seasons in the majors he only once finished even among the top five for the National League MVP award and never hit 40 home runs in a season. Playing with Rose he won the MVP in 1980 and again in '81. He hit 40 or more home runs three times in five years. He walked more often. He drove in more runs. He kept winning Gold Gloves. He became, almost indisputably, the best player in baseball, just as Rose was telling everyone.

When Schmidt went into the baseball Hall of Fame in 1995 he praised Rose during his induction speech. He credits him as being both a beacon and a support beam in his career. Over the years of Rose's banishment,

Schmidt has gone in person to commissioner Bud Selig to appeal for Rose's reinstatement. Pete Rose has disappointed any number of people in his life, but Mike Schmidt is not one of them. Schmidt spoke with me about Rose on two occasions and then, after we talked briefly at an event in Cincinnati, he sent an e-mail. Here, verbatim, is what Schmidt wrote:

I grew up as a young fan of the Cin. Reds
Saw Pete play his first game and become Rookie of year.
Had a poster of him on my grandmother's bedroom door where I spent weekends.
She tailored my little league and high school uniforms to look just like his.
When I worked my way into pro ball and became a major league player of course meeting him was huge.
He was a fun guy, always joked with the opposition before the game, but nobody played harder to win.
Playing against him elevated my game as he pushed everyone around him to be better.
The Reds and Pete set the bar for excellence in those mid 1970 years.
Pete then became a free agent and ended up as a teammate in Philly.
Right away our games were elevated by watching him everyday. First to the park . . . last to leave.
He was our new spokesman which took heat and pressure off me.
He constantly spoke to the media about my ability and how I was the best he ever played with.
He told me daily I was the best, in fact he got everyone to believe they were.
He was a winner and settled for nothing less than championships.
We should have won it all in 1981, our best team, but the strike year stopped our momentum.
We went to the Series in 1983 as well and should have won.
Then Pete was let go and the Phillies started a youth movement.
The best years of my career were the ones spent with Pete, 1979–1983
—Mike Schmidt

Chapter 10

Cincinnati, Forever

HE TV commercial struck just the nerve a Presidential candidate would want to strike. First there was a boat moving across a river, a city skyline twinkling in the background and a waterbird flying across a predawn sky. "It's morning again in America," a man's voice said. "Today more men and women will go to work than ever before in our country's history." The narrative continued in this way, the voice measured and soothing, and beneath the words came images: a farmer steering a tractor, a kid throwing a newspaper on his paper route, a man in a suit joining his office carpool. This was in the summer of 1984 and the ad was put out by the campaign to reelect President Ronald Reagan. The narrator spoke about the economy's newfound health—inflation and interest rates were down, employment was up—as clips ran of a family moving into a new home and of a young couple getting married.

"It's morning again in America," the voice said once more and a man standing in his front yard hoisted a United States flag to the top of a flagpole as children watched.

The ad was brilliant, appealing to the value of good, hard work, and the idea that such work would pay off in the end. When election day arrived Reagan—not just on the strength of this commercial, of course, but riding exactly the spirit that both the ad and the man himself sought to project—won reelection with 525 electoral college votes, more than any candidate has ever received. He took 49 states. The truth of it on the ground was that a lot of folks in the U.S., including the kind of folks who had the inclination to go to ball games in Cincinnati, were feeling pretty good about themselves.

PETE WAS back! He had shucked a brief baseball exile to Montreal and been repatriated by the Reds as both player and manager—in short as the man asked to reinvigorate the franchise that had sagged and stumbled while he was gone. It was August of 1984 and who knew what Rose, 43 years and four months old, had left as a ballplayer? For three months after his '83 season with Philadelphia he had been a free agent out of work and lightly courted. The specter of Cobb before him, Rose said he would play any position for anyone, but the interest around baseball (the Mariners considered him, as did the Angels) proved modest. When the Expos finally signed Rose, for half of what he'd earned the year before, they tabbed him for leftfield. In welcoming him, Montreal's players spoke less of Rose's skills and more about what he might do as an intelligent leader and motivator on a young team, the ethic he could provide. He was the oldest player in baseball and fan polls split on whether the Expos had been wise or foolish to sign him. *National Lampoon* magazine ran a cover illustration of Rose, gut bulging through his uniform, leaning on a walker to get down the first base line. "Pete Rose Hustles After Ty Cobb's Record," read the caption.

Not that Rose was daunted in the slightest, not that he—and this is unquestionable—gave a hairy crap what anyone else thought. His confidence in public and in the privacy of his batting cage at home had not dimmed. He could make up for the steps he had lost, he figured, with his smarts. "I'm going to win Comeback Player of the Year," he said.

In the Expos' 1984 home opener, standing in against the Phillies and Jerry Koosman, who as a Met had thrown too close to Pete back in '73, Rose lined a double into the rightfield corner for the 4,000th hit of his career. When the ovation had died down and the game resumed, he scored on a pop fly single, a pure heads-up play made possible when Phillies centerfielder Von Hayes gathered the ball nonchalantly, assuming that Rose would stop at third.

He hit pretty well for a while, up around .320 and scoring some runs into the middle of May, but he injured his elbow and his heel, and it became clear that leftfield was not for him anymore. The Expos, contenders, needed a player with power at first base, which meant there was no room for Rose in the lineup even after he healed. In the clubhouse Rose got into a scuffle with a Montreal radio host who had chided him on air. (After 21 seasons such a confrontation was a first for Pete.) Another time he and catcher Gary Carter traded barbs over Rose's playing time—Rose saw Carter acting selfishly, Carter saw Rose the same way. By the time August came around, Rose's average was down into the .260s, he was serving only as an occasional pinch hitter and there was no way he was going to catch Cobb, still 130 hits away, if he stayed in Montreal.[1]

It was Pete himself who got on the phone late that summer with Reds president Bob Howsam—the same Bob Howsam of the Big Red Machine—and they spoke for nearly two hours. Dick Wagner had been let go as G.M., a good riddance as far as most Cincinnati fans were concerned, and Howsam wanted Rose to come home, to replace Vern Rapp as manager. The Reds had finished in last place two years running. Rose said he would do it—but only if he could return as a player too. He swore he could still hack it, swore they couldn't blow the fastball by him, said he wouldn't need to play every day. Pete could be convincing and Howsam knew what a game-changer it might be if he delivered Rose home to lead the team. Besides, with a record of 50–70, and attendance

---

[1] In 1981 a historian at *The Sporting News*, Pete Palmer, had discovered that Cobb's career hit total was actually 4,189. (A two-hit game in 1910 had been mistakenly double counted.) Though most statistics houses agreed with the finding and adjusted Cobb's total two hits down, Major League Baseball, and commissioner Bowie Kuhn, said it was too late to change the number seven decades after the fact. So Cobb's total remained 4,191—just as it remains today—according to baseball's official tally.

dropping year after disappointing year, what did the Reds have to lose? In the trade that brought Rose home from the Expos, Cincinnati gave up only Tom Lawless, a utility infielder.

"He's as good a candidate to be a manager as any player ever was," said Phillies reliever Tug McGraw after Rose took the job. In interviews, Rose talked about the managers who had influenced him—Sparky Anderson, Fred Hutchinson, Dave Bristol. Sparky, managing the Tigers, called from Detroit to wish Pete luck and give a few words of advice, fatherly in a way. Back when Harry Rose died in 1970, Sparky had been managing the Reds for about a year. He'd always felt a certain vested interest in the kid.

Rose heard the noise around him and the debates. Could a great player ever be a good manager? Could anyone be a player-manager in this day and age? Would he have the clarity to pinch-hit for himself when the situation arose? Rose declared that he had just two commandments, his golden rules of baseball and of his own life: Be on time and play hard. He wanted to instill enthusiasm in the Reds, he said, get the players excited to come to the park every day. The way Rapp had run things, stern and stuffy, was not for Pete. Before managing his first game, he had the TV put back into the clubhouse lounge. And sure, he said, it was fine for players to drink a beer or two on a team flight. He did not much care what his players did, Rose added, so long as they played the game right.

"He's not like the rest of us," said Sparky. "Nobody will ever know him completely. Can't know him." Anderson had been asked about Rose's prospects as a manager. "He thinks about baseball day and night," Anderson went on. "He can't sit five minutes in a chair and talk to you about anything else. He'll get up. Baseball is all he thinks about. He'll never leave the game. He'd die first."

HE LIVED up in Indian Hill then with Carol, who had in her belly a little Rose. They had been married in a small and private service, April of 1984, when Pete was an Expo and the team was in Cincinnati for three games against the Reds. They held the ceremony in an attorney's office at 8 a.m. and a few hours later, Rose went out and played in the 12:30 businessman's special at Riverfront. The honeymoon was basically Carol flying back to Montreal with Pete and the team, but even still it was just as well they got married when they did. Tyler Rose—that is, a baby Ty, named after you-know-who—was born on Oct. 1, not six months after the vows.

Indian Hill. This was not the West Side of Cincinnati; this was 21 miles northeast of Braddock Street, the other side of the Queen City's great divide, and a world away. Pete bought a house with five fine acres, much of it fanning out flat and into woodlands out back, and set up a state-of-the-art stable to keep a couple of horses. The house looked like a ski chalet, dark wood and skylights in the roof. Tall evergreens and stocky Japanese maples shaded the circular driveway out front and an awning extended over the front door. Pete would take out the black Porsche, or occasionally the white Rolls, and drive through the neighborhood on his way to the ballpark, passing the huge, sprawling lawns, the horse fences and the pastures. Fawn was at Franklin College in Indiana then and sometimes she'd come over and saddle up, canter on the trails back of the house.

The streets in Indian Hill had names that sounded rich and special—Redbird Hollow, Camargo Pines, Sugarun Lane—and the men and women around there had voices full of money, which to Pete's ears provided an inexhaustible charm, a cymbals' song. Not that he was out to mingle with that gilded class; they weren't roguish enough, and he was not a canapés and cocktails type of guy. But still, Pete could chitchat at the stoplight with anyone—talk Simonizing, maybe—and the setting around him was sweet. You'd pass a Mercedes in one driveway, a Jaguar in the next. Men wore their golf clothes on Saturday mornings. To Pete the only real paradox of where he now lived lay in his address, top of the hill on Given Road. *As if*, he would say laughing with that self-assured swagger, as if he hadn't busted his red-blooded ass to earn his way up here. *Given* was never part of the deal, he'd tell you. The kitchen in the house had an island at the center of it and the living-room couches were deep and plush, and Rose put in a satellite dish so he could keep an eye on the out-of-town-games.

When Dave came up from Florida to live in Blue Ash, another suburb north of Cincinnati, and work at the Gold Star Chili, he would do odd jobs for Pete around the house on Given Road. He would stop by when

Pete was on the road and groom the horses, lead them out for a bit, make sure they were well watered. He'd check on the cars in the garage, go over to the house and see that it was O.K. It was worth being careful. Pete tended to have a lot of cash around, banded together in stacks sometimes or in brown paper bags.

Pete had arrived at Riverfront Stadium two days after leaving the Expos, and put himself right into the lineup, an Aug. 17 Friday night game against the Cubs and the first time Pete had pulled on a Reds uniform in nearly six years. He was batting second, back of Gary Redus, ahead of Dave Parker. The manager's office was full of hastily mailed good wishes, gift trinkets and bouquets everywhere. Florists in Cincinnati had come up with the "Rose's Dozen"—14 in every bunch—and Pete had a lot of friends who were buying. When he saw all the flowers, Rose cracked that maybe the manager's office was actually the site of his own funeral.

President Reagan called to congratulate Rose on getting the player-manager's job, and also, by the way, to see whether Pete might want to come to his campaign stop that week at Cincinnati's Fountain Square—Johnny Bench would be there and an old Bengal, Bob Trumpy. But Rose declined. He didn't think sports and politics should mix like that, he said. "Anytime you wanna call, though," Pete told the President, "I'd be happy to talk to ya."

Some of the players, not to mention coach Don Zimmer over in the Cubs dugout, wore T-shirts that read PETE'S BACK as did many among the Riverfront crowd of 35,038, about double the Reds' norm. The game had to be delayed 10 minutes for the crush of walk-up sales, and once it started, Rose was getting ovations whatever he did, just for catching the ball at first base during the Cubs at bat. Then in the bottom of the first inning, after Redus singled to lead things off, Rose came to bat amid the roar at Riverfront. He took a strike, bluffing as if to bunt, to let Redus steal second base. He let a ball go by. And then on a 1–1 pitch from right-hander Dick Ruthven, Rose lined a clean single into centerfield. When Bob Dernier had trouble with the baseball out there, letting it get away, the old man never slowed, rounding second, bullying ahead at his relevant pace toward third and then—would he? Yes!—launching himself airborne into a headfirst slide. Down in a spray of dirt. Safe!

The crowd shook and shook and shook, everyone feeling the years fall away, and in the press box there was an odd silence, reporters shaking their heads, even the cynics among them. Many of the team employees wore rosebuds in their lapels and wherever you looked around the stadium you could see some kind of banner hung out to welcome Pete Rose home. Catcher Brad Gulden was in his first season with the Reds and Davey Concepción was in his 15th and both of them later allowed that standing in the dugout in that first inning, seeing the way Rose went into third like that, they had in spite of themselves felt tears come to their eyes, and that looking around they knew they were not alone. It was morning again in Cincinnati.

Over the weeks that followed Rose would, at least temporarily, change the dialogue about himself. He batted a hard .365 in 26 games for the Reds and he seemed to be on base every time you looked up. The long listless team awoke to win 15 of its final 27 games, and 12 of the last 16 in which Rose played. There was no debate about whether Rose was finished. There was instead hope that he could make the team a contender again after so many lean years and there was the certain knowledge that with 94 hits to go to reach Ty Cobb—*just 94*—Rose would be back to play a 23rd major league season, for the Reds, in 1985.

THE MADNESS—that is, the marketing, the leveraging, the baseball hoopla that only a Rose could love—began immediately. Before the 1985 season, Mizuno sponsored a press conference at which Rose stood before a calendar and made guesses as to the date on which he would get the Ty-breaking hit (late August, he predicted). Rose met with the king of memorabilia dealers, Barry Halper, to see what he might wring out of the chase and, as a 44th birthday gift, Halper gave Pete an 80-pound bronze bust of Cobb. Pete kept it around the clubhouse and had it on the road (the bust became a talisman for an early season winning streak) and sometimes the guys would put a Reds cap on Cobb and dress him in Rose's uniform, number 14.

The selling of Rose in this frenzied time was too much for Reuven

Katz to handle on his own so he hired a firm—Taft Merchandising, with offices in Cincinnati and New York—to figure out the best ways to capitalize. Soon Rose's face was on an array of T-shirts and mugs, matchbooks, key chains, posters, buttons, pennants. Official items and knockoffs. You could buy an autographed photo collage, sold through *The Sporting News* for $175. You could purchase Rose-engraved medallions of gold, silver or bronze. You could pay months ahead of time for a commemorative 4,192 coin. The price for Rose's jersey went up at the Reds' team store, and on the highways approaching the stadium, there he loomed, billboard beautiful, so much larger than life. "I'd like to have a statue of myself in front of the park," said Rose, talking about the period after he retired. "I always get the chills when I see the Stan Musial statue outside Busch Stadium."

In July the Cincinnati Art Museum commissioned Andy Warhol, for a reported fee of $25,000, to create a portrait of Rose. He had in the past done Elvis and John F. Kennedy, Marilyn Monroe and Muhammad Ali. When Warhol was approached about this one, he asked "Who's Pete Rose?" The cluelessness had a certain symmetry about it because when Rose was told by Katz of the impending portrait he had two questions himself: the first being, "How much money do I make on this?" and the second being, "Who's Andy Warhol?"

The idea had been that Pete would pose for Andy at his studio when the Reds came to New York to play the Mets in late July. But Rose never made it over there so the museum instead sent photographs and baseball cards for Warhol to work from. After looking at them for a while he called in to Cincinnati and said he was confused. "In some photos he has the bat on his left shoulder and in some photos he has the bat on his right shoulder, and I am wondering why that is," Warhol said.

"It's because he is a switch-hitter," Warhol was told.

At this, Andy Warhol, then 56 years into his unique and bohemian life, burst into uncontrollable laughter for minutes on end, dropping the phone, being as he was well acquainted with the term, of course, though he had not until that moment known its origins. Pete Rose a switch-hitter! Imagine that.

Along with the master portrait—which would hang not only in Cincinnati but, decades later, in the National Portrait Gallery in Washington, D.C.—Warhol produced 50 additional silkscreen prints, available for $2,500 (to museum members) or $3,000. Forty-five of the prints sold almost overnight, long before they were even finished. The other five were set aside for Pete to keep or sell as he wished.

At times during the season there were new grumbles, by sports columnists mainly, that Rose was putting himself in the lineup too often, that the Reds would be better with a younger, stronger bat in there more regularly. Yet no change was about to come. Rose played himself against righthanded pitching and sat down against lefties.[2] Any number of bench players might have provided more punch on a given night (Pete rarely drove the ball anymore) yet he was still contributing in ways seen—a hot stretch brought his batting average above .300 in early June, and Pete remained tough to strike out—and unseen. With his chatter and intensity and his unceasing attention to detail Rose had the Reds playing better than they had in years, comfortably over .500 and contending in the NL West, just as he had vowed. Exactly how often Pete played, and the fact that he had a lousy slugging percentage, was a matter of inside baseball. To the country, Pete shone bright. He was always on TV somewhere, the *CBS Morning News* or *Face the Nation* or doing a spot for Ted Turner on TBS. When the Reds played in Los Angeles, Frank Sinatra came out to a game and called Rose over to chat.

He was always moving—hustling still. He met with players about their roles on the team and worked the phones to talk trades. He took his early batting practice and his extra infield. He went to the racetrack home and away. (When the Reds played in Philadelphia, Pete had a losing night at the Garden State Park track over in Cherry Hill.) He fed the media before and after games and he stayed up late to watch the West Coast teams. He ate steak and salad and drank iced tea. He was endlessly fiddling with his bats—his stable of black Mizunos, model PR4192— sanding them and

---

[2] The other half of the platoon was Tony Perez, also brought back to the Reds for 1984 and, at 43, the second oldest player in the league after Rose.

scuffing them, taping the handles and writing 14 on the knob (and occasionally on the head) and invariably keeping his gamer by his side.

Whatever criticism Pete took, no one suggested anymore that being both manager and player was too much of a job for one man, not for this man anyway. If anything, it seemed, Rose had appetite to spare. Through all the nonstop energy and thrill of 1985, of the chase, of the new job, of being a Red again, there could sometimes be an edginess to Rose, a kind of shifting restlessness as his teammates recall it. It was not that he seemed put upon by all the demands in his life, but rather the opposite, that he still, somehow, seemed unsatisfied. That even in this heightened time he wanted, or needed, something more.

By September, with Cobb fewer than 10 hits away, the media assigned to the Rose Watch, those following his every game, had swollen to a cast of more than 100. Most were in Chicago on Sunday, Sept. 8, a day that began with Rose at 4,189 career hits and scheduled to ride the bench against the Cubs and their lefthanded starter Steve Trout. This was the last of six games on the road and while Pete Jr. stayed with the Reds working as a batboy, others in Rose's personal entourage—Carol and Tyler, Fawn, Reuven Katz—had headed back to Cincinnati. The most that Pete could do, everyone assumed, would be to get a pinch hit and close within one. Reds' owner Marge Schott was preparing for some serious turnstile revenue when the team got home.

On the morning of the game at Wrigley Field, however, Rose learned that Trout would not be pitching—the story was that he had injured himself when he fell off his bicycle while out riding with his family—and righthander Reggie Patterson, a sometimes reliever whom Pete had singled off of two days before, would get the start. So Rose put himself into the game, batting second as usual, two hits away from Cobb in a ballpark where crowds had pelted him with abuse, and cups of beer and once, even, with a crutch hurled down from the high seats. Pete singled his first time up, hit number 4,190, and the baseball went straight into the vault. All season long in '85, the Reds saved the ball from every hit Pete got.

Word reached Schott that Rose was playing in the game at Wrigley and she became so agitated she got up and left her seat at the Bengals game, needing to find a place to pace and stew. She tried to call Pete to tell him to sit his butt down and save the record for home, but she never got through. There were 28,000 fans in Wrigley Field and hundreds more peering from the rooftops on Sheffield and Waveland, and everyone was standing when Pete came up in the fifth inning. He ran the count to 3–2 and then Patterson threw a screwball and Rose lined a hard single into rightfield, sending the crowd into a chant of "Pete! Pete! Pete!," and an ovation that lasted for more than three minutes, never mind the animosity that Cubs fans had shown him in the past. Out in rightfield Chicago's Keith Moreland applauded into his glove. Pete was at 4,191, dead even with Ty Cobb.

Rose's pursuit that summer unfolded against a hard backdrop in baseball: the drug trials in Pittsburgh. A cocaine dealer named Curtis Strong was among seven men being prosecuted, and many of Strong's clients had been major leaguers. Twelve players were summoned to testify in front of a grand jury and by the end it was clear that cocaine was far more prevalent in baseball than anyone outside the game had known. In early September former Pirate John Milner, whose cousin Eddie Milner, coincidentally, was playing centerfield and leading off for the Reds in '85, said he had bought cocaine in the bathroom of the Pirates' locker room. Outfielder Lonnie Smith testified that he had snorted coke with his Cardinals teammates. Several players implied that they had been high on cocaine during games. A few days after Rose tied Cobb at Wrigley Field, Cincinnati's star rightfielder Dave Parker flew to Pittsburgh to testify about his own cocaine usage during his seasons with the Pirates.

Rose's wholehearted chase seemed unspoiled by such seaminess and served as an antidote to the Pittsburgh mess, baseball fans agreed—and so what if Rose, hitting in the high .260s, was hanging on a little longer than he might have? Hadn't Mays? Hadn't Musial? Didn't Rose, after all that he had given to the game for all those years, deserve that anyway? The fact that Rose had played himself against the Cubs because they were pitching a righthander, not altering his strategy in deference to the record, not being swayed, that is, by the appeal and the potential fruits of breaking the record at home, was seen as a sign of unbending integrity. In his final two at bats at Wrigley after the Ty-tying hit, the crowd up and screaming each time, Rose grounded out hard to shortstop, then struck out. Marge Schott had her reprieve.

Along with all the gewgaws being peddled that season, there were audio and video highlight tapes of Rose on sale, and books by and about him were either out on the shelves or in the works. *Pete Rose on Hitting*, an instructional manual of sorts, appeared in early May, and throughout the season Rose collaborated with writer Hal Bodley and *The Sporting News* on a collection of daily diary entries that would be packaged into a paperback called *Countdown to Cobb*. Meanwhile, *The Cincinnati Enquirer* had decided to do a bookazine and the newspaper dispatched a young metro reporter, John Erardi, to write it.

"My very first day covering the team, Pete waved me over and asked who I was and what I was doing," recalls Erardi. "When I told him about the project and asked for some time with him, he said to me, 'What do I get paid?'"

"I told him, 'Nothing, as far as I know.' And he said, 'You better make a phone call.'

"Well, we didn't pay him, and he was under contract to do that book with *The Sporting News* anyway, but as the season went on anytime I went into Pete's office to talk baseball he talked with me like I was his best friend. He never shut me out."

During his research, Erardi interviewed LaVerne. She was LaVerne Noeth by then, having remarried after Harry's death, and she had recently been widowed for the second time. She lived in Thonotosassa, Fla., not far from Tampa and she had an autographed—not personalized, but autographed—poster of Pete hung up on her wall. LaVerne and Erardi were "shooting the breeze," as Erardi recalls it when LaVerne suddenly volunteered something he will never forget, "You know," she said, "Pete lost a bundle on the Series last year."

She was talking about the 1984 World Series between San Diego and Detroit, won by the Tigers in five games. Pete, LaVerne was saying, had bet on the Padres.

"I had just come over to sports from metro so I wasn't 100 percent clear on the rules," says Erardi. "But I was pretty sure that he wasn't supposed to be betting on baseball, even if it wasn't his own team.

"I was pretty taken aback, but I sort of danced around it. After she said it, I just said 'Oh yeah?' and Pete's mom said 'Yeah.'"[3]

THE EVENING of Sept. 11, 1985, was unseasonably cool in Cincinnati, chilly even, and some fans wore sweaters in the stands. They'd come out to the game the night before as well, more than 50,000 strong, only to see Pete go 0 for 4 against San Diego, an event that disappointed everyone except Marge Schott. With Rose still at 4,191, Riverfront Stadium would be full up for at least another day.

Despite the hitless game, which could sometimes wreck him even still, Pete got a pretty good night's sleep. Carol made him French toast for breakfast, and he read the sports pages while he ate. He kootchy-cooed Tyler for a bit and then he left for the ballpark. "Since the moment he woke up," Carol would say later, in the aftermath, "I knew it would be the night he got the hit."

From their hotel in Fountain Square many of the Padres players walked to the stadium. The sun was out. "It was like a playoff atmo-

---

[3] Any wager on San Diego was an underdog play. The powerful Tigers, Sparky Anderson at the helm, had won 104 games during the regular season and swept the Royals in the playoffs. Detroit's deep roster included a rookie utility player named Barbaro Garbey, who was intriguing for reasons beyond his potential at the plate. In 1980 he had come over from Fidel Castro's Cuba; though he had been a rising star there, playing on the national team, Garbey had fallen into disgrace over his participation in a game-fixing operation: He and two dozen other players faced a ban for life from Cuban athletics. In the U.S., Garbey rose through the minor leagues and, while playing for the Tigers' Triple A team in 1983, he acknowledged to *The Miami Herald* that years earlier in Cuba he had indeed taken money in exchange for trying to keep his team from scoring too many runs. Major League Baseball investigated and responded by placing Garbey on probation. He was not suspended, and in 1984 he made it to the Tigers where, in 327 at bats, he hit .287 and knocked in 52 runs. Garbey went hitless in 12 at bats during Detroit's Series win over the Padres and he wound up playing in just two more major league seasons. He later became a hitting instructor, working for a number of years in the Cubs' minor league system.

sphere soon as you stepped out the door," says Padres second baseman Jerry Royster. "The whole day there was a buzz and people were milling around. It was the middle of the week [a Wednesday] but it felt like a holiday. It didn't matter that it was a little cold, there was already a crowd around the stadium when we got there."

Ticket scalpers outside Riverfront, including those lined up along the stretch of road that would soon be renamed Pete Rose Way, were commanding as much as $100 for an $8 seat.

"What I remember is the sky," recalls first base umpire Ed Montague. "It was a gorgeous pink, just perfect, like something you would see in a movie—a still, golden-pink sky and the Goodyear blimp was up there floating in it."

"I took my son Mickey to the game," says Mike Shannon, a fine baseball writer and editor who lives in Cincinnati. He also has children named Babe, Casey and Nolan Ryan. "Mickey was six months old and I took him with me even though I knew there would be a crazy, noisy crowd and I knew he of course wouldn't be able to make sense of anything or remember any of it. I just wanted him to be there. This was once in a lifetime, you know? I was only glad the Reds didn't charge me to have him sitting on my lap—they were so cheap then under Marge Schott you didn't know what they'd do.

"Sometimes now Mickey will be talking baseball with someone and he'll say, 'Oh yeah I was at that game,' and you'll see the other person look surprised and start figuring in their head—is he old enough? Yes, he's old enough. He doesn't have that game in his mind like the rest of us who were in the crowd do. We'll never forget it as long as we live. But Mickey was there. He can always say that."

Pitching for the Padres was Eric Show, a slim 29-year-old righthander with decent stuff. Show was not popular among his teammates. He was intelligent but also distant and he would sometimes go out into the hotel stairwell and play his guitar by himself. He belonged to an extreme right-wing organization called the John Birch Society, and in the clubhouse he would start talking, to no one in particular, about the role of government and what he thought it should be. "He was not a bad guy," says Kurt

Bevacqua, who was the Padres' third baseman. "But he was a very strange duck." Some San Diego players were also unhappy that Show had a tendency to hang his head and point fingers at others when things were not going well during a game.

As far as being the pitcher facing Rose on this potentially historic night, Show said that he believed the excitement over passing Cobb was a "media creation." It was possible that he might be the one to give up the hit, but he said that that was neither here nor there. He did not care. "In the eternal scope of things," Show said, "how much does this matter?" [4]

The crowd was already on its feet the moment Rose walked out of the on-deck circle in the bottom of the first inning. There was no score in the game and the bases were empty with one out. Bruce Bochy was catching for the Padres and Lee Weyer, a well-respected veteran umpire who had for more than three years been forecasting for Pete that "the night you get past Cobb I am going to be behind the plate," was indeed, by coincidence, behind the plate.

The first pitch from Show came in high and away and Rose let it go by. Ball one.

"Before the game we were talking about what we would do if we wound up with the ball," recalls Royster. He and shortstop Garry Templeton and Bevacqua were saying how if Rose singled into the outfield, they would jostle all over one another to try to catch the throw back in and be the one to bring the ball to Rose. "Or maybe I will just take it and run out the tunnel and never come back," Bevacqua said.

Show's next pitch was a fastball, on the inside part of the plate, and Rose fouled it straight back. The noise out of the crowd was loud and constant. Most everyone in the place knew that Pete had grown up seven miles to the west, by the river. "If you have a lump in your throat,

---

[4] Less than a decade later, Show's story took a tragic turn. Shortly into his retirement it became known that, along with his erratic behavior, he had a heavy addiction to drugs. In 1994, three years after pitching his final major league game, Show was found dead at the age of 37, in a rehabilitation center on a morning after a night in which he had ingested cocaine and heroin.

you're only human," said the Reds broadcaster Ken Wilson over the air.

"Carmelo Martinez was our leftfielder and he was talking with us before the game too," Royster recalls. "Carmelo was saying how if he got the ball he wouldn't throw it into the infield at all, he would just run the ball back in and give it to Pete himself."

The third pitch was low and inside and Rose laid off. Two balls and a strike. It was exactly to the day 57 years since Cobb had appeared in his final big league game.

Show wound up and threw a slider, once again over the inside of the plate, belt high, and Rose was right on this one, knocking it into left centerfield—a clean single. The ball took a high hop on the turf and Martinez gloved it. His plan to carry it into the infield was foiled, though, when Rose rounded first base aggressively, ready to try for second if Martinez didn't get the ball in quickly.

This was it. 4,192.

Fireworks exploded in the Cincinnati sky and paper streamers fell onto the field and the sound from the stands was like nothing you had heard before. People yelled full throat and hugged one another. Dave Rose wrapped his arms around his mother and jumped up and down. LaVerne had been living back in Cincinnati for six weeks by then, waiting for this moment, staying with Pete's sister Jackie at the house on Braddock Street.

The Reds players poured out of the dugout and ran in from the bullpen and surrounded Pete at first base. John Franco and Ted Power, Buddy Bell and Nick Esasky, Petey the batboy, Billy DeMars the hitting coach—every Red in uniform that night. Bobby Brown, a lightly used and little-known Padres outfielder burst out of the third-base dugout and ran across the field to get a piece of Pete. It was Templeton who had taken the throw in from Martinez and he came to present the ball. Show walked over and shook Rose's hand. Within the Red sea, Perez and Concepcíon hoisted Rose onto their shoulders. Marge came on the field and at her beckoning a candy-apple red Corvette appeared, driving slowly toward first base, a gift to Pete.

Those moments all passed in a heady bliss—too quickly for anyone's liking—and even after the players and Marge had gone in and the Corvette had been driven away, there was absolutely no quieting the crowd. Many people were in tears at their seats. Nobody was ready for the game to start again. Show sat down on the mound to wait.

The fans kept cheering. Four minutes after he had stepped into the batter's box, nearly three minutes after the hit had landed, Pete stood alone on first base, the game on hold. Already he had saluted the crowd several times. He took his helmet off of his head and he slapped himself playfully on each cheek as if to show that he was not dreaming. Then he put his helmet back on again, and clapped and nodded and swung his arms.

Later Pete would sell the bat that he used to get his hit. He would sell the red Corvette, and he would sell the T-shirts that he wore beneath his uniform. But right now he was not selling anything. Other people, though, were seizing the situation to sell other things, to push some product in the American way. The TV announcers were Wilson and Joe Morgan, who was less than a year out of his playing career and who wished more than anything, he said, that he could be down on the field with Pete.

"Pete, this Bud's for you," said Morgan. And then the cameras showed Morgan and Wilson standing beside one another in the booth, each with a can of that beer in his hand—a drink, it might be noted, that Pete never drank—and clanking them together. Wilson added, "This Bud's for Pete Rose and baseball because this, Joe Morgan, is what it's truly all about."

Now, more than five minutes after they had gotten to their feet the fans suddenly began to roar even louder, a new burst, as if realizing that it was up to them to make sure that this moment did not end. Pete grinned and blew out through his mouth and raised his helmet to acknowledge the crowd yet again. He could see the faces in the stands. Carol. Karolyn. His children. His mother. His sister. His brother. So many others that he knew. But then, beneath the stadium lights, that detail would blur away and what Rose saw was not the individuals but more of a single, rippling mass—wide and moving and infinite—like looking at the ocean from the shore.

He stood uncomfortably with his left foot on the bag, his hands upon his hips. He looked up into the sky. He looked down to the ground. He blinked and shook his head and worked his chewing gum across both sides of his jaw. And then, there it was. With the crowd some six minutes into its full and unchecked embrace, Pete could not contain himself any longer. He would say later that he had given in and wept because he had seen Harry looking down upon him from the heavens (though Pete had never been religious in that way, or in any way). And as he stood there, after all that he had now done in his baseball life, all those hits he had gotten, all the money he'd made, all the fame he'd achieved and, at the core of it, the singular way he had competed on the baseball field—Harry would have taken note that Pete had rounded first base hard and alert just minutes before—he could feel, he could *know*, that his father would have been proud.

Whatever may have been going through Rose's mind, he knew something else then too. He knew there were also many things he had done of which his father would not have been proud at all, things that would have made Harry stern and angry, and even ashamed. If that knowledge lived always like an invisible little pickax inside Pete's chest, usually, almost unfailingly, he could bury it away. Pete did not linger on feelings. He did not linger on thoughts. He was not an emotional kind of guy. Only now, here, with the crowd cheering and cheering, his own Cincinnati crowd, the all of it—the good, the great, the bad, Harry—fell upon Pete with a force he could not hold off.

He grabbed onto the first base coach, his old friend Tommy Helms, and put his face into Helms's shoulder, and when Petey came out to first base again from the dugout Pete clutched him and held him in a way that he never had. Over the travails in the years to come for Rose, the unraveling of so much of his life, the many chances he would have to show contrition or sadness or regret, or really any emotion at all, anything but defiance, he would not shake like this in public again—not, that is, for another 25 years.

Finally, close to nine minutes since he had begun that walk toward home plate—and to truly understand how long a nine minute-ovation is, one needs to stand in a room, clapping, and time it—there was calm and resolve enough to let the game begin again. Padres first baseman Steve Garvey, the former Dodgers' glamour boy whose poster Fawn had pinned as a teenager on her bedroom wall, came back to his position pounding his glove. Just before getting into his fielder's stance, Garvey winked over at Pete. "What happened, did I miss something here tonight?" he said grinning. "What did you just do?"

ROSE LINED a triple late in the game, hit number 4,193—"When he got to third base he started chattering about the pitch he'd just hit, about the situation in the game, like it was any other night," Bevacqua recalls—and he came in to score on a sacrifice fly. The Reds won. Afterward, during the ceremony on the field Cincinnati radio voice Marty Brennaman read aloud a statement from baseball commissioner Peter Ueberroth: "Not only has he reserved a prominent spot in Cooperstown," Ueberroth had written of Rose, "he has reserved a special place in the heart of every fan alive today." Marge came back out and gave Pete a silver cup-and-bowl set, and he took the microphone and thanked her and thanked especially the fans and said that by the way, he would just as soon call the color of the new Corvette "Cincinnati Reds red." He got everyone cheering again when he said he planned to come back and play another season. People held up signs that said, only, PETE.

President Reagan phoned in again, and Rose took the call on the field, practically used to this by now and as at ease and unadorned as ever. "You missed a good ball game tonight," he told the President.

Years earlier Andy Warhol had advanced an observation about America, something he had noticed about how popular products and popular culture could bridge a class divide.

"What's great about this country is that . . . the richest consumers buy essentially the same things as the poorest," Warhol wrote in an autobiography. *"You can be watching TV and see Coca-Cola, and you can know that the President drinks Coke, Liz Taylor drinks Coke, and just think, you can drink Coke, too. A Coke is a Coke and no amount of money can get you a better Coke than the one the bum on the corner is drinking . . . Liz Taylor knows it, the President knows it, the bum knows it, and you know it.*

"In Europe the royalty and the aristocracy used to eat a lot better than the peasants. . . . It was either partridge or porridge. . . . But when Queen Elizabeth came here and President Eisenhower bought her a hot dog, I'm sure he felt confident that she couldn't have had delivered to Buckingham Palace a better hot dog than one he bought her for maybe twenty cents at the ballpark. Because there is no better hot dog than a ballpark hot dog. Not for a dollar, not for ten dollars, not for a hundred thousand dollars could she get a better hot dog. She could get one for twenty cents and so could anybody else."

Which is, in a way, how it was with Rose. It's as if Warhol had Pete's number long before starting on the portrait. You'd get the same Pete Rose whether you were Ronald Reagan or a fan in the leftfield bleachers. Whether you were Marge Schott or a bookmaker; a trackhand or the commissioner of baseball; the third baseman on Pete's team or the third baseman on the other team. You could be a guy mooked up on steroids running shitcan errands for Pete or a gentleman in his tennis whites up on Given Road. Dugout, green room, box seat, back alley. For better and for worse, everyone got the same Pete Rose.

He taped the Phil Donahue show at the Riverfront Coliseum the next afternoon, more than 5,000 people in the arena seats, and he played into the hometown feeling, saying that of the 50,000 people who had been in the ballpark, "I've probably had an iced tea with 35,000 of them." He said he had gone out to the Precinct, Jeff Ruby's hot place, for steak after the game the night before. "I got home about a quarter to four," Rose told Donahue. "But I had to get up at six and do *Today* and *Good Morning America* and CBS. You're asking me how I slept? Like a dog named Schottzie."

He needled Marge some more and he praised Perez (both of them were there) and Donahue went through the crowd with his microphone, taking questions. A man stood up and said he was proud that Pete "always recognized your fellow players." A woman held a sign that said THANKS PETE. AMERICA NEEDS HERO'S. Each time Pete said something the people liked they broke into applause.

Petey, 15, sat quietly in the audience wearing a Reds cap, and Donahue turned the conversation his way for while. Junior gave short answers to a couple of questions and the worried look about him eased only when the camera swung back to his father. At one point in the broadcast, Rose autographed some baseballs and Donahue, in his shirtsleeves now, tossed them into the crowd.

That same day in Washington, D.C., a federal resolution was passed: "That it is the sense of the Congress to commend Peter Edward Rose on the achievement of becoming the alltime Major League leader in base hits and to recognize all the accomplishments and the inspirational manner in which Pete Rose has played the game of baseball, the National Pastime."

It all amounted to a dizzying stretch of hours, both enormous and precious. "Someday, when things are going bad," Rose had said during the postgame of 4,192, speaking as if he somehow already knew, "I'll be able to reminisce about tonight."

Chapter 11

Cooperstown, 2012

ALKING AROUND Cooperstown on induction weekend you can see the darnedest things. Such as a pair of slight, white-haired men in flannel baseball uniforms intently flipping baseball cards outside Doubleday Field, or 68-year-old Denny McLain (of all people) signing autographs in front of a memorabilia shop called (of all things) Paterno Brothers Sports.[1] McLain weighs about 100 pounds more than he should, and he tends to give a merry dose of live-for-the-day optimism with every signature.

McLain's extravagant success on the baseball field, his 31-win season in 1968 and his back-to-back American League Cy Young Awards, gave way to a life touched by almost Biblical distress—a lot of Judas and a measure of Job. His rap sheet includes convictions for racketeering, conspiracy, mail fraud, money laundering and attempting to distribute cocaine. He has been to prison twice. A judge at a bond hearing once

---

[1] The store owners at Paterno Brothers bear no blood relation to the late Penn State football coach Joe Paterno.

called him "a professional criminal." Out of jail, McLain has suffered through a fire that destroyed his home (as well as his Cy Young Award trophies), personal bankruptcies (he had to sell off his *replica* Cy Young Award trophies) and, most tragically, in 1992, the death of his 26-year-old daughter Kristin in a car accident.

McLain first made the wrong kind of headlines after he invested in a sports betting operation while pitching for the Tigers in the late 1960s. McLain, like Rose later, was investigated by Henry Fitzgibbon, the former FBI man turned baseball's head of security. Commissioner Bowie Kuhn wound up suspending McLain for three months in '70. Although he has committed crimes far more wide-ranging and sinister than Rose ever has—McLain once robbed the pension plan of a small business—McLain, like Pete, had the roots of his troubles in a powerful weakness for gambling. And his public trajectory from baseball superstar to pariah has made McLain the closest thing, from a public perception standpoint that is, to a poor man's Pete Rose. That can be read literally or figuratively.

"Pete and I have a bond," says McLain, who broke into the big leagues in 1963, Rose's rookie year. "The two of us share something. And we both like to bet. I've been a gambler all my life."

When McLain signs a jersey he adds beneath his name: 31–6, 1968/Cy 68–69/MVP 68. Although his body of work is far from Hall of Fame-worthy (over the last three of his 10 seasons he won just 17 games while losing 34), McLain was, in 1978, on the ballot and as eligible for election that year as were Eddie Mathews, Duke Snider and Gil Hodges. McLain received one vote that season and three in '79. Although there were heavy suspicions that some of his cohorts in that 1960s bookmaking scheme wagered on baseball, any connection between McLain and baseball betting proved speculative. Commissioner Bowie Kuhn, in levying that three-month suspension, said, "There is no evidence that [McLain's] activities in any way involve the playing or outcome of baseball games."

"The big difference between me and Pete when it comes to gambling," says McLain, failing to note that his list of crimes committed and his swindling of innocent people out of their retirement funds is another big difference between them, "is that he bet on baseball and I did not." There it is. The cardinal sin.

––––––––––––

GAMBLING HAS circled around baseball from the game's rough-knuckled start, intertwined with its early popularity and immediately a concern for the governors of the game. In 1858—a time when, as baseball's supreme historian John Thorn has written, bookmakers worked the sidelines of league games, adjusting the odds as the score changed, and taking wagers from fans and players—the National Association of Base Ball Players laid out the rule: "Betting prohibited. No person engaged in a match, either as umpire, scorer, or player, shall be directly or indirectly interested in any bet upon the game."

By the time the National League began, in 1876 (and then the American Association six years later), the consequences, as specified in the rulebook, were clear: "Any player who shall, in any way, be interested in any bet or wager on the game in which he takes part, either as umpire, player, or scorer . . . shall be dishonorably expelled, both from the club of which he is a member and the League." Betting on a baseball game that you weren't directly involved with meant expulsion for a year.

Those stipulations form the basis of Rule 21 (d), also known now as the rule that Pete Rose made famous. The language has been honed and codified over time and has for many decades included "any club official or employee" among those forbidden to bet. (This covers managers of course.) The rule has also, since the time of Commissioner Kenesaw Mountain Landis, who came in on the heels of the 1919 Black Sox scandal, stated that such betting involvement would result in becoming "permanently ineligible."

That is the ineligible list that Rose has been on, now alone among the living, since Aug. 23, 1989.

The risk of a dishonorable expulsion was not always a deterrent in the early years. There were sporadic attempts (some almost certainly successful) to fix games throughout the late 1800s and well into the 20th century. Gamblers made overtures to fix the first modern World Series, in 1903, and numerous players, as well as an umpire and at least one manager, were banned over the years either for betting on games or attempting to influence an outcome on the field. It was in the '20s that Cobb and Speaker were investigated for wagering on a game; Dodgers manager Leo Durocher was set down for the '47 season in part for having consorted with gamblers suspected of betting on baseball. Other incidents arose.

For the general public, wagering on baseball continued, through the decades and still today, to hold a broad appeal—the same appeal that the NFL, it's worth noting, has long embraced as a key to its popularity.[2] Although the betting lines on baseball games were not published in the 1940s and '50s, as they were for fights, football games and golf matches, all the local bookies knew the odds. In so many neighborhoods across the country you could lay a bet with the butcher or the baker, with the grocer, the tailor, the tobacconist. By the 1950s more people bet on baseball than on horse racing, and the occasional police raid found daily odds written and annotated on chalk boards—at the back of a barber shop in Harlem, N.Y., at the back of a barroom in Covington, Ky. It was not unusual for gamblers to cold-call a major league clubhouse seeking information, and for the longest time managers refused to reveal, in the days before a game, who the starting pitcher would be. Giants manager Alvin Dark, for one, held to that practice into the '60s, believing the information to be tantamount to a gambling tip.

Rose's entrance into the majors coincided with an exceptionally prom-

---

[2] The many by-products of the NFL's allegiance to the betting world include the league's strict demands on each team to divulge the precise nature and severity of its players' injuries each week. Although this puts those players at risk—in football, of course, a weakened body part is open to legal attack—the league is not about to put player safety ahead of being on the up-and-up with bettors. "[Disclosing injuries] eliminates an opportunity for someone to benefit from inside information, as it might relate to gambling activities," NFL spokesman Greg Aiello once told me. This is in distinct contrast to hockey, the other major North American sport in which violent body contact is routine and encouraged. There's not nearly as much betting on the NHL and there is no kow-towing to it. NHL injury lists, especially in the playoffs, allow teams to be vague and noncommittal. "Pulled groin" might mean "injured ankle" or "sprained shoulder." The players love the camouflage (it keeps them less vulnerable on the ice) but it introduces uncertainty into a wager.

inent sports gambling case, not in baseball but relating to two highly visible NFL players: the Green Bay Packers' Paul Hornung and the Detroit Lions' Alex Karras, both of whom were suspended indefinitely for betting on NFL games, including games involving their own teams. Commissioner Pete Rozelle levied the ban—which created front page news coast-to-coast—on April 17, 1963, just as Rose, living on Braddock Street and reading each day the newspaper that Harry brought home, was finishing his first homestand as a Red. Hornung had been the NFL's Player of the Year in '61. Karras had been an All–Pro on the defensive line.

Hornung, 27, got news of the ban over the phone from Rozelle while sitting on his bed in Louisville and with his mother standing in the doorway. He was contrite and forthcoming, detailing how he had indeed placed bets, at $100, $200 or more a game, with his friend Bernard (Barney) Shapiro, a slot-machine and pinball baron with interests in Las Vegas. The two men spoke a couple of times a week during football season and Hornung said he answered questions for Barney along the lines of "How are you doing?" and "What do you feel about the game?" Hornung would respond with things like: "We're a good bet on an eight-point spread."

Both Hornung and Karras, who in addition to the betting was cited for spending time with "known hoodlums," had violated their contracts' clearly stated prohibition of gambling on football.[3] Commissioner Rozelle made a point of saying that neither player had been found to have bet *against* his team, although Hornung allowed that there were some games on which he did not bet at all, not feeling quite as confident as he usually did in his Packers. What Barney Shapiro or any other bettors might have surmised from Hornung's nonbet, no one could really say.

In his first public appearance after the ban Hornung was teary and red-faced, telling the press, "I made a terrible mistake. I realize that now. I am truly sorry." Although Karras was initially defiant, saying "I'm not guilty of anything. This isn't over yet," he eventually relented, accepting the ban and acknowledging what he had done. Rozelle said that both

---

3 A U.S. senator from Arkansas, John Little McClellan, led a federal investigation of the case but, satisfied with Rozelle's punishment, did not prosecute.

Hornung and Karras would be considered for reinstatement after the 1963 season but that for the time being they were out of the league and on a kind of probation. He laid forth a guideline for how the players needed to behave to have a chance at getting back in: "They must avoid the things they were found to have done before—gambling and associations."

Hornung blossomed during his suspension, honing his public speaking skills during a run of 28 banquet appearances. He worked on television and radio (the *Paul Hornung Show* aired in 22 states). He emceed a car show and he made in-store appearances for the sportswear company Jantzen. Karras stayed active too. Just 10 days after being banned he went through with a previously scheduled pro wrestling match against Dick the Bruiser (a ring villain and a retired Packer) at Detroit's Olympia Arena.

Both players were reinstated before the 1964 season, and both continued to have productive careers. Karras made All-Pro again while Hornung won two more NFL titles with Green Bay before retiring after the '66 season. In '86, after 15 years of eligibility, Hornung was inducted into the Pro Football Hall of Fame, the length of his wait attributable not to voters' squeamishness about his betting history but because, over the whole, his raw statistics were not overwhelming. Quipped Hornung when he went into the Hall: "Statistics are for suckers. Ask any bettor."

Hornung—who was raised 100 miles from the Anderson Ferry and who was surrounded by low stakes sports gambling throughout his Kentucky youth—got to know Rose in the 1960s. They kept up a relationship over the years; Pete sometimes went on Hornung's radio show in Louisville and Hornung went on Rose's show at the Ballpark Cafe in Florida during the 1990s. They also played a fair amount of golf together around that time. Says Dave Rose, who sometimes joined a foursome with those two and Dave Thomas, the founder of the Wendy's hamburger chain, "Between Paul and Pete there were some bets going down on the course. You could definitely say that."

The two stars have also been hired to do events together and in 2010 they appeared as guests of honor at a sports stag for a high school on Cincinnati's West Side. Rose lit the spirit of what would be a lively, laugh-filled night, when, standing on stage, he gestured toward himself and

Hornung and said into the microphone, "This looks like a meeting of Gamblers Anonymous up here." The crack brought down the house. One refrain in Rose's calibrated appeal for public sympathy is to remind people that in the sin of gambling he is not alone among his athletic peers.

––––––––––––––––––

THE MOST notorious gambling case in baseball history is, of course, the fixed World Series of 1919, when White Sox players agreed to take money from gamblers to throw the games to the underdog Reds. Eight players were later permanently banned by Commissioner Landis and the one among them whose name most often comes up in discussion of Pete Rose is Shoeless Joe Jackson. Shoeless Joe was one of baseball's greatest players and the only one, aside from Rose, who would be in the Hall of Fame if not for his gambling-related sins.[4] Over the course of a 13-year career, Jackson, a splendid outfielder and dynamic base runner, batted .356, the third-highest career average ever. Ty Cobb called him "the finest natural hitter in the history of the game." Babe Ruth, who said that he modeled his batting stance after Jackson's, labeled him "the greatest hitter I have ever seen."

Jackson was never judged to have actually bet on baseball games, or even suspected of it, but simply to have been in on the Series fix. The Sox, heavily favored, lost the best-of-nine series to Cincinnati five games to three and the revelation that the players had lain down rattled the country immediately and for many years afterward, blossoming into popular culture and imagination long before the 1963 book and '88 movie *Eight Men Out*. Covering the grand jury investigation into the fix in 1920, a

––––––––––

[4] Another banned White Sock, infielder Buck Weaver, sometimes gets mentioned as a Hall of Fame candidate, but he's really not. Solid and even excellent in many ways, Weaver played just nine seasons, producing a meager .307 on-base percentage and high error totals. Aside from those White Sox, the other high-level player of the gambling sort is first baseman Hal Chase, who played for five teams and was later found to have bet on games *and* having tried to fix them. Chase batted .291 over 15 seasons (1905–19) with decent power, good speed and some flashy glove work, yet he too falls far short of Cooperstown-level caliber.

newspaper man from Chicago reported the first version of the immortal exchange outside the courtroom: a small boy confronting Jackson and demanding, "Say it ain't so, Joe!"

Baseball was a far-reaching and immensely popular game, and the sabotage of its championship, wrote F. Scott Fitzgerald a few years later, proved powerful enough to "play with the faith of fifty million people." It's an early and undeniable sign of the moral imbalance of Jay Gatsby— born fully formed from Fitzgerald's mind in the 1920s—that he consorts with Meyer Wolfsheim, "the man," as Gatsby puts it, "who fixed the World's Series back in 1919."

Some historians then and now have presented Jackson as more victim than perp in the scandal, defending his name primarily on the grounds that 1) he batted .375 over the eight games of the Series and he swore that he had tried his hardest, and 2) he was illiterate and so, perhaps, not entirely witting as he entered into the agreement. Yet it remains hard to get past some of the things Jackson said under oath to the grand jury in Cook County:

Q: Did anybody pay you any money to help throw that series in favor of Cincinnati?

A: They did.

Q: How much did they pay?

A: They promised me $20,000 and paid me five.

And, from later in the testimony:

Q: Then you went ahead and threw the second game. . . is that right?

A: We went ahead and threw the second game.

Later still, when Jackson is asked what he did with the $5,000, he answers: "I put it in my pocket."

It does seem clear that Shoeless Joe was a follower and not a ring-leader in the fix, and although he and the other players were acquitted at trial (jurors carried some of the Sox around the crowded and jubilant courtroom on their shoulders), Commissioner Landis, aware that the integrity and perhaps the solvency of the game was under threat, banished every one of them.

In 1951, less than 10 months before Jackson's death, the House of Representatives in South Carolina—Shoeless Joe lived much of his youth and his postplaying years in or around Greenville—passed a resolution to appeal to baseball for his reinstatement. The appeal was denied. The South Carolina House appealed again in '85, this time to new commissioner Peter Ueberroth who had reinstated Mickey Mantle and Willie Mays, players banned for their casino associations by Ueberroth's predecessor Bowie Kuhn. ("The world changes," Ueberroth said.) Ueberroth also rejected Jackson and so the state tried one more time in '89, appealing to commissioner A. Bartlett Giamatti amid the heat of the Rose gambling investigation. Three weeks before signing Rose's lifetime ban, Giamatti officially denied the Jackson petition, writing in part: "I, for one, do not wish to play God with history."

Rose's case (along with *Eight Men Out* and the 1989 movie *Field of Dreams*) helped revive interest in Jackson's situation and also moved the emphasis onto the question of his suitability for admittance to the Hall of Fame. Earlier debate around Jackson had centered more generally on the clearing of his name and the restoration of his legacy; Cooperstown itself moved to the forefront only after Rose was barred. When fans in South Carolina rallied behind Jackson once again in the '90s, they had the Hall in mind, and it was in those years that Hall of Famers Ted Williams and Bob Feller publicly took up the cause. Williams pleaded directly with Bud Selig—unsuccessfully—on Shoeless Joe's behalf. "Damn it," Williams, then 80, told friends of his Jackson advocacy, "I'm going to keep it going until I'm gone."

Linked by their banishments, Jackson and Rose—as Cincinnatians can tell you—are also linked by the city itself. Much of the 1919 scandal came together in Cincinnati, the site of Games 1, 2, 6 and 7. On the eve of the Series opener, shops and street corners swirled with rumors that the fix was in and later, after all the games were done, the Reds' World Series win seemed not a victory at all, but a sour and unwanted gift.

"When everything was going on with Pete, there was a lot of talk about 1919 around here," says Jeff Ruby, the Cincinnati restaurateur who was close to Rose during the late '80s. "The idea was that a gambling situation in baseball was hitting us hard again. It was 70 years later—70! One thing I've learned since coming here"—Ruby arrived in Cincinnati in 1970 as a young man from the East Coast—"is that in this town history really matters. People have long memories."

For all the linkage of their fates, and the fact that both of them greatly endangered the game through gambling, Jackson and Rose committed very different sins with different implications. Jackson's fix appears to have been an isolated case in his life, while Rose's gambling was heavy and chronic. Unlike Jackson, however, Rose was never, even after exhaustive investigation, accused of attempting to throw or alter the outcome of a game. Nor was Rose ever charged or even suspected of giving anything less than full effort with full intent to win in every one of the 3,562 major league games in which he played.

PETE ROSE and Denny McLain are not friends, though they've been closely coupled at various times in their lives. In 1969, the two were credited as coauthors on a paperback manual, *How to Play Better Baseball* (not to be confused with Bud Harrelson's *How to Play Better Baseball*, published in '72). Later they appeared at card shows together, and in 1988, when McLain was working as promotions director for the Fort Wayne (Ind.) Komets pro hockey team, he hired Rose to do an event at the rink. "Pete Rose Night" went very well (thousands lined up for autographs) and during the visit Rose and McLain went out for dinner. A quarter of a century later, McLain recalled that dinner as he sat in front of the Paterno Brothers store—in between signing for the fans and greeting passersby on their way to the Hall of Fame.

"Pete had his guys out with him that night," said McLain. "Every rat in his cage. They were such talkers and such amateurs. As the night went on [some of Pete's friends] started talking about doing a cocaine deal. I could hardly believe it." Less than five months earlier McLain had left the Federal Correctional Institution in Talladega, Ala., having served 29 months of a 23-year sentence for several crimes including extortion and an attempt to distribute three kilos of cocaine. His prison time had been drastically reduced because in an appeal it was determined that procedural errors had been made during the original trial.

"I took Pete aside at one point and said, 'What are you doing with these guys?'" says McLain. "He said, 'Nah, they're my friends.' I tried to talk him away from it. These guys were amateurs, clueless. I said to Pete, 'Do you know what could happen to you if you get caught? Look at what happened to me. You do not want to end up there.' He started talking about how, Yeah but I'd gotten my case reversed and all, which to me was ridiculous logic."

This dinner in Fort Wayne was also mentioned in a phone conversation that became evidence in the Dowd Report, which also included a separate and well-detailed suggestion that Rose was near to and aware of cocaine dealings. Rose, though, has never been charged with a drug-related crime and he has firmly dismissed any suggestions of involvement with cocaine.

"I have no idea what ended up happening with all that," McLain said. "But it was right out there on the table. I said to him, 'Pete you are fucking crazy. You're crazy. What are you doing with these guys? You're Pete Rose.'"

Chapter 12

Petey

July, 1997, Central Georgia

THE OLD bus traveled northward through the night, making time on I-75, whirring up and inland toward Chattanooga. The seats were full of ballplayers, the members of the Double A Chattanooga Lookouts, a Cincinnati Reds affiliate that had just played a game in Jacksonville. Among these teammates was a third baseman of inevitable renown: Pete Rose Jr. That summer Petey—to everyone he was Petey—was having the finest season of his career, batting comfortably above .300 and with newfound power. He was on his way to a Chattanooga total of 25 home runs, 31 doubles and 98 RBI in fewer than 450 at bats. No one could say for sure, but there were whispers around the club that the time was drawing near, that, finally, when the Reds roster expanded in September, Rose Jr. would get his chance to play in the major leagues.

Now the hour was late and the air inside the bus hung stale and dense. Here and there yellow foam rubber worked its way out through tears in the faded fabric of the seats. A TV screen above the aisle flickered silently. Someone belched. Jacksonville to Chattanooga meant seven and a half, maybe eight hours in all—more than 400 miles to ride.

Rose Jr. was well familiar with this kind of trip. He was playing in his ninth season in the minor leagues, seven of them spent at low-rung A ball. He knew not to take even an uninterrupted bus ride for granted (he'd endured roadside breakdowns in five states over the years), and he had long since learned that in the minor leagues you get your sleep whenever and wherever you can.

He zipped up his ball jacket and folded his arms across his chest. Wedged into his window seat, he grew tired of the rhythmic monotony, the blur of yellow-orange highway lights and the ceaseless black road. The bus rolled past Waycross, Dixie Union, mileage signs to Atlanta. Soon Petey's eyes fell shut, and his neck went slack. It was a warm midsummer night. Pete Rose Jr. was 27 years old, and in his sleep he had a dream.

He is at Riverfront Stadium in Cincinnati, the cradle of his boyhood and youth, and he is stepping into the batter's box. The crowd is thundering all around him and there is a pitcher, faceless and nameless—irrelevant—on the mound. His father is in the stands. Suddenly it is quiet, and the pitch is thrown. And in his dream Pete Rose Jr. is aware that this is his very first at bat in the major leagues.

He swings at the ball, and he hits it hard, and he can feel the clean, weightless ricochet off the bat and see the ball on its path, a white streak going into rightfield, curling toward the foul line and an outfielder moving toward the ball, and all of it, as he would recall more than 15 years later, "vivid. Very, very vivid, as vivid a dream as I have had in my life."

He begins to sprint down the first base line. He is wearing the red number 14 on his back. He can hear the crowd again, and the fans calling out his name, "Petey! Petey!" as they stretch their necks and peer down toward rightfield and the ball as it drops fair to the grass. And now he is angling toward first base, and making the turn, and the ball is being gathered in by a rightfielder (also nameless and faceless); now he is nearing second base, knowing that the ball is coming there too and that there will be a play on him. And so he leaves his feet, all Pete Rose Jr. of him., and he goes hard into the bag, arriving headfirst and safely in a spray of dirt.

It very nearly came true, "that crazy, real, strange dream that"—Rose Jr. says—"I sometimes still think about." He arrived to the big leagues less than two months after that bus ride, getting there Sept. 1, 1997, nine years to the day after he signed his first professional contract. In his second at bat for the Reds he pulled a ball to the right side and it bounded off the glove of the Royals first baseman, Jeff King. Rose Jr. turned at first base and held there with a single. The camera showed his father, in the front row behind home plate, fleshier than he might have been at age 56, sunglasses and ballcap on, standing up and clapping, a grin on his face. "For Pete Rose Jr. only 4,255 more hits to go," a television commentator would say.

Petey had come to the park that day from his in-laws' home in Cincinnati, driving along the same streets he had so often traveled as a child with his mom or dad—a piece of Glenway, a stretch of Queen City Avenue, a few miles down I-75 to Second Street and the side road now called Pete Rose Way—and pulling into the players' parking area at what was now Cinergy Field but would always be Riverfront to him.

He dressed beside the locker with his nameplate on it, and bantered with Bernie Stowe and the other clubhouse men. There was still the same old carpet, but some of the lighting was new. In all, the clubhouse seemed a changed, familiar place. He had been awake in his room until 5 a.m., he told people, "with nothing on, doing my stances in the mirror."

He buffed his shoes and buttoned his white jersey. Until now, the number 14 had been taken out of circulation, no longer available to any Reds player, but Petey's dad had said it would be O.K. for him to wear it. He tarred up his bat and when he jogged onto the field the early crowd leaped forward. Before it was announced that Rose Jr. would play, the Reds had sold about 16,000 tickets to the game. After the announcement they sold 16,000 more. Red-white-and-blue bunting hung around the stands as if it were Opening Day, and a helicopter clucked loudly overhead trailing a sign that read WELCOME HOME PETEY. This was one of the largest crowds of the season in Cincinnati; the Reds were out of the pennant race and on their way to a losing year.

"I haven't been to a Reds' game in seven years, since Pete was banned," one fan told a newspaper reporter from West Virginia. "But I saw Pete's first game, at Crosley Field in 1963, and I'm here to see Petey's first game."

Petey took batting practice just as he had at the same home plate under the same cage during the 1980s—as a teenage ballplayer at Oak Hills High, tagging along to work with Dad—but this time he was being paid a prorated portion of the big league minimum, $150,000 a year. This time Petey was hitting in a group with the other starters in the Reds lineup.

After BP, after a game of catch and some infield, after he'd gone back inside, pulled on a clean shirt and buffed his shoes one more time, he was in the dugout, standing at the rail beside Eduardo Perez, Tony's son, another kid who'd been raised in this same clubhouse, raised by the Big Red Machine. Eduardo was Petey's age, almost exactly, and already in his fifth big league season. In the 1970s they had played Wiffle ball together in the tunnels at Riverfront, more times than either of them could count. It was 12:56 p.m., about nine minutes before the start of the game and Petey turned to Eduardo and said, "My dad just got here."

Yes. Big Pete, up from Florida, was striding through the ballpark gates then with his wife Carol, stopping first to greet Reds owner Marge Schott with an embrace. Some 32,000 fans in the house, another payday Rose and Schott could congratulate themselves on. Marge took a drag on her cigarette, and Rose made a joke about how he might just leap the railing and pinch-hit. Below, on the bench, far out of sight and earshot, Pete Jr. had the familiar cold feeling wash over him. "All kinds of chills," he says. It's a feeling he often gets when Big Pete is near, even before he has seen him, before, it would seem, he could be certain his father is there. "I know," he says. "I get the feeling and I just know. I am always right."

The crowd stood and applauded a few minutes later when Pete Rose appeared in the stands and made his way down to his seat at the rail—waving to folks he knew—and the applause began anew when Petey ran out to third base for the top of the first inning. He bent and with his index finger wrote "HK 4256" in the dirt by the bag, the HK standing for Hit King, the inscription being what he scrawled onto the baseball field before every game he played. He gathered in a few warmup grounders from tall Ed Taubensee at first base. And then with

Petey pounding his glove and fielding-ready at third, Reds lefthander Mike Remlinger threw his first pitch to Kansas City's Johnny Damon, making it official: Petey was a big leaguer.

He was hitting seventh in the lineup, and his first at bat came in the bottom of the second inning, the Reds trailing 1–0, the tying run on second base. He carried to the plate one of the black Mizuno bats that were custom-made for Big Pete to use during the home stretch of his pursuit of Ty Cobb in 1985, and on Petey's way to the batter's box, he called out to his father, "This one's for you." He had been saving this bat for this moment since he was 15 years old.

Though Petey normally stood straighter in his batting stance than Big Pete had, with his hands higher and his feet wider apart, for that first pitch he got down in his father's old crouch, the black bat low over his shoulder in tribute. He followed the path of the pitch (a fastball) out of Kevin Appier's right hand and he looked the ball all the way into Mike Macfarlane's catcher's mitt, just the way his dad had taught him to do when taking a pitch. *Understand how the pitcher is trying to get you out.* The fans were tingling and abuzz, getting what they had paid to see.

Petey struck out that first at bat, high fastball away, but then came the base hit, leading off the bottom of the fourth, on a 3-and-2 count. Petey would play all nine innings, make a nice backhand play at third base, draw a walk. And though he went down on strikes a second time and though the Reds lost the game, Pete Jr. recalls this day as the best day of his 21-season playing career. When the media surged around him afterward, he kept tugging on the 14 on his chest as he spoke and he grinned and nodded a lot. "The nine years of bus rides, bad food, bad hotels, bad fans. It was all worth it," he said.

He met his dad after the game too—outside the players' tunnel, near the media entrance—and his father hugged him. And though it really *was* the best day of Pete Rose Jr.'s long and winding baseball life, it was a day darkened too.

"I'm the only guy to play his first game in the big leagues, and my dad wasn't allowed in the locker room," Rose Jr. says. He is saying this more than 15 years after that day. "Every other guy you ask: Did your dad come to your locker after your first game? The answer is yes. My dad? I wasn't even allowed to leave passes for him. It was miserable.

"Imagine if he could have come in, if we could have walked out of the clubhouse and onto the field the same way we always used to do, only now I'm the one playing and he's the one watching. And after the game he could have come over to my locker instead of the way I used to go over to his. I know, I get it. I guess I understand why he wasn't allowed, but even so, couldn't they have just let him in? What was he going to do, come in there and be some crazed bad guy? Come in and start taking bets on the game? He would have just come in and talked baseball with everyone. That's what he does. He could have just come in and been with me. My dad. But he wasn't allowed in. Why did *I* get penalized? What did I do?"

August 2012, Bristol, Va.
One of the most popular nights of the year at Boyce Cox Field, home of the low A Bristol White Sox, is Mayberry Deputy Night, a takeout from the old *Andy Griffith Show*. It features a Barney Fife impersonator—a local man of local renown named David Browning—who meanders among the crowd, handing out summonses for miscues and infractions. Say, being bald. "Guess you went from Head and Shoulders to Mop and Glo," the putative Fife will say, writing a guy up. If someone calls out "Hey, Barney, where are your bullets?" He pulls them out of his breast pocket. Just like on *Andy Griffith*. The BriSox, as they are affectionately known, typically draw about 550 or 600 people per game. On Mayberry Deputy Night several hundred more turn out.

This is the field where in 2011 at the age of 41, Pete Rose Jr. began his professional managing career. The 30 or so BriSox ballplayers dress in close and spartan quarters: metal benches, gym-room lockers. Some are mid-to-late twentysomethings hanging on for the last of their baseball lives, others are teenage bonus babies on their first professional stop. To pass the time before a game, players will gather around and do card tricks or take turns making mouth-farting noises. Later at night a group will sometimes go to the State Line Bar and Grille, the only joint open, and try to meet some girls.

In the outfield at Boyce Cox, the home run fence looms 16 feet high and is plastered top-to-bottom with sponsor signage: Blevins Tire & Recapping Co.; Appalachian Orthopaedic Associates; McDonald's; VFW Post 6975; Walgreens; Walmart; Addilynn Memorial United Methodist Church; and so on. A large American flag flaps on a pole behind centerfield, and beside it a stand of tall pine trees into which the best of the young sluggers might lose a baseball. If you were to sit on one of the orange plastic chairs beside the first base dugout where Rose Jr. liked to sit with his coaches during games, you could see past the trees and into the surrounding neighborhood. A battered red Chevy truck might roll down Division Street, turn onto Elmo and pull into a driveway where the driver shuts off the motor and goes inside his home. In the infield the base paths run 90 feet each and the distance from the mound to home plate is 60 feet, six inches.

A fair number of notable baseball figures have stopped in Bristol, the bottom rung on the Chicago White Sox's organizational ladder, on their way up through the ranks—future American League All-Star Carlos Lee as a player in 1995; the major league's former single-season saves leader Bobby Thigpen as a manager in 2007 and '08 to name just two— but the arrival of Rose Jr. as Bristol's manager created a level of excitement of an altogether different order; folks around the team were ecstatic. Each year on the eve of the season the team holds a Meet the Sox night in which fans, especially the bundles of children who come to games seeking autographs and foul balls, can chat with the team. Before the '11 and '12 home openers, there was a twist in publicity: The stadium marquee read, "Meet Pete Rose Jr. and the Bristol Sox." Bristol is about a six hour drive south of Cincinnati.

His was the autograph that the kids in the crowd coveted more than any other. A prospect such as first-round draftee Courtney Hawkins— who signed for nearly $2.5 million in 2012 and who did a memorable televised backflip on draft day—might have strolled to the parking lot unbothered but not Pete Jr. "These kids have stacks of Pete Rose Jr. autographs at home," says Tim Hayes, a reporter for the *Bristol Herald Courier* who began covering the BriSox in '02. "I know. I grew up here. I have about 16 Carlos Lee autographs that I've kept to this day. Rose Jr. is the biggest attraction in Bristol in my time."

He wore number 14, and the door to his bare, uncarpeted office was always unlocked. Through the record-hot summer of 2012 Petey went out with the young team hours before each game, hitting fly balls, showing a batting grip, teaching baseball under the Southern sun. The BriSox play about 65 games a year.

For the 2013 season the White Sox moved Pete Jr. half a step up to another short-season rookie ball team—this time in Great Falls, Mont., another dot on the sprawling baseball map of the United States. Great Falls is well-known for its UFO activity, and Pete Jr.'s team, the Voyagers, is named for a never satisfactorily explained sighting of two flying disks in 1950.

As a manager Rose Jr. emphasizes fundamental play and the importance of knowing the situation, of knowing yourself and your opposition. Because many of the offensive players on instructional league teams are so fresh-faced and so often easily frustrated when they don't dominate as they did in high school, Rose Jr. hammers home the truths of the game—notably the importance of learning to accept failure. He teaches this old and enduring baseball lesson as only he can. "Who has the most hits in major league history?" Rose Jr. asks an assembled group of new players. After a moment or two someone calls out, "Your dad."

"Right. And who has made the most outs in major league history?"

To this there is no reply. The players peer in quietly.

"That's my dad too," Rose Jr. says

It is in places like Bristol and Great Falls that Pete Rose Jr. has spent his baseball career—his life, really—both before and for many years after his stirring Reds debut. Rose Jr.'s major league experience, accumulated entirely in that September of 1997, amounts to 14 official at bats over 28 days. And yet he played professional baseball from '89 through 2009. Twenty-one years in the minor leagues. He made 31 stops and played for 27 teams. He played winter ball in Puerto Rico, Nicaragua and Colombia. He came to the plate 8,160 times in the minors, got 1,924 hits, drove in 1,058 runs, scored 915, walked 751 times and struck out 855.

All told Rose Jr. appeared in 1,972 minor league games over those 21 years, and here are the most remarkable facts of all: More than a third of those games were played for independent clubs with no major league affiliation. And only 166 of his career games—less than 9%—were above the level of Double A. This catalog of minor league numbers is unlike anything the game has ever seen.[1]

"Off the charts," says Bob Hoie, a leading minor league researcher for SABR. "It's astounding, really. No one in the past 50 years has had a career even close to that. To play in that many games is extraordinary. To play so many games in low-level leagues? That is unheard of."

HE WAS born on Nov. 16, 1969, six weeks after Pete Rose had laid down a two-out bunt hit to edge Roberto Clemente and win his second consecutive batting title. Peter Edward Rose II read the birth certificate. (The "Jr." just came about, naturally, and stuck, sounding less pretentious than "The Second.") He wasn't the first Rose child—Fawn, born late in '64, would at age four and five play in the so-called father-son game with the Reds—but from the start, he was the one ordained. "Did Pete ever love that boy!" recalls Karolyn Rose. "It used to be baseball first, then Fawn, then me. But when Petey was born he jumped to the top of the list. After baseball I mean."

Official major league baseballs were placed in Petey's crib (he liked to rub his tiny fingers along the stitches) and before he had learned to walk his father had taught him to hold a bat in a stance. The 1971 Reds media guide featured Pete Jr., 15 months old, on its cover—no one else, just Petey in a triptych of poses, cherubic in a roomy Reds uniform, preening before a camera and seated before a typewriter like a hard-

---

[1] A very small handful of present-day players have even appeared in more than 1,500 minor league games with scant major league reward—first baseman John Lindsey (1,908 career minor league hits) and third baseman Mike Hessman (389 home runs) among them. And all of those have played the majority of their games at the Triple A level, where the hotels are decent and a solid living can be made. Such Triple A players earn many times what a Class A or independent league veteran makes.

boiled reporter, a bottle of milk, straight-up, on the table beside him.

When Petey was five years old a Baltimore Orioles scout—the Roses' friend Jack Baker—wrote the kid up a mock professional baseball contract as a lark, specifying that Petey was to become the highest paid player on the O's. Big Pete laughed loud and hard when he saw the contract and Karolyn had it framed.

All through the mid-1970s, at the height and sway of the Big Red Machine, little Pete and other players' sons—Ken Griffey Jr., Eduardo and Victor Perez—spent long parts of days and countless stretches of night at Riverfront. Fawn was there too, a determined tomboy in those years, and Petey likes to say that when it came to the Wiffle ball games, "she was better than all of us."

The kids would grab their gloves and zip around the field and the clubhouse, darting up the tunnel and back just because they could, yelping out to hear their voices echo along the way. They'd clown around with Joe Morgan and eat too many snacks and try on all the batting helmets and sometimes throw a ball around together for a while, down the foul lines, before the team came out on the field.

Petey was always in uniform. He would dress before a full-length mirror, pulling on his regulation Reds issue: double-knit fabric, built-in sash belt, fitted hat, shoes polished just so, his name stitched—not ironed—on the back, above the number 14. Petey was ready to play. "No!" he'd shout if any sort of facsimile outfit were offered up. "I'm not wearing that! I'm wearing what Dad's wearing!" Karolyn ordered a couple of extra uniforms for little Pete in case one was in the wash.

There was the time that Griffey Jr. threw up after eating too much corn on the cob, and the time when Big Pete said that, Sure, the cackling pitcher Pedro Borbon could take a whack at cutting his son's hair; Petey emerged from the clubhouse with a new hairstyle of a sort—call it Dutch-boy punk—that took weeks to grow out. When game time neared and they were supposed to go sit in the stands with their moms, the kids might hide in the umpires' dressing room, noodling with stuff until clubhouse uncle Bernie Stowe came and pulled them away. After the games the boys could come to their dads' lockers, but only, and on this score Reds' manager Sparky Anderson would not bend, only if Cincinnati had won the game.

In a locker room of stars (Morgan, Perez, Bench, Concepcíon...) Petey's dad was *the* superstar, the face of the team, the face of all of baseball, the darling of all media and a swaggering pitchman in TV commercials. There was no bigger life in Cincinnati in those years. Rose might drive Petey and Fawn to the ballpark in his Porsche; Karolyn sometimes showed up to get the kids from school in the family's Rolls-Royce. For a while the Roses had a dog named King Tut. Everybody knew little Petey by name and people called to him in greeting wherever he went.[2]

"He was our leader, really confident even as a young kid," says Eduardo Perez. "We'd play ball, imagining we were big leaguers. We'd be going against the Big Red Machine and of course we always won. Petey organized us, set the rules. I don't want to say he was cocky—he has never had that quite the way his dad has it—but Petey was the kid who figured things out.

"I'll never forget my six-year-old birthday party," Eduardo goes on. "My parents strung up a piñata in our yard. We were all knocking at it with a plastic Wiffle ball bat, but nothing was happening. Then it got to be Petey's turn, and you could see he was thinking about what to do. He had it in his head to get that candy. He *loved* candy. Well, he goes and grabs a *wooden* bat. One swing and that was it. Candy everywhere."

Rose Jr. remembers the sweetness of those early years, and the high jinks, with a laugh. (By the time he and Eduardo were in their early 20s they would reminisce on those days in the manner of rocking-chair ancients gazing back on their prime: "Remember when we were young. . . . ") Yet what endures, the moments that Rose Jr. says he carries with him, that hold him steady in his path, are not about the romping and the playing, but about the baseball and his dad. Driving to the park together, arriving hours early when there were just a few other folks around. Sitting

---

[2] As the years went on, Fawn often seemed forgotten by Pete—an afterthought, and heartbreakingly so. Karolyn recalls reporters or acquaintances running into her and Fawn at the ballpark and saying with surprise: "I didn't know Pete had a daughter!"

at the locker side by side. Usually Big Pete had work to do—extra hitting, sharpening his bunt defense, testing the ground after a night of rain—or he would go off and make a phone call for a while. Petey knew not to bother him then, just waited for those moments in the dugout when his father would pound his glove and nod over at him—*Let's go*—and the two of them would bound out onto the bright green grass in front of the Reds dugout to play catch. "Right to my chest," Big Pete would say holding up his glove for a target. "Put it right here."

When the time was right, closer to the start of the game, Big Pete might gather a few of the kids and a Reds teammate together and get a little game of pepper going behind home plate. "It was just about being with my dad, wanting to be where he was," says Pete Jr. "That happened to mean playing baseball. Isn't that just how it is? If your dad is a cop, you want to be a cop."

In the backyard at home, morning time usually, Petey would stand with his bat and Big Pete would throw batting practice, always with a hardball, always pitching overhand, even from the earliest years. There was one particular day, and both father and son still recall it fondly, when Big Pete was a little wild and kept bouncing pitches in the grass, until Petey, exasperated and maybe four years old, finally called out: "Hey, Dad, get this crap over!"

HE WAS narrower in build than his father, and ruddier in complexion, and yet, by nine and 10 years old, unmistakably Pete Rose's son. When Petey was nine, his dad was in Philadelphia, playing for the Phillies and it was the summer of '79. "We were staying on Locust Street," Rose Jr. says, "and we would get on the subway and take the Broad Street line right to the ballpark. People would look at us and say, 'Hey, it's Pete Rose and his kid!' Everyone knew us. But it was kind of normal too. We were just riding the subway to work."

At Veterans Stadium, Petey occasionally served as a batboy and a clubhouse gofer. He'd shag flies during batting practice (sometimes alongside Ruben Amaro Jr., who was four years older and who would grow up to become the Phillies general manager), and he'd throw on the sidelines with his dad. In the dugout in the middle of a game, he'd go up to a player, Mike Schmidt maybe or Greg Luzinski, and ask questions like: "What pitch did that guy throw you?" Even with his prepubescent voice Petey could sound a lot like the other Pete Rose. Once Rose Jr. and Bud Harrelson's kid, Tim, got into a fistfight around the batting cage, just like their fathers on the field at Shea Stadium in 1973.

"Pete Junior had this way about him," says Greg Gross, a Phillies outfielder. "It was like he had been in the big leagues for a while."

Most of the time Rose played in Philadelphia, though, Petey didn't live with his dad but in Cincinnati with Karolyn and Fawn. The marriage fell apart late in 1979, finally undone by Pete's extravagant philandering, and after the divorce in '80 and the lawyer battles over alimony and child support and who would get which house and which cars (Karolyn kept the Rolls and a Jeep; Pete kept the Porsche), Karolyn would tell the story of the last straw. One day Petey had come home from being at the racetrack with his father—in Cincinnati, Big Pete used to take them over the river to Latonia, put a little money down, get some dinner—and said, "Guess who I saw today, Mom? Dad's girlfriend!" That wasn't the only time; Petey had seen the girlfriend at the ballpark too.

Karolyn had known about Pete's parade of other women from the start, had accepted it as a curse of loving the s.o.b. she loved. She had weathered, barely, Pete's fathering a child with another woman and then the paternity suit against him. But this was too much. Life seemed to be getting away from her. "Flaunting it in front my kids? That's not going to work," Karolyn says. "I could handle what I could handle—my own reasons. But I did not want Fawn and Petey to grow up and think that what Pete was doing was acceptable, as if that was something you could do to your wife." The girlfriend whom Petey saw turned out to be Carol Woliung, who would become the mother of two of Pete's children.

Petey came to Philadelphia only from time to time, on school breaks and parts of the summer, when Big Pete called for him. During the 1980 World Series, Petey flew with the team to Kansas City. He'd hardly seen his dad in months—divorce proceedings were ongoing—and Big Pete had

had to wrest Petey from Karolyn with a court order. Karolyn said that she'd resisted letting Petey go to the Series out of indignation and anger that Big Pete had not invited Fawn as well. *How could he leave her out? How could he exclude his daughter?* Pete, in the midst of that $800,000-a-year Phillies contract, explained that he had nowhere for Fawn, as a girl and now a teenager, to comfortably stay.

So it was Petey who slept in his father's hotel room during that World Series, who saw his father up and pacing, bat in hand, by morning's light. During games Petey sat in the dugout, wearing number 14, cheering on the team and calling out "Get a hit" to his father before at bats. In the clincher, back in Philadelphia, Rose singled three times.

"I spit, I chew sunflower seeds and gum," Petey said then to a reporter. "I go between innings to get Tootsie Rolls. This is the best thing to happen in my life."

The nation saw Petey then, just as they saw him when he was brought into one of his father's Aqua Velva aftershave commercials. The two of them stand on the steps of the dugout wearing their Phillies whites and looking out toward the field. Petey has his slim arm across Pete's back: "Hey, Dad?"

"Yeah?"

"When do you think I'm going to start shaving?"

Big Pete, inspecting the face: "It's going to be a few years, Son, but when you do you've got something great to look forward to."

"Aqua Velva, right, Dad?"

They give one another jokey little buddy-pal punches on the chin. "Aqua Velva," Big Pete says, "it makes a man ... " and Petey finishes, "feel like a man."

In 1982, when Petey was 12, he appeared on a big league baseball card, Fleer number 640. It's a candid shot, middle of a game. Petey is on one knee by the on-deck circle and Big Pete crouches beside him, bat in hand, doughnut on the barrel, pine tar rag by the handle, looking out at the pitcher with fingers raised to make a point, telling Petey something about what's going on in the game. The photo is labeled PETE & RE-PETE. The back of the card tells of Rose's fine season and .325 batting average the year before, closing with this paragraph: "On

August 10, 1981 Pete surpassed Stan Musial's alltime National League hit record with 3,631 hits. Cheering him on throughout his great career is his faithful and loyal son, Pete Rose II."

BIG PETE didn't make it to Petey's Little League games during the Philadelphia years, of course—even when the family was intact in Cincinnati he didn't get to them, playing his own ball games with the Reds—but even in his absence, his presence was felt. There was always someone around to remind Petey whose son he was. "Hey, what's the matter with Pete Rose's kid?" an opposing player's parent would crack, chortling if Petey struck out or dropped a ball. "No wonder his dad got out of town!" Then brassy Karolyn, at every game with snacks for the kids, would rumble over and tell the parent in her convincing hellmouthed way to shut it. And shut it the parent invariably did.[3]

Petey's strikeouts weren't all that common though. He could play, could handle himself on a ballfield. When Big Pete came back to lead the Reds in August of 1984, it meant Petey was back too—back in a Cincinnati uniform and back in the clubhouse with a half-sized locker all his own. Being batboy was just the nub of it. Petey came early to the park, hit in the cage, went out and got some hacks off Tommy Helms or whichever coach was throwing BP. He'd get in line near the bag at first or third and take ground balls, circle under pop-ups. He played pregame catch with any Reds player who needed to get warm and he was always ready to shoot the bull about that night's game. "I think he thought he was actually on the team," says Buddy Bell, the Reds' third baseman in those years. "You know, he kind of was."[4]

---

[3] Bill Giles, the longtime Phillies executive, tells the story of standing in an elevator in a Florida hotel with his father, Warren, the National League president, when Karolyn and Petey stepped inside. Petey was about nine and Warren mussed his hair and said to Karolyn: "He's so cute, I just love this kid." To which Karolyn replied: "Yeah, but he cusses too goddamn much."

[4] At Opening Day in 1987 a reporter approached Pete Jr. on the field before the game and asked him how he felt about losing his starting shortstop job to Barry Larkin. The writer had confused Petey, then 17, with 21-year-old Reds' infielder Kurt Stillwell.

Of course Petey's life was not whole, not with his father now remarried. An underlying sadness inhabited him, an emptiness. The three of them—Petey with Karolyn and Fawn—were in a new house now, on Neeb Road. Petey didn't have Big Pete throwing batting practice to him in the backyard anymore. He hit off a pitching machine. "He was still our same Petey, still full of energy, ready to play ball," says Karolyn. "But he was different. Sometimes, I would see him looking around in a way that I hadn't seen him do before, his eyes moving this way and that. Like he was unsettled." Later Petey would describe the divorce as being mystifying to him, and unexplained. One day his mom had packed up their things and they'd left without his father for Puerto Rico. They stayed at the Perezes' place for a while, and when they came back to Cincinnati his father's stuff was out of the house.

Big Pete couldn't stand even talking to Karolyn, although Petey and Fawn knew that the feeling did not go both ways. As angered as she was—and it was she who had demanded the divorce—Karolyn still had a thing for Pete. It felt like she wanted him back. "I think she still loves him," Fawn said a few years after the split. But there was never even a hint toward reconciliation. It was after that 1984 season that Big Pete and Carol had named their infant son Tyler after Ty Cobb, the figure who loomed larger than any living being in Big Pete's life.

Petey knew that things would never be the way they had been, that life at home would not again be the way he wished it could be. But at the ballpark? Well, that could be a kind of home for Petey. That could work. At the park, Petey was in the throes of that wonderful, anticipatory summer of 1985. His father was the Reds' player-manager, and the team, crummy for three years straight, was suddenly winning and fans were coming to the ballpark, and it was all because of Pete Rose. He was about to do something that no one had thought could ever be done. He was stalking Cobb's alltime hits record, full of the chase and keen to the record on every front, right up to the night of Sept. 11, 1985, when he had 4,191 career hits and needed one more, and nearly 50,000 people packed Riverfront Stadium to see what Pete Rose could do.

Eleven-month-old Tyler Rose may have been in the stands swaddled in Carol's arms, but it was Petey who was in the dugout beside his father, down by the bat rack before the game. They had their gloves on and when his dad gave that familiar nod—*Let's go, time to toss*—Petey loped up the dugout steps and out onto the field. He was growing tall, closing in on six feet, and even if you were in the very first row behind the Reds' dugout, and particularly if you were among the thousands and thousands behind that, you looked onto the field and saw that number 14 jersey and naturally thought that this was the man himself.

Cameras flashed like a light show and the crowd erupted in huge cries, standing and clapping and calling out the name: "Rose!" "Pete Rose!" "Tonight's the night, Rose!" It was unlike anything Petey had ever heard, louder than a World Series game. He punched his glove and turned to look for his father. But Big Pete had stayed in the dugout instead of coming onto the field. Petey looked in and caught Big Pete's eye and saw that big familiar grin, and Petey realized, as he stood out there naked and awed under the stadium lights, what his father had given him: this moment before the crowd on this night so that he could feel the thrill of it, the joy, the electricity and the weight. So that for a moment he could stand in his father's shoes.

When Big Pete stepped out of the dugout himself a few moments later, the crowd surged again, understanding now that they would see the two Roses play catch. Petey recalls the first ball his father threw to him arriving as if out of a rifle, a much harder throw than usual and the powerful *thwock!* in his glove another reminder that this night was different from all others. Petey could hardly see through the tears in his eyes. He felt nauseated almost. His throw back to Big Pete sailed too high. The next time he got the ball Petey threw it almost straight into the dirt. It was as if he had never played catch in his life and his legs felt weak and unsteady.

Through the pregame and the top of the first inning the crowd's hum rose and fell, and then Rose stepped to the plate, bottom of the first, and drove that clean opposite-field single—yes, indeed, hit number 4,192!—that made the game, and all the world it seemed, come to a stop. Pete Rose Jr. was 15 years, nine months and 26 days old. He went out onto the field with the Reds' players and hovered on the outskirts of the celebration as so many teammates—Perez and Concepcíon, Browning and Franco, Hume and Murphy and O'Neill—gathered around Pete at first base and hoisted him onto their shoulders. Marge Schott appeared, escorted out by a policeman, and put her arms around Big Pete. Even after she and all the Reds players had left the field, Petey along with them, and with umpire Lee Weyer back of home plate seeming inclined to resume the game, the volume of the crowd did not wane. On and on it continued. Six minutes, seven minutes, eight. . . . Petey saw his father standing alone at first base. Helms, the coach at first base, draped an arm around Big Pete and turned toward the dugout, and Petey heard the catcher Dave Van Gorder say, "You should go back out there."

Petey felt unsure. For all his father had given him on the baseball field, all the access and freedom, all the tutelage, there were still the many things that his dad withheld; there were borders around Big Pete that Petey was not supposed to cross. Fawn and Karolyn stood beside one another in the stands. Petey's grandma and his uncle Dave were there too. All of the huge crowd was cheering. And even as Petey summoned his resolve and did it, as he ran out of the dugout and onto the field toward first base, he wondered how it would turn out, whether his arriving at first base would be O.K. with Dad.

He would say later that this was the first time that his father had ever hugged him, really hugged him, a tree trunk of a 44-year-old man to Petey's green stalk, not letting go. Petey could feel that his father was weeping, his body racked—and that too was a first—and he could feel his father's heart beating, and he could feel his own heart beating and now in their first moment together since Pete Rose had taken it away from Cobb, since he had become the Hit King, he said into Petey's ear, "You'll catch me." Petey couldn't say anything to that, not one thing. He only stayed in the embrace and patted his father on the back, the way macho old buddies do upon greeting, or the way a woman might pat a man to signal that an embrace is chaste. There was a stiffness in the way Petey held on to his father, although in Big Pete at this moment there was no stiffness at all.

What Petey would say—and he would say this too on camera in a doc-

umentary film, so it was not a personal detail that he had a mind to hide—
was that he was so very happy to have gotten that hug from his father, on
television, before all the masses of people at Riverfront. And he added that
for all the roaring in the stadium and all the many eyes that he knew were
upon them, as he stood out there in that strange, first true embrace, the
crowd was in fact not there at all, and that when he and his father were together at first base, "There was nobody there but me and him."

Chapter 13

Suspended Belief

A CROWD OF 55,438, a regular-season record for Riverfront, had come out for this Opening Day against the Cardinals. Rose was beginning his fourth full season as the Reds' manager, and now, April 4, 1988, it seemed at last safe to say that he would not be getting in the batter's box again. He was 10 days shy of his 47th birthday, 20 months removed from his last at bat. This was the 26th Opening Day that Rose had been in a major league dugout and the 107th straight opener in the continuum of Reds history. The team wore black armbands to remember Ted Kluszewski, the brawny Cincinnati slugger of the 1950s and the batting coach for the Big Red Machine. Big Klu had died a few days earlier. "I never heard a bad word said about him," Rose said after attending the funeral. "He was a prince."

Rose's final appearances as a player had passed quietly in the summer of 1986. He'd started that season, his first as the Hit King, on the 15-day disabled list with a nasty flu (just the second stint on the disabled list in his career) and had slumped terribly once he came back—playing through a steady hum that he should hang it up. Fan polls suggested as much and so did commentators. Rose was not chasing Cobb anymore, and as a player he was hugely diminished, no longer helping the team. He had more miles on him than anyone in major league baseball history—by a long shot—but still Rose found it too hard to pull away. In May and June and into early July, he kept putting himself into the lineup at first base, batting second, just about every time the Reds faced a righthanded pitcher—singling softly here and there, fighting to keep his batting average above .200. "I don't want to be around him when the end of his career comes," Joe Morgan once said. "I know what it will do to him . . . It is his life. . . . When I'm through, I'll still be Joe Morgan. He won't be Pete Rose and I worry about that."

On Aug. 11 of that 1986 season, Rose got five hits in five at bats in a home game against the Giants, four singles, a double, three RBI. "That was the 10th five-hit day of my career," he said in his crowded manager's office after the game, correcting a reporter who'd gotten it wrong. Six days later, a Sunday at Riverfront against the Padres, Rose went up as a pinch-hitter to face Goose Gossage in the eighth inning. Gossage threw three fastballs and Rose struck out. Rose was 45 years, four months and three days old, his batting average stood at .219 on the year, and that, it turned out, was the last of the 15,890 times he came to the plate in the major leagues.

Rose, though, never said, "I'm done." He couldn't. He didn't put himself into a game the rest of the year, but he didn't announce his retirement as a player in the off-season either. He wasn't on the roster when 1987 began, though the possibility persisted that season that ol' Pete, as manager, might activate himself at any time. He did nothing to discourage such talk. Up on Given Road, he loaded up the pitching machine and hit for long stretches after the games. At the ballpark he watched pitchers, deconstructing, as he always did. Weeks and then months went by but Rose would not rule out a return, no matter his age or faded skills. He kept his black bats around him in the clubhouse. Maybe, he said, the Reds would need a pinch-hitter late in the year. "I know I can hit the bleeping baseball," he said. Not really, though. Not in a way that Pete Rose or Harry Rose could be proud of, and Pete knew that deep inside. Fawn said at the time that her father bore a perceptible resentment toward Pete Jr. "Petey has the one thing Dad doesn't have now," Fawn said. "Youth."

It was only a couple months after the end of that 1987 season, at base-ball's winter meetings, that Rose allowed to a few reporters—no press conference, no big declarative statement, it was almost an aside—that he was through playing the game. He did not want any kind of farewell tour, he said, no send-off at Riverfront, no to-do, no fuss. "Don't people understand I'm not retiring?" he said. "I'm just moving into a new posi-tion. I still have a uniform on."

Yes, he was still in and into the game and the Reds players, most of them, though not quite all, loved him as a manager. He bustled around as he always did, energy unbound, and he let loose his peppery ragtime of talk. He managed the team with great attention to detail, reminding players of the particulars of each umpire's strike zone, telling them which grounds crew cut the grass high or low. He was loyal to the Reds who worked hard for him and he always knew what time it was in each of his player's lives. "He messes with me just like he did when he was playing," said pitcher Bill Gullickson. "You can clown with him but you respect him." Added outfielder Eric Davis, "He is one of us."

That Rose was sometimes accompanied at the ballpark by a coterie of neckless and decidedly unpolished men (often with pagers clipped to their belts) did not jar his players. Pete knew everyone in Cincinnati, they fig-ured, and he was the type to gather the street life around him. Although Pete often talked about the football games and horse races he had won or lost money on, the players did not know and few suspected—"It never crossed my mind," says Rob Murphy, a Reds reliever from 1985 through '88—that Rose was during those years wagering heavily on the Reds, if not every night then close to it. They did not for the most part find it surpris-ing or out of character that he watched out of town ball games so intently.

"Well, there was this one time," recalls Reds pitcher Tom Browning. "There was a Padres-Giants game on TV in the clubhouse." Browning at one point casually questioned a Padres pitching decision (*had they left the starter in the game too long?*) and Rose became irrationally angry at him. "What do you know? You're a manager now?" he snapped. Browning be-lieves Rose was so on edge because he had money on the game.

Rose managed splendidly, though, showing a patience that belied his otherwise insatiable style. He accumulated and retained subtle and valuable details about opposing players, and he made in-game decisions that the players understood and generally agreed with. Cincinnati hadn't climbed back to first place, but the Reds seemed on their way. Under Rose they were winners, finishing second in 1986 and '87 (as they would again in '88) and were a lot better off than before he'd taken the job. "Pete was like God to us," says Browning. According to analytics done by stats emperor (and devoted Rose supporter) Bill James, Rose had become, "one of the most impressive and intriguing [managers] in the league . . . just as much a tactician as an emotional leader."

ONE MONTH into the 1988 season, on the last day of April, Rose clashed with umpire Dave Pallone. Pete had run out to argue a ninth-inning call that cost the Reds a game against the Mets in Cincinnati and in the heated face-off that followed Pallone unintentionally jabbed Pete's left cheek. In response Rose pushed Pallone once and then, more subtly, again. Pallone ejected Rose from the game and before long the Riverfront fans began heaving things onto the field. Finally, for his safety, Pallone went inside, leaving just three umpires to work the game's final outs. Two days later Rose got the news from the league: a $10,000 fine and a suspension of 30 days. This was the first suspension of his life. No manager had been banned for that length of time since Durocher got kicked out for a year in 1947.[1]

Rose howled that his suspension was way too severe and others echoed on his behalf. Pete was no repeat offender, after all—umpires liked him and Rose had a reputation for being fair. Besides, Pallone had poked him first. The man who suspended Rose, however, National

---

[1] Along with his associations with the big-time gamblers Memphis Engelberg and Connie Immerman, Durocher had been having an affair with the married movie actress Laraine Day, upsetting the Catholic Youth Organization enough that its Brooklyn chapter threatened to boycott the Dodgers. Those events, along with some unpleasant things that Durocher said publicly about Yankees' owner Larry MacPhail, led baseball commissioner Happy Chandler to suspend the Dodgers manager for that entire, historic season.

League president A. Bartlett Giamatti, did not bend. "Such disgraceful episodes are not business as usual, nor can they be allowed to become so," explained Giamatti, adding that the league would not "countenance any potentially injurious harassment of any kind of the umpires." And another thing, Giamatti said, "I hold managers to higher standards of behavior." When Rose, his agent-attorney Katz at his side, came to baseball's Park Avenue offices to appeal the case, a committee of three team executives denied him and upheld the ban.

Giamatti had taken over at the National League in 1986, directly off an eight-year tenure as president of Yale University. He had been a scholar of high prestige and a literature professor of enormous popularity, and was also a man who loved baseball in a way that he loved few things. He'd grown up in small-town New England, a deeply devout Red Sox fan, and a few months before accepting his appointment as the youngest president in 200 years at Yale, he had commented, "The only job I ever wanted was to be president of the American League." (Rose, upon hearing of the remark during the Pallone fallout, said, "I wish he'd gotten what he wanted.")

Giamatti wrote beautifully about baseball and in 1977 had done a piece for *Harper's Magazine* in which he likened the Mets' trading of Tom Seaver to the Masaccio fresco on a wall of the Brancacci Chapel in Florence, the *Expulsion of Adam and Eve*. Giamatti believed in the sanctity of baseball and in the value of its purest tenets, and he believed as well in the power of punishment as a deterrent.

The season before the Rose-Pallone incident Giamatti had suspended Phillies pitcher Kevin Gross for 10 days after Gross was found to have glued sandpaper onto the heel of his glove, ideal for scuffing a baseball. Giamatti's written denial of Gross's appeal is well-admired for its clarity, intelligence and thoughtfulness, and is included in a collection of Giamatti's writings, *A Great and Glorious Game*. In his ruling Giamatti declared that he viewed cheating as categorically more serious than most physical transgressions (abusing an umpire, say, or an opponent). While an impulsive act of violence on the field "can never be condoned or tolerated," Giamatti wrote, it might be seen as an outgrowth of the "aggressive, volatile nature of the game." Cheating on the other hand is "cool, deliberate, premeditated" and antics such as Gross's, "seek to undermine the basic foundation of any contest declaring the winner."

The extraordinary length of Rose's ban did not follow from Giamatti's code. His shove of Pallone was certainly not premeditated, nor cool, nor a threat to undermine the foundation of the game. There was nothing cheating about it. The shove might have been seen as an extension of an exchange in which Rose was physically provoked. Still, the incident was bush and thuggish and by any reckoning intolerable, and it came up against another core of Giamatti's beliefs and mission—he felt charged to protect and enforce a respect for the game and its explicit rules. So, a 30-day ban it was for Rose, and on top of the fine another $82,000 lost from his half-million-dollar Reds salary. (Baseball warned Schott not to pay Pete during the ban.) Rose, along with Katz, had gotten a first, up-close sense of Bart Giamatti and of the convictions and thought-lines that guided him.[2]

ROSE'S GAMBLING had intensified, in season and out (the NFL, of course, and college sports too) and some of the men around him in the mid-1980s, Tommy Gioiosa and Paul Janszen and the event organizer Mike Bertolini, among others, were at the heart of the group that placed bets for Pete and would be connected to his downfall. Rose spent time working out at Gold's Gym, which had become a seat of illegal steroids, cocaine activity and bookmaker gambling. Gioiosa worked as a manager at Gold's and everyone still thought that he looked a lot like Pete, only juiced. Janszen, a steroids dealer, well-muscled and comfortably over six-feet, acted as a kind of bodyguard at some of Rose's autograph sessions.

---

[2] Another telling mark of Giamatti's tenure came in advance of the 1988 season when he ushered in strict enforcement of a long overlooked feature of the balk rule by approving language that called for a pitcher to come to a "discernible" stop—as opposed to just a stop—in his set position. The amendment led to a 260% percent jump in balks (from 356 to 924) over the 1987 season, as well as to a lot of booing and cussing. The rule was rescinded after the one season.

"All of a sudden I've got to go through him to get to Pete," complained Willie DeLuca, a Cincinnati restaurateur and bookie who had known Rose since the early '70s.

Before the 1988 season Rose was summoned to see baseball commissioner Peter Ueberroth. The commissioner had heard about the heavies who sometimes hung around with Rose at Riverfront and wanted to explicitly warn him to keep unauthorized people out of the clubhouse. After that meeting, Rose told people close to him that he was relieved Ueberroth hadn't asked him about his gambling.

At home, Rose watched a gargantuan television set, along with two smaller ones, keeping tabs on several games at once. Janszen came over a lot with his girlfriend Danita and she and Carol would talk while the men followed the sports. When games were on that he had a stake in, which was much of the time, Pete could become intensely reactive and even more tightly wound than usual—he would be suddenly overjoyed, then suddenly irritated, just as Browning had seen in the Reds clubhouse. Some of Rose's friends felt then that the gambling had gotten to be too much. "But he was going to be the last to see it," says Jeff Ruby, who opened his upscale Covington restaurant, The Waterfront, in 1986 with Rose as a key investor. "It's like my daughter telling me I'm addicted to cigars and I say I'm not. But I was. She knew. We all saw things in Pete, but he wasn't going to hear it."

Late at night after home games, Pete sometimes went over to Sorrento's, a family restaurant on Montgomery Road in Norwood, and sat at the bar. This was DeLuca's place. Willie was a warm, friendly and enormous man, with an extraordinary ability to balance objects on his nose—a football helmet, a chair, a samurai sword. Willie always had a big salad and a Diet Coke waiting for Pete when he got there. West Coast ball games played on the satellite TV and it was understood that the guys hanging around the bar might have a little something riding on them. Willie would take a wager on just about anything—no betting slips, you were on your honor. Everyone loved Willie and everyone enjoyed having Pete around. He was easy to talk to and he'd sign autographs for free and chatter about sports and put down his fork and smile for the camera whenever someone came over to take a picture with him. He was seen as smart money too. One day Pete might be rooting for the Dodgers, the next day he'd be rooting against them, and not for reasons that had anything to do with the Reds' place in the standings.

IN THE ballpark, that 1988 Opening Day went very well for Cincinnati. Giamatti threw out the first ball and though St. Louis, the defending National League champions, took a 4–1 lead, the Reds buckled no further. Trailing 4–3 in the seventh inning Rose put in Jeff Treadway to pinch-hit, then called for a bunt play that led to the tying run. Rose used four relievers in the game, and none gave up a run. He ordered three intentional walks and each time the move paid off. Finally, in the bottom of the 12th inning a two-out single by Reds' leftfielder Kal Daniels won the game. The huge crowd was delighted—this was Cincinnati's sixth straight Opening Day win—and for Rose the victory came with sweet icing: Daniels had stroked his game-winning hit off Larry McWilliams, the pitcher who, as an Atlanta Brave in 1978, had helped to stop Pete's hitting streak at 44 games.

Rose did not know it then, as the fans dispersed happily into the spring evening and he jabbered happily in the clubhouse—"We're going to be a tough ball club," he predicted—but at that very same time, a phone conversation was taking place that would dramatically reorder his life, that would, along with others of its kind, bring his transgressions and indiscretions home to roost with a severity of consequence he had never imagined. The phone call, its transcript later appended to John Dowd's report to the commissioner of baseball, began quite simply. Like this:

Janszen: "Hello."

Bertolini: "Paulie."

Chapter 14

T HE DOWD REPORT, *In the Matter of: Peter Edward Rose, Manager Cincinnati Reds Baseball Club*, runs 228 pages, mostly double-spaced. It's heavily footnoted, with many of the notes referring to the accompanying trove of evidence and supporting material gathered over the course of baseball's, and John Dowd's, investigation into Rose. Straightforward and carefully reasoned, the report provides a streamlined account, a cogent narrative meant to be easily digested by new baseball commissioner Bart Giamatti, his deputy Fay Vincent and the others who would read and reflect upon it under heavy pressure during the spring and summer of 1989.

The report's attendant exhibits, however, are raw and sumptuous and largely unedited—they include depositions, transcripts of phone conversations, court documents, canceled checks and much more. Bound in hardcover books, the exhibits bring the physical output of the investigation to 13 hardbound volumes that together take up 23 inches of shelf space, weigh about 54 pounds and total more than 5,100 pages. The legal fees associated with baseball's Rose investigation have never been released but if you were to guess "astronomical" you would be in the right ballpark.

Rose had been up to many things that you would not want a major league player or manager to be up to, but the central trouble, of course, was that he had bet, and bet frequently, on games involving his own team. Although this fact—and its dangerous implications—is borne out and verified in numerous ways and by numerous people and documents in the exhibits, it was the decision by Paul Janszen to come forward to the authorities and the media, and to come forward with such potent material as his taped April 4, 1988, conversation with Mike Bertolini, that put baseball's investigation in motion and sustained it. If not for Janszen, might Rose have gotten away with what he did? "You know, yes, he may have," says Dowd. "Pete might have actually walked at that time. But it would have caught up with him. There were too many people who knew too much, and several witnesses ready to roll. Once we started hearing names we just followed up on them, and then it was one person after another verifying what we knew."

Throughout the investigation, all of the evidence, testimony and other uncovered information was, per commissioner Giamatti's directive, immediately made available to Rose and his team of lawyers. Some material got to the media. More than six weeks before Rose was banned, for example, *Sports Illustrated* ran an excerpt from Dowd's deposition of an Ohio bookmaker named Ronald Peters, which included this sequence:

Q: And in 1985 what sports activities did [Pete Rose] place bets on?

A: He bet college basketball, professional football and major league baseball.

Q: And that continued into 1986?

A. Yes.

Q: And when [he] bet baseball, did he bet on the Cincinnati Reds?

A: Yes he did.

Transparency was a crucial tenet of the process. "The world will see what we do and how we do it," said Giamatti. Yet that transparency did not always lead people to see things that they did not want to see. Though the finished report went out to the media right away and many of the exhibits were made available soon after, many reporters, as well as many fans, continued for years to believe (or to say that they believed) Rose's claims that he had not bet on baseball. Those people simply must not have read the Dowd Report. For someone to spend even a short time paging through the document—which includes, over one 72-page stretch, a game-by-game breakdown of Pete's bets on the Reds during the first half of the 1987 season—and still maintain Rose's innocence is to be a subscriber to the most elaborate conspiracy theories. It is to believe that the '69 moon landing was a hoax and that the earth, never mind what Copernicus, Galileo or, well, satellite photos might say, is obviously flat.

The power of the Dowd Report traces to its thoroughness and also to its all-knowing tone—one that anticipates the Rose camp's inevitable attempt to discredit and vilify what was found. As the report marches along, often pointing up contradictions in Rose's testimony, its language is dusted with the bluster of righteous conviction. There's a subtle edge to the text, an underlying feeling that another "gotcha" moment is coming up and then, yes, it does. Dogged, intelligently crafted and occasionally, to Rose's annoyance, smug, the sense and quality of the report provide a reflection of Dowd himself.

––––––––––

JOHN DOWD is a large man. About 6' 5" and full across the chest and belly. Even in his early 70s he looks as if he could throw you across the room and that if the need arose he would not mind doing so. He is bluff and gesticulant, and a former captain in the U.S. Marine Corps. One thing that first impressed Dowd upon meeting Rose, when both men were in their late 40s, was his size and muscularity. "Pete was just solid, right through. Strong," Dowd says. He long ago adopted the habit of immediately sizing people up.

Dowd is easy to talk to and good with a story the way Pete is, and he abides by a self-defined sense of fairness that he prides himself on. He has an emotive, appealing face—long, heavy cheeks, blue eyes, a thick lower lip. He's much smarter than he might want to appear and his temper, even when you don't see it, is right there. There is a trace of Boston in his speech. From the standpoint of a casting director or a reader of legal thrillers, Dowd is pretty much exactly what you would want a lead investigator to be.[1]

The Rose inquiry—noncriminal though it was—remains the signature case of Dowd's long career, but it's hardly the only time his profile has risen. He's a highly regarded trial lawyer who has done much of his conspicuous work as a defender (perhaps surprising to those who know him only for his prosecutorial role in baseball). Dowd represented Sen. John McCain in the savings and loan scandal in the 1980s (McCain was cleared). He defended Arizona governor Fife Symington against charges of extortion in the mid-'90s (later overturned on appeal), and he defended the billionaire hedge fund manager Raj Rajaratnam, who in 2011 was convicted on numerous counts of securities fraud and conspiracy. During the Rajaratnam trial a visibly worn Dowd told a reporter it would be his last, and after the verdict he was approached by CNBC outside the courtroom. Dowd looked into the camera and barked "get the fuck out of here" then flipped the bird. "That's what I've got for CNBC," he said in a clip that the network played and replayed.

"John's really a big pussycat," says Fay Vincent. "Well, no he's not really. Only sometimes."

Dowd embraces the spotlight and on the wall of his office at the Washington firm of Akin, Gump, Strauss, Hauer & Feld LLP, hangs an excerpt of Theodore Roosevelt's "The Man in the Arena" speech of 1910. Roosevelt famously hails the man with the courage to risk himself, "whose face is marred by dust and sweat and blood" and "who

---

[1] Early on in what would be a daylong interview of Dowd at his Washington, D.C., office in 2012, he suddenly became unhappy with my line of questioning. I was playing devil's advocate to some assertions he had made, asking him to elaborate, checking his version against others I had heard or seen. "What the fuck, who sent you here?" Dowd said suddenly, raising his voice and standing up behind his desk. His face grew red and his eyes had narrowed. "Who put you up to this? Did Selig send you?" It took me a few minutes to reassure Dowd that no one had "sent me," that my intentions were as previously stated—to research this book fair and square—and that countering him with questions and casting a certain skepticism on all sides of the story was, as he of all people surely understood, part of my job. He calmed down and I breathed again, and after that we got along fine.

at the best, knows, in the end, the triumph of high achievement and who, at the worst, if he fails, at least he fails while daring greatly."

A type of book occupies the office shelves: bound volumes of the Dowd Report, along with several war hero tributes—*The Gift of Valor, Medal of Honor*—as well as *Baseball as America*, a glossy companion to the Baseball Hall of Fame's traveling exhibit of the same name. Dowd and Vincent swap reading material sometimes and on the day I was in D.C. to see Dowd, Vincent called and said he was sending down a biography of Dwight Eisenhower. There is a red, Everlast boxing glove on display in Dowd's office and a bumper sticker that says WHEN IT ABSOLUTELY, POSITIVELY HAS TO BE DESTROYED OVERNIGHT, and also a lot of framed photos—the family at Christmas; a wedding; a picture of Dowd seated on a red Wheel Horse tractor with a small laughing child in the crook of each arm.

"I guess I like to be in the World Series," is how Dowd describes his affection for big, well-publicized cases. "And when the commissioner of baseball calls and asks you to take on a case involving Pete Rose, you do it. It is an honor to be asked."

Dowd was living in the D.C. suburb of Vienna, Va., the father of five kids, on the day that call came in late February of 1989. He'd just come back from a few weeks trying a case in Atlanta, and hadn't seen the headlines reporting that Rose had been summoned to New York from spring training to meet with baseball commissioner Peter Ueberroth and talk about allegations of Rose's gambling. Ueberroth was about to step away as commissioner—he would officially resign on April 1—and Giamatti was coming in, with Vincent as his deputy.

"Pete stood in front of us in the commissioner's office and said he bet on other sports but didn't bet on baseball," Vincent recalls. "He said 'I'm not that stupid,' and we all believed him. There was a part of Peter and Bart that did not want to follow up, but there was so much smoke, it was impossible not to."

A day after that meeting the phone rang at Dowd's house at 10:30 at night and it was Vincent on the line. They had known each other since the 1970s when Vincent worked as a securities guy at the firm of Caplin &

Drysdale in D.C. and Dowd worked at the Justice Department. It turned out they each had a place up in Brewster on Cape Cod and during the summer Dowd sometimes ran into Vincent and gave him a lift to the grocery store. By the time of the Rose investigation, they'd been friends for years. "John, I'm here with Bart Giamatti," Vincent was saying now. "And I said to him that as long as we're looking for outside counsel in this Rose case, let's talk to this guy Dowd, because he knows what he's doing."

Giamatti then came on the phone and he spent 40 minutes getting a handle on Dowd—"He is the only man I ever met who could question you for that long without getting your edge," Dowd says. Finally, pleased by Dowd's manner and knowledge and approach, Giamatti asked in closing, "Do you have any conflicts with Rose or the Cincinnati Reds?"

"No," said Dowd.

"Then can you be on a plane to Cincinnati tomorrow morning at eight o'clock?" Giamatti asked.

"And I was off and running," says Dowd. "I did nothing else for six months."

AN INVESTIGATION into Rose had long been underway by the time Dowd touched down in Cincinnati, of course. It had been set in motion by Kevin Hallinan, Major League Baseball's head of security who'd come into the position in 1986, not long after commanding a joint FBI-NYPD anti-terrorism task force. Commissioner Ueberroth liked the FBI background and he wanted Hallinan to do things a little differently in baseball, to be proactive and look at all kinds of things under the security umbrella—stadium operations, crowd control, anything that might impact attendance. Ueberroth was a tough executive, a no-bullshit kind of guy. On Hallinan's first day at the office an assistant asked him what his title should be on his business card. "I don't know," said Hallinan. The assistant went into Ueberroth's office and came back out. "Peter says let's see what you can do first, before we put anything on your business card."

That first year Hallinan spent a lot of time on the road going to ballparks, pressing the flesh, meeting people on every team. He set up an infrastructure, enlisting retired cops in each big-league city to work as stringers. New to baseball's culture, Hallinan was taken aback at how the clubhouse served as a kind of makeshift bazaar before games—guys selling clothes or equipment, players getting haircuts. He didn't like it. He didn't like the distractions and he didn't like not knowing who was milling around in there. So Hallinan made sure that every team kept someone at the clubhouse door before games; anyone coming in had to sign their names. Hallinan kept going around the league checking up on how things were working out. "That was when I just stumbled onto the Rose stuff," he says. "It seemed like wherever I was traveling I kept running into the Reds, either in Cincinnati or on the road. So much so that in Philadelphia one time Pete asked one of the local guys, 'Is your boss following me?' As God is my judge I wasn't following him at all. This was pure coincidence. But when Pete asked that, it did send up a little red flag. I thought, *If he is that paranoid . . .*"

Hallinan had also taken note of the characters that Rose had hanging around him, the muscle guys with the attitudes and the oil slicks through their hair. He had a strong sense about them—they fit into a less-than-savory type that he had come across time and again in his years as a lieutenant in the NYPD. "There's a kind of radar," Hallinan says. "I saw those guys and right away I knew that some of them were no good. And it was plain that they could see the cop in me. The way they reacted to me, uncomfortable right away, and avoiding where I was, that told me something too."

There was talk in Cincinnati about some of the things going on at Gold's Gym, the steroids and the cocaine. Pete went over there sometimes to work out and mingle with Gioiosa and others he knew. Hallinan had heard too that Rose was selling off some of his prized memorabilia—his 4,192 bat, jewels off the Hickok belt he'd won in 1975—hardly a crime (any number of Hall of Fame players have sold any number of pieces of memorabilia) but another red flag, especially since Rose wasn't usually setting up public shop to sell these items but rather appeared to be selling them on the sly. Why? Hallinan wondered. Why would Pete, flush in salary and endorsement dollars, have such an interest in cash?

Hallinan told Ueberroth that he believed he needed to dig further into what he was seeing and hearing around Pete. (Later it turned out that the FBI, tipped off to Rose's gambling, was independently watching him then too.) Hallinan had a feeling he might be getting into some deep water—this was Pete Rose in Cincinnati—so he spread his wings again; getting the O.K. from Ueberroth, he brought in another ex-FBI guy, Joe Daly of Cincinnati. Daly could put his ear right to the ground on those city streets. He knew where to look and whom to ask. Daly was an even-keeled guy, reliable, efficient and sharp, and it was through the work that Daly did that Hallinan first started hearing that Pete was betting with bookies on baseball. On that February day in 1989, when Rose came up to meet with Ueberroth and the others in the commissioner's office—with his hair spiked and wearing a green polyester suit—Hallinan was standing in the very next room.

FIRST, FOR DOWD, there was Janszen, who said he was letting this all spill out because Pete owed him many thousands of dollars (a life savings' worth by Janszen's lights) and also because he had bookies after him for other money that Pete owed. This on top of the trouble he'd already gotten into, the steroid dealing and his conviction for tax fraud. Janszen didn't know what else to do but come out with all the stuff about Pete, he said; he was at the end of his rope and needed to turn his life around. Janszen had called in so many bets for Pete, so many baseball bets among them, and he had been so close with the guy for a while; all in all he provided the investigation with many reams of details. Janszen's girlfriend Danita Jo Marcum also spoke under oath with Dowd and she too talked about placing bets on the Reds for Pete.

Janszen led to Peters and to more specifics and clarity and corroboration. Peters said he had a code name set up for Rose (the cute though barely disguising "14") but that Rose never actually used it. Usually someone else phoned Peters to bet on Rose's behalf and on the rare occasions when Rose himself called, at least as Peters told it, he just announced, "This is Pete." No code, no disguise. There was another convicted bookmaker who turned up early in the investigation, too, a guy named Joe Cambra out of Massachusetts, who'd hung around at Rose's house in Florida, visiting. Of interest to Dowd, among other things, was that Pete had given Cambra two sizable checks (Rose put the value at $19,800) for what the two men described as a real estate deal that never came through.

Dowd's team talked with Don Stenger and Michael Fry, the guys who were moving the cocaine out of Gold's Gym. There were other witnesses whom Dowd and Hallinan sat down with on the record, and others still who came forward but were turned away, Dowd believing their testimony too vague or circumstantial to rely on—for example, more folks who'd overheard Gioiosa on the phone at Gold's talking loudly about placing bets for Pete.

Gioiosa himself never sang, never showed up even after Hallinan sent him a plane ticket to fly in for some discussions. It was only later, after Pete had been banned and Gioiosa sat in Boone County jail starting his sentence for conspiracies to distribute cocaine and to defraud the IRS—the latter related to winnings from a 1987 Pick-Six horse racing bet that Rose had been in on—that Gioiosa too began to open up about Pete's betting on the Reds.

Turned out Dowd and Hallinan didn't need Gioiosa. Within two weeks of landing in Cincinnati, Dowd had nine people who said Rose had bet on baseball. Then he had a dozen. And the hard physical evidence was starting to come in. Rose's handwriting on betting slips. (His fingerprints all over them too.) Canceled checks. Phone records. "Like shooting fish in a barrel," Dowd says. "In terms of getting information this was as easy as could be. There were so many people out there."

One of them was Mike Bertolini, a massive young man—obese or close to it—with a truly glorious mouth: He was out of Brooklyn, full of charisma, and you could hear the *fuhgeddaboutit* in everything he said. The first time Hallinan and Dowd met with him, in a diner, Bertolini ordered up six hard-boiled eggs to snack on. While the order was in, though, the three men got to talking and Bertolini began to grasp the depth of what Dowd and Hallinan already knew, started to get a clear picture of what was at stake and what could happen. When those hard-boiled eggs came to the table, Bertolini didn't eat a single one.

In Dowd's offices he and the other lawyers sometimes listened to the tape of Bertolini and Janszen for pure amusement. "We were rolling on the floor, the way this guy talked!" says Dowd. Bertolini couldn't say hello without a four-letter word attached, and the conversation was soaked with exchanges like:

> *Bertolini:* "Uh huh. I fuck'n, first of all, I ain't been able to call you because I fuck'n been trying to fuck'n think of your number and shit and I fuck'n just remembered it today."
> *Janszen:* "Did you ever get settled up with Pete?"
> *Bertolini:* "About what?"
> *Janszen:* "The money?"
> *Bertolini:* "Fuck'n, we're working it out and shit. I don't know, the fuck. Did you ever?"

As entertaining as the dialogue was—a dash of salted Runyon, a heap of Paulie Walnuts—what really got Dowd and Hallinan's attention were the weightier parts, the passages when Janszen and Bertolini talked about money that they say Pete owed:

> *Janszen:* "Did he ever get . . . wait a minute, he was up to you for how much total?"
> *Bertolini:* "What me or all together?"
> *Janszen:* "No, the guy . . . the bookies in New York, how much did he"
> *Bertolini* "Don't talk like that on the phone, I hate that."
> *Janszen:* "Alright, how much did he owe you, owe them?"
> *Bertolini:* "All together between me and them about 2 . . . 2 and a quarter."
> *Janszen:* "Jesus Christ."
> *Bertolini:* "But we're forgetting them, he's just gonna take care of me."
> *Janszen:* "What do you mean you're forgetting them?"
> *Bertolini:* "Forgetting them, they don't get nothing."

Janszen: "What are they gonna do to him?"

Bertolini: "I don't know. We're not gonna worry about them."

Janszen: "Oh my god, Mikey. You're gonna have some people after him."

And a little later:

Janszen: " . . . how much did he wind up paying them total?"

Bertolini: "Paying them that they've gotten, cash?"

Janszen: "Yeah."

Bertolini "About 150-200."

And:

Bertolini: "They got him for enough. You know what I'm saying, it's not like they got 25 and then we started this and now we're gonna screw them out of this. What he owes, they already got that much in previous loss."

Janszen: "Yeah."

Bertolini: "Know what I'm saying. Man, fuck'n, they already raked the guy, fuck it, man."

And later still, Bertolini saying of the debt Pete was in: "Then it got so high and shit and fuck'n, you know, it was like he said, man no matter how good I do, it's like I never go down."

There was also another Janszen tape, of a phone call with a guy named Steve Chevashore that had a lot of betting discussion on it and which appeared to trace money that Pete owed back to bosses in New York. When Hallinan and another investigator met face-to-face with Chevashore, he seemed very nervous, they say, and reluctant. And when they tried to get to him again a few days later he wouldn't talk anymore—he was suddenly suffering from a broken arm. "Playing baseball," Chevashore said in explaining how he'd broken it, although he also allowed that he had not played baseball in many years.

"There was no doubt in our minds that these bets were ending up with organized crime," said Hallinan. "There was a connection there that you could not miss."

Things turned up about Pete's being near the cocaine dealings and about all kinds of undeclared cash and about the depths of his bookie betting. Lead after lead after lead. The investigation could have gone on and on. And it was everywhere, in the news, bigger than anything happening on the baseball fields. The media milked every drop of information. Reporters followed Dowd and his team into hotel lobbies. They lurked around the Cincinnati airport. They showed up at restaurants. When Dowd and Hallinan came out of the MLB offices on Park Avenue, they sometimes saw rows of TV trucks idling three deep in the street—and then suddenly had microphones in their faces. Hallinan started slipping out a back door when he left.

Dowd seemed confident, undeterred. He zeroed in on the baseball betting and went after particular dates, in 1987 mainly, and concentrated on putting it all together as neatly and quickly as he and his team could. Baseball's club owners wanted the Rose thing out of the headlines. Dowd answered to everyone in some sense—to Giamatti, the owners, the public, Rose's counsel—but, truly, he answered to no one but himself. He steered the ship in the manner he saw fit, through foul winds and fair.

"I'd worked with U.S. attorneys," says Hallinan. "I'd worked with Frank Hogan"—the longtime New York D.A. famed for his incorruptibility—"I'd worked with enough attorneys to fill a ballpark, and I'll tell you that John Dowd had all the qualities you could want for this job. Brilliant, driven, committed, honest. A man's man. And I was not easily impressed. I'd seen them come and go. There was so much pressure on this case, and Dowd never blinked."

Media folks were all over Rose too, of course, wearing at him every damned day as he plowed ahead, pestering him with questions, questions, questions, on the field or in his office or in the parking lot before he got into his Porsche. Reporters showed up at the house in Indian Hill. He didn't talk about the investigation with his players in the clubhouse—"Not once," says reliever John Franco. "He was all business about managing the team"—but Rose grew edgier, more brusque and more defiant with each passing day. *Sports Illustrated* kept breaking big news out of the case, and *The New York Times* dug stuff up too, and so did the newspapers in Cincinnati and in Dayton. Pete showed up on the TV news just about every night.

He couldn't understand how unyielding the media was, how they had pressed him so hard from the moment the investigation was known. Reporters Rose had been acquainted with for so many years, along with the many newer faces suddenly assigned to his case. Why couldn't they all just lay off him some? And how could they believe what they were hearing from other people and doubt him? Didn't those reporters owe him something for all the years he had been so good to them, win or lose, good times and bad, filling every notebook with his candor, his insight, his humor, his inimitable talk?

Pete's family felt it, too. Pete Jr., playing minor league ball, could barely breathe from the heckling. Fawn heard it at graduate school. Karolyn, tending bar at the Wagon Wheel Cafe, shook her head and barked back when customers brought up Pete. (Which they did and did and did.) Carol looked out the windows before she and Tyler left the house each day, checked her rearview mirror when she pulled out onto Given Road. LaVerne was living in Delhi on the West Side, refusing all requests to talk specifically about the case involving her son. She had a two-bedroom apartment where she lived by herself and she hadn't gone to the ballpark to see Pete manage the Reds for a couple of years. LaVerne told people that Pete was not the tough guy he was being made out to be in the papers, that he had really been a mama's boy. And when someone asked why she didn't have a single picture, or even a news clipping, of Pete anywhere around her place, she cackled and said in her twinkling rasp: "I don't need pictures, I know what that brat looks like!"

Dave Rose was working his short order job at Gold Star Chili and just about every time he left work, someone followed him—a baseball investigator or an FBI guy or a reporter. Sometimes all three. They thought they might see Dave run a bet, or go meet a bookie on Pete's behalf. No one got anything by trailing Dave, though. He didn't have anything to give. "I was completely out of the loop," he says. "Not that

I wanted to be. I just never knew what Pete had going on. He didn't even tell me what he wanted me to say when baseball came to talk to me, which they did a few times. The Dowd thing, the betting, this wasn't something I could even ask Pete about. He was not open to it. He told the papers he did not bet on baseball, and that's what I believed."

When Dave was working the chili kitchen, he sometimes heard customers talking about Pete (a large photo of him hung on the wall by the counter), with some of them speaking approvingly and defiantly on Pete's behalf and others saying nasty things, saying how he should be kicked out of the game. If a customer got a good sight of Dave, though, that talk usually quieted or stopped—he looked so much like Pete with that barrel chest and the mouth, and Dave could cut you with a glance.

The hounding by reporters meant that when Dowd and Hallinan sat down to talk with Rose, to get him on the record, they had to find someplace out of the way to do it. They couldn't just get together in Katz's office in Cincinnati, say, or call Rose to New York in the middle of the season. You might as well just order the circus into town. That's how the deposition ended up taking place in a convent in Dayton, in the cafeteria of a little Catholic school where the press never found them. "Which one of us is doing God's work?" one of Pete's lawyers joked, observing the surroundings. There were 10 people in the room: Dowd and two other lawyers from his D.C. law firm; Hallinan and Daly; a court reporter; a paralegal and Pete Rose with his counsel, Robert Pitcairn and Roger Makley.

The deposition started on the late afternoon of a late-April off-day for the Reds. The team had gotten back to Cincinnati that morning on the redeye, after playing the Dodgers in L.A., and Makley asked right away for Dowd to forgive Pete if he was a little weary, being as he had only slept for about three hours. "An hour and a half," Rose interjected.

Dowd started by asking Rose to lay out who he was and where he was from, the details of his baseball career and his position as manager of the Reds—basic material for the record. Then he asked about the bookmaker Joe Cambra, and Rose said that he had gotten a chunk of cash from the guy, cash back from those checks for the soured real estate deal. "And what did you do with the cash?" Dowd asked, and Rose responded, "Put it in my pocket."

They talked about a recent winning Pick-Six ticket from Turfway Park, worth more than $250,000 and why Rose as one of the winners hadn't cashed it himself, or ever reported the income. Rose said how his pal Arnie Metz, a stadium ops guy for the Reds who so often went to the track with Pete and ran bets up to the window for him, had signed for the ticket, really as a matter of convenience. Pete said that he himself had gotten $109,000 in winnings, and that another bettor on the ticket, Turfway Park owner Jerry Carroll, had gotten about that same amount and that Arnie had gotten some of the rest, as a tip. That was one of the other aspects of that Pick-Six ticket—that Carroll was on it. Some people around Cincinnati wondered whether a track owner winning big like that signaled something fishy. Some people thought that Carroll shouldn't be betting like that, Rose said, "because he could have five out of six and go down in the jocks' room and tell them who should win the sixth race."

Rose was eager in the deposition, eager to talk and explain, to parry and justify, and sometimes Dowd had to put the reins on him, "Let me finish my question, please," Dowd said, "and then I'll let you answer." He said "let me finish" numerous times over the course of the deposition and if it came off a little terse at times, Dowd also abided by a degree of formality. Through the early going he always called him, "Mr. Rose."

"Please, call me Pete," said Pete. "Mr. Rose is my dad." Dowd apologized and said that he was just trying to be respectful. "I understand that," Rose said, adding, "I'm going to call you John."

This was the first time that Rose and Dowd had ever met or interacted, and the way that the ground rules were being set and the way they kept feeling each other out—circling one another, mannered and tentative, then full bore in a rush, jousting here and there, trading niceties, stiffening up, suddenly cheeky or flip, then relenting or consenting—it was as if each of the two men had a keen sense of how the other might come to impact his life.

THE DEPOSITION lasted for about three hours that evening, and when they came back to the convent at 8:30 the next morning, Dowd picked up where he'd left off. The Reds would play the Astros at Riverfront that night.

They covered a lot of ground—Rose discussed memorabilia shows that he did for cash and autographs that he signed, and how he'd had Gioiosa sign for him when he was squeezed for time. They talked about all kinds of money being exchanged and about the numerous Pete Rose checks written for $8,000, the figure under $10,000 so as to help the casher avoid having to file papers with the bank. They talked about checks written to Mike Bertolini and to Mike Fry, about checks given to Gioiosa and about checks with Pete's signature on it that were made out to fictitious names. Checks cashed at the dog track. Checks cashed at the horse races. Checks, checks, checks.

They talked about expensive cars that Pete had owned and those that he had sold to certain individuals—a BMW, a Porsche, and also an M-1 that was bought by big Don Stenger. They talked about just what exactly was the nature of Rose's association with Stenger and the other guys over at Gold's Gym. Rose said that he liked going over there to work out at nine in the morning when it wasn't too crowded and that he hadn't known anything about any cocaine until much later on and that he had absolutely nothing to do with that.

The main issue, of course, the matter at which the deposition and the whole investigation aimed, was Rose's extensive sports betting, which he admitted to, and specifically his betting on baseball and the Reds, both of which he denied. When the topic of Pete's heavy betting in the early part of 1987 came under discussion, Rose recalled how Gioiosa had passed along a threat from a bookmaker that "the guy was going to burn my house down and break my kids' legs if I didn't pay him." Pete said that he had owed some money after having lost a run of football and college basketball bets and that the bookie's threat is what led him to write a check for $34,000 and settle things up. A little later Rose cracked a few jokes and said he hadn't been worried at all about that threat, that "those guys are all talk."

In the deposition Rose conveyed a solid and even intimate knowledge of bookmaking. He was clear about the collection schedules and the vigorish and how the odds are laid. He said that he didn't know any bookmakers in New York, however, and that he certainly had never bet with them. He did not place bets with any Steve Chevashore, he said, and he could not explain why there were phone calls to Chevashore from his house, nor why there were also calls to the bookmaker Ron Peters from his home as well as from the Reds hotel. Maybe Janszen had made the calls, Pete said. As for all the calls that Janszen had made *into* the Reds clubhouse, those, Pete guessed, might have been Paulie looking for tickets to the game. The calls had nothing to do with wagering on ball games, that is.

He had never ever bet on baseball, Pete maintained, and he stuck hard to it. And if things didn't always seem square in his testimony, if Rose's version of events sometimes seemed to fly up against evidence already collected, or against the testimony of others, Pete offered an alternative answer, a plausible explanation for everything. He was often quite good at answering Dowd's yes-or-no questions without actually saying yes or no, a skill that got under Dowd's skin.

On key points, Dowd could be highly persistent and even, it seemed, intentionally dense. "I'm sorry" or "forgive me" or "it's an education" he would say upon honing in and asking for clarification of some basic detail for the third time. Dowd says now that he, in fact, liked Pete and that he even felt a little sorry for the guy—not that he would ever let that sympathy show or let it translate into any kind of mercy or forgiveness. It was just a feeling Dowd had upon seeing Rose tripped up by the evidence set plainly in front of him. Rose was given exhibits to look at (checks, documents, letters) and, a few hours into the second day, Dowd played for him the Bertolini-Janszen conversation of April 4, 1988.

"An amusing tape," Rose said when it finished. He agreed that some of the things in the conversation were true but said that the critical parts were made of lies and that he "did not owe anybody a dime." Rose's contempt for Janszen was complete and, he said, "That tape don't mean diddly-squat to me."

"O.K. Well, I will tell you, Pete, it means something to us and we're troubled by it," Dowd said in response.

All told, Rose was in that convent before god and man for seven hours. At times an expression of profound unpleasantness came over his face, a look that not even his fierce defiance could wipe away. As if he had eaten some lousy seafood. Several in the room noticed it: At times during the deposition, Pete Rose started to look a little green.

Chapter 15

Fable

HEN MEMBERS of the Reds brass get to musing about Pete Rose (and it's inevitable that they do), they will sometimes liken his story to the parable of the Scorpion and the Frog. It is an old tale, ancient, and in other versions, a turtle, a fox or a small boy stands in for the frog. Sometimes a snake subs for the scorpion and in one quasiadaptation of the fable, an Aesop's rendering with a moral about comeuppance, a mouse and a frog get set upon in the water by a predatory hawk.

No single origin of the Scorpion and the Frog is definitively known, but an outstanding work of scholarship by Arata Takeda—written when he was an assistant professor of comparative literature at the University of Tübingen in Germany—traces the seeds of the fable to the centuries-old Indian tales of the *Panchatantra*. More specifically a clear version of the story surfaces in the 12th century as told by a pair of truth-spewing jackals in the Arabic version of the *Panchatantra, Kalila and Dimna*. Takeda's 2011 paper, written in German and titled as an inquiry into the rambling, East-West journey of *Der Skorpion und der Frosch*, suggests that ancient stories from the Orient and passages from the Koran influenced the creation of the fable as well.

The Scorpion and the Frog has gained wide cultural purchase in recent decades, beginning perhaps with its telling by the title character in Orson Welles's strange (and strangely gripping) 1955 film *Mr. Arkadin*. In *The Crying Game* (1992) a blindfolded British captive relates the story to his IRA guard, as a means of appealing to the guard's inherent kindness. The fable has been unspooled on the deck of the *Voyager* in a classic, two-part episode of *Star Trek*, and it appears, told in unique fashion (the frog is a woman, the scorpion a snake) by a Native American man in Oliver Stone's *Natural Born Killers*.

Just as the fable has accommodated different characters, its moral can be interpreted in a number of ways. It can be seen as a parable about the dangers of risk-taking or gullibility or tempting fate. It's also about not trusting enemies, or friends or strangers. There's a lesson about Schadenfreude in the story. At times the Scorpion and the Frog has been adopted as an allegory about suicide bombing, and about difficult human relations in a contentious region of the world. In this rendering the river that the animals cross is the Jordan and the Scorpion's final, explanatory line is, "This is the Middle East!"

The clearest and most potent moral though—the message that has made this fable endure and resonate as it has—comments on man's inescapability from himself. A person is who he is, inevitably limited or undone by his own shortcomings and unable to change his essential self even in the face of dire consequences. This is the gist the folks with the Reds have in mind when the story comes up as they are talking about Pete Rose's fate and ongoing plight. They tend to tell the fable with a crocodile instead of the frog, but the basic, familiar story is intact and the scorpion, in this case, represents Pete:

The Scorpion and the Frog

A scorpion is out for a walk on a warm summer's day when he comes to a river that he would like to cross but can't because he doesn't know how to swim. The scorpion looks around and sees a frog on the bank by the water's edge.

"Mr. Frog, would you let me climb onto your back and swim me across the river so that I can reach the other side?" the scorpion asks.

"No way," says the frog. "If I did that you could sting me with your poisonous tail and I would die."

"Oh, I would not do that," the scorpion says. "If I were to sting you, you would sink and then I would drown as well."

The frog considers that logic for a moment and then consents to give the ride. "Okay Mr. Scorpion," the frog says. "Come on board."

The frog is swimming along, about halfway across the river, when he suddenly feels a searing pain in his side. The scorpion has stung him.

"Oh, no! Why did you do it?" says the frog with his final breaths. "Now we will both die."

To which the scorpion replies: "I could not help myself. It is in my nature."

BART GIAMATTI might have avoided sitting in judgment on the Rose case altogether, and instead might have spent his months as baseball commissioner in other ways and doing other things. Ueberroth, before officially resigning as commissioner, had offered to see the Rose investigation through—either to try to wrap things up slam-bang or to stay on and oversee the case as a consultant even after stepping down. Giamatti, though, wanted to take it on. He welcomed the responsibility, he said, and he welcomed the challenge of doing it right.

Giamatti, it's worth noting, adored Pete Rose as a player and as a baseball figure—"Isn't he marvelous?" he had once said to the writer Roger Kahn, as they watched Rose gathering baseballs around the Reds' batting cage in spring training—but that did not hold sway against his convictions. Giamatti had been unsparing in suspending Rose for his umpire clash in 1988, and as the Dowd investigation bore in, the commissioner did not like the feeling that Rose saw himself as being above baseball's laws. Had Rose come to Giamatti early on, contrite and showing a desire to change, Giamatti might have opened his embrace as wide and warm as any mama bear's. He was a man forgiving of many vices and many sins, but hubris and dishonesty were not among them.

"Pete thinks of himself as a national treasure, and we agree," Reuven Katz said to Fay Vincent during the months that baseball was working the case. To which Giamatti responded, "I'll show him who the national treasure is." For Giamatti, the treasure, what had to be protected at any cost, was the game itself.

He stayed awake to all hours, at the commissioner's office, or in his room at the Yale Club, and he pored through the information he received from Dowd and through the miles of Rose-colored type in so many newspapers. Giamatti had during his time as president of Yale been at the center of controversies—late in his tenure he weathered a high-profile and feverishly pitched strike of clerical and technical workers—but nothing had prepared him for what was happening now. Not for the unending media push, not for the waves of public second-guessing at any move that baseball made, and certainly not for the sensation of opening an anonymous letter to read in an unfamiliar hand or answering the telephone to hear in an unfamiliar voice these words: "If you put Pete Rose out of baseball, we will kill you."

"One day, late afternoon, my father came to the restaurant where I was working," says Marcus Giamatti, Bart's eldest son. Marcus was in his late 20s and tending bar at McAleer's, a wood-floor-and-Naugahyde-booths pub on the Upper West Side of Manhattan. "He told me I had to leave my job because it wasn't safe for me. He was getting too many death threats and threats against his family too. My dad was worried about my mom, and my sister and brother, all of us. I wouldn't quit my job but they started having an unmarked police car park outside the bar when I went to work."

The commissioner, though, did not waver from his task. How could he, knowing what he knew? Whatever small holes there might have been in the case, whatever details might have been still in question, the evidence against Rose was overwhelming. The FBI knew what he had done, baseball knew what he had done. Yes, when Rose had denied betting on baseball in the commissioner's office they had believed him, but in the weeks and months that followed, that belief proved impossible to maintain. The investigation needed to proceed in its thorough way, of course, and Rose had to be given every opportunity to state his case, and every word of testimony against Rose needed to be tested and retested before it was accepted as truth. But the fact was that Rose's guilt was plain. And that gave Giamatti all of the confidence and moral conviction that he needed. Reuven Katz was flat-out wrong in his assessment of the man: "This guy was just a college professor," he said of Giamatti when the investigation was young. "We're going to roll right over this guy,"

After Ron Peters had given his deposition to Dowd, Giamatti wrote a letter to the U.S. sentencing judge in Peters's cocaine case, hailing Peters for having been "forthright and truthful" with Dowd. It was, in effect, meant as a thank you to Peters for the critical information he had helped to provide. The sentencing judge, however, chafed, saying the letter was out of line and that he thought Giamatti had a "vendetta against Pete Rose." In the minds of many, the letter confirmed that Rose was being "railroaded" and the Rose camp seized on that notion. Pete was being prematurely and unfairly judged, they argued, and false assumptions were clouding the truth of his innocence.

Yet neither Rose's lawyers nor Rose himself nor any in the discontented public maw could explain *why* Giamatti or baseball might want to railroad Rose like this. Why would the commissioner, or anyone in baseball, want to unfairly bring down Pete Rose? Everyone understood what a sturdy ambassador Rose was for the game and knew that there were few who had brought more attention and joy to the sport. For Giamatti and his team, the fact that Rose had done something that so acutely threatened the game, that obligated them to respond, was a bitter blow. Even in the heat of Dowd's chase that year (and that is at times what it felt like, a chase) and even in the thrill of new discovery, there was always something sad and lamentable about the work. Proving Rose's guilt did not feel like it would be a real victory at all.

The Rose camp fought back at every turn, discrediting the witnesses, assailing Giamatti, cooperating with Dowd in slow, calculated and incomplete ways. When baseball officials privately asked Rose whether he might step aside as manager while the investigation was going on—to perhaps minimize the aggravation and the constant media exposure—he refused. He was not going to let go of what was his without a battle. He never had and he never would.

Baseball's hearing on Rose was set for late May of 1989, but just before the date Rose asked for more time. Giamatti postponed the hearing for a month. A few weeks later, Rose sued to prevent Giamatti—with his allegedly prejudiced view—from presiding over the hearing. The suit failed but it bought Rose a couple more weeks. Rose's lawyers filed other procedures and raised other objections and gummed up the system for as long as they could.

In mid-June the Reds had begun to lose more often than they won, and by late July the team had fallen to fifth place and out of the pennant race entirely. For the first time there were hard lines set upon Pete's face each day as he stepped onto the field, a sullenness. For his part, Giamatti was gaining weight that he could ill-afford to gain, and he slept badly and he smoked as few men could smoke. "There is only one thing at which I am truly world-class," Giamatti told Vincent, "and that is smoking cigarettes." Some days he went through five packs.

At last, in late August, there were no options remaining for Rose and his lawyers, nor did they have the tools with which to combat the case against them. They had no serious counter-evidence, no alibis, no alternative reality. They had nothing at all. It was then that Rose agreed to forgo a hearing altogether, to instead sign a document saying that he agreed and submitted "to the sole and exclusive jurisdiction of the Commissioner." As Rose's lawyers explained it to him, bowing out of the hearing had helped them win a clear concession: the document included the provision that "Nothing in this agreement shall be deemed either an admission or a denial by Peter Edward Rose of the allegation that he bet on any Major League Baseball game."

As concessions go, though, this was extravagantly slight—irrelevant and wiped out by the agreement's most central determination. This: "Peter Edward Rose is hereby declared permanently ineligible in accordance with Major League Rule 21 and placed on the Ineligible List."

The only relevant part of Rule 21 that mandates permanent ineligibility is the subset d), which concerns baseball club employees who bet on their own team. From Rose's perspective signing the agreement, as he would gradually come to realize, was a pure and terrible miscalculation. It was true that he would be eligible to apply for reinstatement after one year, but that is a right that baseball bylaw affords to any player or official who is suspended indefinitely. Nothing was gained by putting his signature on that paper. In fact, one could argue, everything was lost.

Rose received and signed the document on the morning of Aug. 23. Carol had given birth to their daughter, Cara Chea, the day before and Pete had been there, in the delivery room at Cincinnati's Jewish Hospital. He had left the Reds in Chicago after managing them to a 6–5 win over the Cubs in what would be his last game in a major league uniform. He had not told his players or his coaches anything about the agreement or the pending suspension. The Reds would learn of his banishment from bulletins on TV, or over the radio in their cars.

Four men signed the five-page banishment document: Rose, Katz, Giamatti and Vincent, and the next morning, at 9 a.m. on Aug. 24, 1989, the commissioner's office faxed a copy to every team in the major leagues. Pete Rose was out of the game.

The settlement stipulated that "Neither the Commissioner nor Peter Edward Rose shall be prevented by this agreement from making any public statement relating to this matter so long as no such public statement contradicts the terms of this agreement and resolution." That explains why Rose at a press conference that day continued to forcefully deny that he had bet on baseball, and also why when Giamatti was asked at his own, separate press conference whether he believed Rose had bet on baseball and bet on the Reds he answered, "Yes."

Giamatti appeared worn that day and was somber when he spoke. Pete too had a deep sadness about him, and had to control his quavering voice when, at the start of his press conference he said, "Baseball is my life." Soon, though, Rose's natural feistiness took over, his recalcitrance and his optimism. He vowed that he would be out of baseball for only a "very short period of time," that he would apply for reinstatement after a year and that he would surely get back in. That evening, for the second night in a row, in an appearance that, to many, seemed at odds with the circumstances of his life, Rose went on the TV shopping network CVN. He offered for purchase autographed bats and jerseys and mounted photos of him on the night he'd passed Ty Cobb, and he chatted car-salesman-style with prospective customers who called in.

Giamatti was less conspicuous in the aftermath. He got away from New York and worked for some days from his home in Martha's Vineyard. And it was there, on Sept. 1, 1989, just over a week after he had closed his press conference statement by saying "Let it also be clear that no individual is superior to the game," that an extraordinary thing happened: Giamatti died of a massive heart attack. He was 51 years old and his death made international news and caused widespread sorrow. His wife Toni and the family received many bags of mail, so many condolences and appreciative words, from intellectuals and executives and politicians, as well as from clubhouse guys and doormen, sanitation workers and a particular hot dog vendor from the ballpark in Anaheim. Bart Giamatti, it was said, could just as easily be friends with the man who owned the building as with the man who swept its floors. He was buried privately, before family and friends, at Grove Street Cemetery in New Haven, where Yale presidents are traditionally laid to rest.

He had been overweight and a chain-smoker and unhealthy in many ways, and no one could rightly say that the Rose investigation, even with the months of high stress, had been what killed Giamatti. He had not taken care of himself physically and his doctors were not entirely shocked by his fate; an autopsy suggested that Giamatti had suffered a separate, minor heart attack at an earlier time as well. What people around him could and did say, and as Marcus Giamatti will still say today, is that, "The Rose case did not kill my father, but it definitely did not help." And for those who would go on to preside over the game and to hold the fate of Rose's continued banishment in their hands—namely the commissioners Fay Vincent and Bud Selig—the sudden death of Bart Giamatti has been another reason that it has been so difficult to ever forgive Pete Rose.

Years later, with his investigation having stood the test of repeated inquiry and reexamination, and with Rose having finally admitted to its crucial findings, John Dowd says that he has only one regret about how the whole matter unfolded. He wishes, he says, that sometime during that spring or summer, long before the banishment document was drafted and signed, he could have gone away with Pete for a day or two. Taken Rose out of the dugout, out of Cincinnati, away from his agent and his lawyers. He and Pete would have gone to Cape Cod and walked together there along the beach, Dowd imagines, just the two of them laying their footprints among the tidal pools on the Brewster Flats, perhaps, or into the soft sand against the high dunes over on the ocean side.

They would have worn bathing suits—and so would have had nothing to hide, no tape recorder, no one listening in, nothing to get in the way of the truth. And Dowd would have laid it all out for Pete, explained everything his team knew and just what the repercussions could be. He would have done it in a gentle, clear fashion without lawyers interjecting or engendering confusion about what was real and what was not. There would have been no misunderstanding and no one looking for a loophole; Pete would have gotten it straight.

Then, Dowd says, he might have offered him a safe passage home. Speaking on the commissioner's behalf, Dowd would have told Rose that if he would come forward and admit his guilt and take his medicine, agree to quit all his gambling cold turkey, and to do some clinics for kids, talk to them about the dangers of gambling and then to just sit quietly on the sidelines awhile and let baseball recover from the wounds, then, Dowd would have said, baseball would in turn have done some things for him. They would, if needed, help to swab out the gambling debts, just a one-time fee for Pete then no more payments he couldn't ever get down. And they would have set a path and a timetable for him to get back into the game. Dowd knows that Pete might have laughed all that off, stuck hard to his denial, told Dowd to forget it. But maybe, alone there with Dowd, seeing the waves crashing inevitably into the shore, Rose might have agreed. He might have saved his own life.

"I'll always believe that I could have turned him around," says Dowd. "That I could have made him see the error of his ways, and to see how to make it right. He might have still thought I was a prick, but I think he would have understood what had to be done. And if he had done it, had owned up and accepted a punishment, well if you ask me, he could be managing the Cincinnati Reds still today."

As it was, of course, Rose and his people were not having any of that. Pete was never alone anywhere with Dowd or with any baseball officials or investigators. His lawyers played defense, desperate defense, for as long as they could and Rose himself never budged. As baseball bore down, he only barked in defiance, just as he would bark at his suspension, scornful and dismissive, arrogant behind his bulwark of lies. He maintained a defense for himself throughout the investigation and then for so many, many years afterward, the same stubborn and unchanging defense that in essence and tenor boils down to five words: "Fuck you. I'm Pete Rose."

Chapter 16

Main Street to Marion

T HE HALL of Fame's half-century anniversary celebration began in Cooperstown on June 10, 1989, 50 years almost to the day after the building had first opened its doors and a little more than two months before the banning of Rose. An event across from the post office unveiled a Lou Gehrig stamp; Hall of Fame president Edward Stack presided over the ribbon-cutting for the museum's new $7 million wing; and, in the downtown parade, firefighters, girl scouts and veterans joined a line of convertibles stocked with Hall of Famers. The parade route followed a familiar, Rockwellian path of streets (Chestnut to Main to River to Church to Pioneer . . .) and American flags flapped everywhere. Bart Giamatti sat on the reviewing stand beside New York governor Mario Cuomo watching the procession roll by. Later the Hall of Famers and other old-timers played a ball game at Doubleday Field.

That anniversary spirit was still very much in the air six weeks later on induction weekend. Red Sox outfielder Carl Yastrzemski was going into the Hall of Fame as was Johnny Bench, a Red for 17 seasons and Pete Rose's teammate for 12. Bench had been named on a remarkable 96.4% of the ballots—then more than any inductee ever save for

Ty Cobb and Hank Aaron—and Cooperstown was thick with fans from Cincinnati and Boston. The Reds and Red Sox had been slated to play an exhibition game until the Reds' plane had mechanical trouble getting out of Montreal, forcing the team to cancel its trip. Even before that, Rose, in the crosshairs of baseball's investigation, had said he would not make the trip to Cooperstown with his club, feeling he would be a distraction.

He'd got that right. For all the excitement of the weekend, the swarm of more than 25,000 fans that Cooperstown mayor Harold Hollis called "the largest crowd ever" and the many Hall Famers on hand ("Ted Williams is John Wayne," said Bench, and pitcher Bob Gibson announced that he would spend the day *getting* autographs, not giving them), the topic of the weekend, without question, was the ugly news swirling around Rose, and the uncertainty of his fate. Discussion and debate about Rose has, at varying levels of intensity, been part of every induction weekend since.

Bench didn't like the Rose buzz one bit. He said he thought Pete had made a "great decision" to stay away from Cooperstown. "He [Rose] said it was my day, my glory," remarked Bench, pointing out that he himself had once stayed out of Rose's limelight by not going on the field to celebrate at Riverfront on the night of the Ty-breaking hit.

When Giamatti was introduced before the Sunday induction speeches, some in the big crowd chanted "Pete, Pete, Pete" and booed the commissioner. "Boo some other time, folks," Bench later admonished the gathering. "This is a time for celebration."

Rose and Bench were never peas and carrots as teammates—around the clubhouse they could needle one another with an edge—but through an angling rivalry, there was a symbiosis, an on-field camaraderie and a clear respect. They were deeply linked, the Big Red Machine players with the brightest names on the marquee, and they became, and remain, the two most beloved ballplayers in Reds history. Irksome to Bench, there has never been a doubt about who on the ground in Cincinnati is No. 1.

Even as Pete embarked on his exile, continuing his lies to everyone, wading into too many cesspools, his place in the hearts of most Cincinnatians could not be dislodged. He remained the everyman. Their everyman.

"The difference between the two of them is that if you run into Pete outside the Skyline Chili, he'll talk with you and bring himself right to your level—look you in the eye, crack a joke," says the longtime Cincinnati writer Mike Shannon. "When you meet Bench you feel as if he is extending his hand in your direction and saying, 'Kiss the rings.'"

It was not lost on Reds fans, nor on those who played with him, that Bench got through his entire induction speech in 1989 without thanking or even mentioning any of his teammates. Seventeen seasons in the major leagues and no mention of a single one.

"There would be no chance of that happening with Pete if he ever had an induction speech," says Joe Morgan, who himself went into the Hall of Fame, in 1990. "Pete spends half his time talking about what the players around him did."

Over the years Bench has made it publicly clear that he was not in favor of Rose's being reinstated to baseball ("He broke the rules!") and at times he bristled when he was asked for comment. ("It has nothing to do with me.") In 2000, Bench approached Marty Brennaman the day before Brennaman was to receive the Ford C. Frick Award at the Hall of Fame for his work as a broadcaster; Bench, saying he was speaking on behalf of aging Hall of Famers Bob Feller and Ralph Kiner, told Marty that he was not to mention Pete Rose in his speech. Brennaman did mention Rose, briefly but in kind terms, and soon afterward Bench quit the radio show that he and Brennaman did together in Cincinnati.

The Rose-Bench relationship has mended some in recent years, a conciliation that began in the summer of 2010 when Rose called and then later apologized to Bench for the years of lying, for all the nuisances that had been visited upon Bench because of Rose's sins. Rose would never see his own behavior as a betrayal, in the way that Bench saw it, but he understood that his life had had an unhappy impact on Bench's, and for that, he said, he was sorry.

Even now, one would never stumble upon Rose and Bench sharing an embrace or locked in discussion. But there is at the least a stiff and smiley cordialness that attends them when circumstance lands them in the same place at the same time. In late 2012, Bench organized and headlined a charity banquet and he agreed to let Pete attend and take part as a highlighted guest.

It has been vexing for Bench, and understandably so, that despite the generous public life he has led, the money he has raised to improve so many lives, the reliability he has shown as a baseball ambassador, the respect he has accrued around the game—"If JB calls and asks me to do something, I'm doing it," says Hall of Fame outfielder Dave Winfield, "and a lot of guys feel that way"—and also that he can be sharp and funny on the radio and on the dais, that for all of that it is still Pete's light that shines more brightly. Pete is still the one.

By the end of his induction weekend in 1989 Bench stopped answering questions about Rose and baseball's investigation. "Everything has been said," he responded tersely when asked (and asked again) for comment. As if. As if there would not be so much more to say, and as if Bench, bound forever with Rose, wouldn't be hearing questions about him at most every public appearance he made for the next 25 years. And counting.

ALL THE inmates at the federal prison camp at Marion—the roughly 225 of them—had to wake up around dawn each day, and Pete rose even a little earlier. He made up his cot tight and smooth the way he had as an Army Reserve back in Fort Knox, and he kept his space clean. Breakfast might be a bowl of corn flakes with green bananas, or biscuits and gravy. Hard French toast on the weekends. This was the minimum-security facility in Marion, Ill. Acres of woodland surrounded the grounds and there were no thick window bars or coils of barbed-wire fencing. The idea was that the white-collar types serving their sentences here knew better than to try to leave. If you pulled a walkaway, as the guards called it, or if you got into a fight or other trouble, you'd wind up being sent to a much worse place.

Each morning after headcount Pete and dozens of other inmates were led across the street to work at Marion's federal penitentiary, the super-maximum-security fortress which was sometimes called the Rock because it had gone up in 1963, the same year that Alcatraz was shut down in San Francisco. Now it was the fall of 1990 and the penitentiary contained about 350 very hard men—convicted murderers and rapists, a leader of a Colombian drug cartel, a turncoat spy. Pete went through the sally gate into the penitentiary each morning, through the metal detectors and subject to search. His job assignment had him sweeping up in the welding room; he also helped out on the paint crew for a while. He worked hard and steady, not a lot of standing around like some guys. "Put his head down and got it done," says Billy Guide, an inmate and ex-cop who befriended Pete at the correctional facility. Guide, who'd been nicked in a bribery scheme, spent 10 years of his life in prison, 5½ at Marion. Pete was in for five months.

He had pleaded guilty to two counts of filing false tax returns and for Rose this was clearly a bargain. Both he and the IRS knew there were plenty more Rose violations out there. He had admitted to stiffing the government on more than $350,000 in taxes from cash he'd earned selling autographs and memorabilia (along with some gambling winnings) between 1984 and '87. He had long since gone too far and the Feds, emboldened in part by the way Dowd and baseball had taken on Rose, were keen to get their due. The sentencing judge—U.S. District Judge Arthur Spiegel, the same man who had sent away Ron Peters on tax and drug convictions—levied a $50,000 fine, 1,000 hours of community service, and, along with the five months at Marion, three more months at a halfway house in Cincinnati. It could have been worse: Sentencing guidelines allowed for up to six years in jail. Pete stood up in court. "I lost my dignity, I lost my self-respect," he said, and added, "I really have no excuses because it's all my fault."

Rose checked himself into Marion on Aug. 8, 1990 (two days before Spiegel had ordered him to report), which meant that when Aug. 24 rolled around—that is, the date on which he could first apply for reinstatement to baseball—Pete was just getting used to doing time. Commissioner Giamatti had suggested with deliberate nonspecificity that Pete should "reconfigure" his life before weighing a reinstatement bid and, well, *reconfigured* is what Pete's life certainly was. Headcount happened three times a day.

As far as a reinstatement effort, however, that would wait: "Now," said a Rose representative, "is not the time." The prisoners wore green khaki clothes and Rose, like everyone else, had been assigned a uniform number: 01832-061.

"I can't say enough about him," says Rose's fellow inmate Guide. "He was a regular guy, went to work every day, came back to his room, never asked for special treatment. And people were on him—some of the guards and the other guys. He got a lot of attention as you can guess. He was kind of nervous and he was naive. It's like he thought he was in the locker room; he would leave his stuff out when he went into the shower. His first couple of days there someone stole his commissary card. I had to remind Pete that it's not all good people in that place."

Carol came on Sunday afternoons sometimes, bringing Tyler and little Cara. Tyler was just old enough that the kids at school teased him, he said, about his father's being a jailbird. When Pete Jr. visited, he and Pete talked baseball the whole time, like normal almost, until dusk neared and the guards announced it was time to leave. Petey got up to go and Pete stood too, and as Petey walked away he turned back and saw his father in his prison issue, hand up in a wave, and with an unfamiliar expression on his face—a look of vulnerability and uncertainty. The expression, the whole tableau, rattled Pete Jr. for days after, and has never, he says even now, fully left him.

Jeff Ruby showed up to see Pete at Marion as well, first on his own and then again late in Rose's sentence with WLWT-TV's Jerry Springer. Pete had lost some weight. "That was a different Pete Rose," says Ruby now. "He wasn't exactly comfortable, but he was making the best of things. The first time I saw him he was friendly and tried to make light, but I had the sense he was a little lost, even despondent. I'd never seen that. By my next visit he had brightened up. Pete has an ability to isolate himself from the pressures and troubles around him. It's extraordinary."

Ruby has long carried the belief that he might have saved Pete from his banishment, or at least done something to delay it. Long before baseball got involved, as Ruby recalls it, he knew what Janszen had on Pete and what his plans were for exposing him.

Rose and Ruby went back a lot of years together, back to when Ruby ran bars in the Holiday Inns around Cincinnati and Sparky Anderson and the Reds used to go there. Later Rose (and Bench) backed Ruby's restaurants—his signature steakhouse, the Precinct, opened in 1981— and at the time that Rose was managing the Reds and his troubles with gambling (and with Janszen) were beginning to get away from him, Ruby and Rose were working out together a few times a week at the Scandinavian Health Spa on Montgomery Road.

Outside of the spa one day, Janszen came up to Ruby. They knew one another through Rose. "Pete owes me $30,000," Janszen said. He was using Ruby as an intermediary because Pete wasn't talking to him anymore. Janszen told Ruby that he wanted his money but that Pete wouldn't pay. He also said he had betting slips that could be bad news for Pete if they got out; one day Janszen and Ruby arranged to meet at the Kenwood Mall and Janszen produced the slips for Ruby to see—betting slips with the teams and games logged on them and Pete's name attached.

"Paul is telling me he's going to go to the FBI, he's going to go to baseball, he's going to go to everybody but the SPCA," recalls Ruby. "But when I talked about it to Pete he said, 'That guy's full of it, I don't owe him nothing.' I called Reuven Katz—he was my lawyer too—and asked him what he knew about it and Reuven said Pete says he doesn't owe Janszen anything, and that it would be better for me to stay out of it. So I didn't do anything. I don't know who owed who what, but Paul sounded pretty convincing that he would take those betting slips to baseball. I believed him. I look back sometimes and wish I had just paid Janszen that $30,000 and made him go away. I don't know what would have happened—it turned out Pete was into so much—but things might have gone a little differently."

Ruby and Rose don't see each other much these days, but when Pete is in Cincinnati he might stop in at the Precinct or at Ruby's place downtown—Rose will eat there for free for so long as he lives—and they'll pose for a photo together grinning widely in their brimmed hats. They run into each other at Reds games sometimes too. "We've gotta do a steakhouse together in Vegas," Pete might say. It was, and will always be, Ruby who in the fall of 1990 came into the big room at Marion and took off his cap and sat at the table among the prisoners and their guests and shot the shit with Pete for a while.

At nights in Marion the prisoners were allowed to watch sports on a TV in the rec room, and that October the Reds, managed by Lou Piniella, reached the World Series against the Oakland A's. Pete watched the games a little differently, you might say, from the other men at the correctional facility. He liked to forecast moves that Piniella (or Oakland's manager, Tony La Russa) would make an inning or two ahead of time, and most often he was right. "It was crazy the way he could do it," says Guide. "He could read those games inside and out, he knew the team so well; he knew so much about the guys and the situations."

The 1990 Reds, free of the Rose scandal and the media barrage that had buried them the year before, won 91 games and finished on top of the National League West with room to spare. They beat the Pirates in the playoffs, and although the A's were heavily favored in the Series, the Reds knocked them off in four straight games. "Pete taught a lot of us how to play," said the veteran infielder Ron Oester during the sweep. And by that Oester was referring to an attitude toward the game. "He helped put this together."

Everyone around the club knew that, understood that this championship was something that Rose had helped to build. About seven months before the Series, March of 1990, Pete was in Plant City, Fla., where he owned a house and where the Reds still trained. He was six months into his ban and playing golf at the Walden Lake course with Tom Browning, the lefthanded pitcher who as a rookie had been the winning pitcher on Sept. 11, 1985, the night of 4,192, and who remained an anchor of the Reds staff. Browning stood at the 8th tee when all of sudden the new Cincinnati manager, Piniella, appeared. Lou had seen Browning from the road in passing and thought to stop and say hello. What Piniella had not seen, however, was Rose, hidden from his view by a stand of palmettos. As Piniella came up to greet Browning, he and Rose found themselves suddenly face-to-face.

"There was an immediate and very awkward silence, really so quiet," says Browning. "It felt like 10 minutes." This was a warm and sunny-hazy day in Plant City and birds wheeled overhead. "Finally Lou puts out his hand and says, 'Pete, it's good to see you. I'd love to sit down together and talk about your team.' That's what Lou said, 'your team,' which was classy. And it was also true."

Says Browning, "The whole thing had to break Pete's heart. But he just shook Piniella's hand and said, 'Sure. That would be great.'"

All during the World Series that October the topic came up of how odd and almost eerie it was that Rose, Mr. Red, was nowhere to be seen—except that is, in the historical sections of the Reds media guide, and in the stories some of the players told, and on the backs of the people who wore Rose's jersey in the Riverfront stands. "I've got his address at that place in Illinois right in my pocket," said Johnny Bench, who was working the Series as a commentator on CBS radio. "But whenever I think about writing him, I wonder about what I'd say."

THEY ALL high-fived in the Marion rec room after the Reds won it all, although there was not a cork to be popped, and talk of the Reds filled mess hall conversations for weeks. Pete felt grateful to have Guide, along with a couple of other inmates, to help see him through. In later years Rose was never shy about this gratitude, never ashamed. "Hey, this is my friend Billy," he would say, cheerfully introducing Guide to Mike Schmidt or to Steve Carlton, when Guide came to see him at a show somewhere. "This is the guy who took care of me when I was in prison." Guide met Carol and Tyler and Pete Jr. as well. "Pete did not turn his back on me after he got out," says Guide. "He made me feel good and accepted."

When in November the Associated Press sent Rose a letter at Marion asking if he would answer some interview questions, he declined. He did, however, write back on a sheet of lined paper: "Thank you very much for giving me the opportunity to respond to your questions. However, at this time I'm not ready to talk to the media. I hope you understand and maybe sometime in the near future we can sit down and talk. Sincerely, Pete Rose."

And then he added, still winking, that same Pete Rose: "P.S. Please excuse the stationery."

Rose would get out of Marion on Jan. 7, 1991, and that same winter's day he would arrive (with Carol beside him and riding in a black Jaguar driven by Jeff Ruby's wife, Rackele) at the halfway house, the Talbert House in Cincinnati, where he would sleep on a cot every night for three months. He checked out in the mornings when he left to do his community service—assisting gym teachers at inner city schools—and he checked back in at the end of the day. He sometimes wore a ballcap that read 4,192.

During his final weeks in Marion, though, Pete had already been looking ahead, past the Talbert House and the community service, to a new future, away from Cincinnati. The house in Indian Hill went up for sale and the house in Plant City too. Pete and the family were preparing to move into a new place in Boca Raton. He would do his appearances and work his card shows and make a go of it in the restaurant business. Play golf. Bet the dogs. Things were easier in Florida, he said, "more action, more to do." And Pete knew too, as he swept up the welding scraps each day in the penitentiary or played some handball in the rec area, that even if he wasn't yet ready to try for reinstatement to baseball, at least something else was coming: Late in 1991 (he'd be about 11 months free of Marion), his name was to appear before more than 400 baseball writers on a Hall of Fame ballot. Rose would be eligible for induction for the first time.

Chapter 17

Gate Keepers

T HEY GATHERED together, 10 men in a meeting room in a hotel in the center of New York City, and for eight of those men the purpose and intent of the gathering was clear: Keep Pete Rose out of the Baseball Hall of Fame.

This was a special committee put together by the Hall of Fame's board of directors and led, at least nominally, by Edward Stack, the Hall's president. The committee was stocked with influential guardians of the game: American League president Bobby Brown and his predecessor Lee MacPhail; former National League president Chub Feeney. Sixty-four-year–old Hall of Fame pitcher Robin Roberts was on the committee too and, in a cosmetic gesture, two members of the Baseball Writers' Association, executive secretary Jack Lang and past president Phil Pepe, were also invited to take part. The meeting had not been explicitly labeled as a means for barring Rose, nor had Rose's situation even found its way onto the formal agenda, which included discussion of nuances of the Hall's voting procedure. The idea from the top was to draw less attention rather than more to the committee's true mission.

Rose had been released from Marion three days before this meeting, but plans to deny him his chance at Cooperstown had been brewing since soon after he'd entered prison. There was nothing to prevent a banned player from being elected to the Hall of Fame, and the thought of Rose being celebrated and honored with a bronze plaque after his impudent flouting of Rule 21, after his tax conviction and prison time, and with baseball's leadership still in the long shadow of Bart Giamatti's untimely death, held little appeal to the Hall of Fame's 16-member board of directors. One somewhat notable board member, baseball commissioner Fay Vincent, Giamatti's successor, had said privately and firmly that he believed induction into Cooperstown is best suited to upright and honorable men. With Rose about to appear on the ballot alongside contemporaries such as Tom Seaver and Tony Perez, the board of directors was so determined to block him that it was willing to rewrite the rules.

Among the actual voters, the baseball writers, debate over whether or not Rose deserved induction had begun almost immediately at the time of his banishment from the game. Some writers had vowed that they would not support Rose. (Charles Scoggins of the *Lowell* (Mass.) *Sun* said, "As long as the lifetime ban exists for the commissioner I wouldn't be voting for him.") Others said they would. (Joe Goddard of the *Chicago Sun-Times* said, "It doesn't change what I would be voting for and that is Pete Rose as a player.") It was hard to truly gauge the depth of Rose's support or opposition, and the uncertainty of how the overall vote might go made folks uneasy in Cooperstown and in the Park Avenue offices of Major League Baseball. While it was true that neither the writers nor the Veterans Committee had ever inducted the banned Shoeless Joe Jackson over the many years that they had the chance, there was no way to be sure what would happen with Rose.

It was MacPhail who brought up the motion in that hotel meeting room on Jan. 10, 1991. The group was seated around a conference table and everyone wore shirt and tie. Saying he was "very concerned," that Rose might be inducted, MacPhail proposed that the committee recommend to the board that it add a clause to the voting regulations: "Any person on baseball's ineligible list shall not be eligible for election to the

Hall of Fame." This was later shortened to: "Persons on the ineligible list cannot be eligible candidates."

Lang and Pepe protested strongly but to no avail. The motion went to a vote and came back 7 to 2 in favor of the recommendation. Then Stack added his name to the minority, siding with Pepe and Lang to make the final score 7 to 3. "If it had been 5–4 when it came to Ed there is no way he would have voted to even it up," says Pepe. "It was a calculated vote, for show." (Similarly, Lang said to reporters at the time that Stack "was just trying to make himself look good.") Stack responded by saying that wasn't true—that he honestly believed the writers association should continue to control the Hall of Fame fate of even those players banned from the major leagues. But Stack also claimed that the committee and its recommendation was not meant to target Rose, thus making it hard, in these matters, to take Stack at his word. Said Lang of the committee process: "It was a sham, from start to finish."

Less than a month after the committee's vote, the Hall of Fame's full board officially passed the resolution into its election bylaws. The democratic process had after more than 50 years been abruptly scuttled, and done so in a direct rebuff to the spirit and intentions of the Hall of Fame's founders—no longer would the fate of all players be entrusted to hundreds of veteran writers who cover the game. No longer would the voting necessarily aspire to reflect the feelings of the everyday baseball fan.[1]

The Hall of Fame is a private institution supported by a public trust, and it has at times taken it upon itself to alter and amend certain guidelines. After the death of Roberto Clemente, the Hall permanently waived its five-year waiting period in the case of a deceased candidate. In 1977 the board adopted a resolution to allow for the induction of the

---

[1] Giamatti himself might have been disturbed by the board's dictatorial move. When asked at the press conference announcing Rose's ban from baseball whether the expulsion would have bearing on the Hall of Fame, Giamatti had dismissed the idea, saying he saw no place for intervention: "You," he said, addressing the baseball writers in attendance, "will decide whether he belongs in the Hall of Fame."

old Cleveland pitcher Addie Joss even though Joss had not played the 10 seasons required for eligibility. In tweaking its ballot guidelines in '84 and again in '93, the Hall added grandfather clauses to maintain the eligibility of any players who had been adversely affected by earlier tweaks. What the board did to Pete Rose in '91, however, remains the only time that it has taken measures designed specifically to keep a particular player *out*.

There is nothing keeping this 1991 rule in place; it is hardly etched in granite. Tomorrow, the Hall of Fame's board could pass an amendment to the resolution that says, "Persons on baseball's ineligible list cannot be eligible candidates . . . unless the person is baseball's career hits leader."

Or: " . . . unless the person played in more than 500 games at each of five positions."

Or: " . . . unless the player wore number 14 and sang in an aftershave commercial."

If such suggestions (greeted with understandable chuckles when I presented them on separate occasions to current board members Joe Morgan and Phil Niekro) seem specious, and narrower in theory than the rule that the board of directors passed in 1991, in practice they are not. Consider, after all, the alltime list of players who by virtue of achievement would have appeared on the baseball writers' Hall of Fame ballot but who did not appear on account of being on Major League Baseball's ineligible list. The list is printed here in its entirety: Pete Rose.

When the Hall of Fame ballots were counted in January of 1992, the first year Rose would have been eligible, Rose drew 41 write-in votes, the most write-ins, by far, that anyone has ever received. Those voters supported him even knowing that their votes would not be officially counted. If Rose had been eligible—that year and in the years that followed—maybe he would have still gotten those same 41 votes. Maybe he would have gotten fewer. Maybe he would have gotten more. Maybe he would have received the 323 votes that he would have needed to join the Hall of Fame class of 1992 alongside Tom Seaver and Rollie Fingers. We'll never know.

The Rose resolution was then and remains the greatest disservice to be inflicted upon the Hall of Fame induction process, an injustice not simply to the player and the voters but also to the fans, the people who sustain the institution. There have been other cases in which the voting has for one reason or another seemed compromised—mostly relating to the earliest years of the Hall or to matters of the Veterans Committee— but none other has so deeply stained the procedure nor delivered such a blow to the integrity of the process as a whole.

THE THREE players who were inducted into the Hall of Fame via the baseball writers' vote on July 21, 1991—about five months after Rose had been ruled ineligible for the Hall and about five months before he would have appeared on the ballot—make for an interesting study in themselves: Rod Carew, Ferguson Jenkins and Gaylord Perry.

Carew was a fabulous, precise offensive player who held his bat in the manner of a fly fisherman handling his rod. He won seven batting titles and an MVP, was a daring base runner and retired (with a .328 lifetime batting average) as arguably the best pure singles hitter of his generation. Carew was born in 1945 on a passenger train in Panama, where he lived until age 15 before moving to New York City. Over the course of his 19 major league seasons with the Twins and Angels his teams did not appear in a single World Series; upon receiving his Hall of Fame plaque, Carew kissed it and began to weep.

Jenkins, an exceptionally consistent righthander who won 20 games in a season seven times and pitched to a 3.34 career ERA over 4,500 innings, was in 1980 known as well for a less inspiring reason. While a member of the Texas Rangers, Jenkins was arrested and later convicted after airport officials in Canada found about four grams of cocaine in his luggage. Jenkins, a Canadian citizen and national hero there, would receive no jail time but drew a suspension from baseball that lasted for two weeks. He was repentant, reflective and contrite about his transgression, volunteering to speak with children about drug use. "Nobody'll find any more of that stuff in my luggage," he said. Eleven years later, before giving his induction speech,

Jenkins was asked his opinion on Rose (each of the inductees were asked about Rose, repeatedly); he made his case without even mentioning all the hits: "Pete deserves to be in the Hall of Fame because of his careerlong hustle and because of the influence he had on each of the teams he played with," said Jenkins.[2]

And then there was Perry, perhaps baseball's most noted cheater of the presteroid era. The superb righty won 314 games and two Cy Young Awards and struck out more than 3,500 batters, and did so, he proudly admits, while putting a little something extra on the ball. Perry's autobiography *Me and the Spitter* came out in 1974, 12 seasons into his 22-year career. Part of Perry's effectiveness came from the fact that preoccupied batters believed he was throwing a doctored baseball even when he was not (he fidgeted famously on the hill, irritating hitters; Rose used to yell from the batter's box, "You have to cheat to get me out!"); but Perry acknowledged that at one time or another he had used not only saliva but also wax, K-Y jelly, resin and other substances on the baseball. In '82 he was ejected from a game and suspended for 10 days after umpires discovered him holding a ball greased with some indeterminate muck.

Heavy clouds (but no rain) filled the sky above Main Street in the summer of '91, as Perry and the other inductees accepted their plaques. People in the crowd waved the flag of Panama for Carew and Canadians who had come by the busloads held up the Maple Leaf for Jenkins. Thunder clapped. Lightning flashed. Along with the new Hall of Famers and the other distinguished guests on hand (DiMaggio was there, and Williams), appeared commissioner Fay Vincent, who introduced the inductees. Asked now, Vincent says he does not think that Perry belongs in the Hall

---

[2] Players of various generations were asked about Rose in those years and while some were dead-set against him, by far the majority supported Rose's inclusion to the Hall. "I would let him in," said Ted Williams. "I'm not saying [what he did] is right but it shouldn't deny him something he deserves." Other players, like Jenkins, articulated reasons to support Rose even beyond his formidable stats. "I'd like to see Pete Rose in the Hall of Fame," said Reggie Jackson. "Baseball is so American that I want to see him in there as a guy who loves baseball and America. Pete Rose diving into second base is more important than Pete Rose the man."

of Fame (because of the cheating); but at the induction he offered no objections, smiling and joking gently as he handed the plaque to Perry.

The commissioner cut a strong figure at the ceremony. He posed for photos and greeted the older stars and talked with Stack and some of the writers. He distanced himself from Rose when the topic came up—too hot just then—but in all that he did and said Vincent seemed confident, secure and, behind his horn-rimmed eyeglasses, even wise, the owl-eyed man.

ALTHOUGH VINCENT maintained then and continues to maintain now that he had no involvement in the Hall of Fame's decision to render Rose ineligible—he neither attended the meeting nor voted in absentia when the board passed the resolution, explaining that he did not want the controversy to become "a Vincent-Rose" matter—that has always proved a tough pill to get down. He was the commissioner of baseball and his feelings on Rose were solicited and well-known. He might after all have spoken out against the board's anti-Rose motion (as Giamatti may well have done), but he did not. Major League Baseball and the Hall of Fame were, in the words of Bobby Brown, "kind of one and the same." And, as the president of the Baseball Writers' Association Kit Stier said back then of Vincent's bearing on the Rose resolution, "He's the one I believe who has created this situation."

"No," says Vincent. "I did not push for the Hall of Fame to put in that rule. But I think it is a good rule. I like it."

In the heat of the baseball morality play surrounding Rose's fall, Giamatti and Rose emerged as the Christ and the antichrist. Giamatti set, confirmed and delivered Rose's punishment, firmly casting him out. He was the face and protector of baseball during the investigation, bearing the brunt of the criticism (and the anger and the death threats), as well as large helpings of respect and applause. Giamatti handled himself masterfully in the spotlight, articulating a philosophy of idealism and fairness that elevated himself and the game. Yet even with that context—and even when considering Bud Selig, the commissioner who has in effect held control of Rose's reinstatement prospects for two decades—the person who has proven Rose's most influential and most unwavering detractor, a foil both in deed and in word, has been Vincent.

It was Vincent who led to the hiring of John Dowd for the Rose case, and Vincent who spoke directly with Reuven Katz during the investigation. Vincent wrote Rose's banishment document. The idea for the nonadmission, nondenial paragraph regarding Rose's betting on baseball—that meaningless concession that Rose's team demanded as essential to agreeing to the deal—came directly from work Vincent had done while in the corporate finance division at the Securities and Exchange Commission.

At Rose's 1989 spring training visit to Ueberroth's office it was Vincent who had spoken up in the crowded room and asked Rose, "Did you bet on baseball?" And it was Vincent who continued to press the point that day. Partially paralyzed due to an accident during his college years, Vincent moves slowly and deliberately and in Ueberroth's office relied upon a cane. Rose, after leaving the room, grumbled to those around him: "That crippled guy asked all the questions."

"That comment was my first sense that there was a gap in Rose's armament," says Vincent. "That maybe he was not too bright."

The strong trust and friendship between Vincent and Giamatti—they met in the late 1970s, when Giamatti was president of Yale and Vincent ran Columbia Pictures—was built on a rich exchange of ideas and eloquences that marked and bettered each man and that ultimately led Giamatti to handpick Vincent as his deputy commissioner.[3] On the eve of the Rose banishment announcement the two men were discussing how Giamatti might respond to reporters when they inevitably asked what Rose would have to do to get back in the game. "At the least he'll have to reconfigure his life," Vincent suggested. The phrase stuck in Giamatti's mind and he used it at the press conference, and it has survived as a touchstone remark, one that Rose himself often refers to even now.

Over the more than two decades since he left the commissioner's

---

3 Vincent has never forgotten, as one example, what Giamatti said to him at the funeral of Vincent's father: "When the last of your parents dies you feel particularly pained because that is the end of the line. There is no longer anyone left between you and eternity."

office, Vincent has continued to speak against Rose's reinstatement and against his inclusion in the plaque gallery of the Hall of Fame. He has publicly chastised Bud Selig when Selig has shown or even suggested any leniency toward Rose. In Vincent's reckoning Rose violated not only a cardinal baseball rule but also a principle, a moral boundary. And for those reasons Vincent will never forgive him.

FRANCIS T. "FAY" VINCENT grew up on the first floor of a three-family house in New Haven, Conn., watching Joe DiMaggio's Yankees on a television his father had won at a church raffle. His father, who worked for the New England Telephone Company, was also named Francis T. Vincent and was also known as Fay.

Born in 1938, three years before Rose (and 55 days after Giamatti), Vincent enrolled at age 14 at Hotchkiss, a well-heeled Connecticut boarding school. Fay Sr. had also gone to Hotchkiss—the school had coveted him as a football player—and a scholarship was arranged for his son. At the same time that Rose was pounding a ball into a wall near the Anderson Ferry or grappling with Slick Harmon in the bramble along the Ohio River, Vincent was knotting his tie and going to class to read aloud from the Western canon.

These were deeply formative years for Vincent. More than a half-century after graduating from Hotchkiss he wrote an admiring book about his headmaster, George Van Santvoord, a devoted teacher with unyielding standards. At the school, as Vincent writes, "we followed a tidy and disciplined regimen that carried over to the classroom ... Sloppy dress was unacceptable, as were sloppy speaking and thinking. We learned grammar because we were corrected."

The values imprinted upon him at Hotchkiss guided Vincent as he went on to study at Williams College and Yale Law School, and also in his career—as a lawyer, as an executive at Columbia and Coca-Cola and then, conspicuously, in his jobs at Major League Baseball. The Rose case is certainly not the only issue on which Vincent adopted and stuck to a hard line, which is a large reason why, after inheriting the commissionership from Giamatti, Vincent lasted only three years before base-ball's owners forced him out.

During his brief tenure Vincent publicly admonished owners for having colluded to control player salaries in the 1980s; he banned Yankee owner George Steinbrenner after an investigation (conducted by Dowd) revealed that Steinbrenner had paid a known gambler to dig up damaging informa-tion about Yankee outfielder Dave Winfield (Steinbrenner was reinstated two years later); Vincent also gave a lifetime ban to pitcher Steve Howe, a repeat drug offender, and when Yankees manager Buck Showalter testified on Howe's behalf Vincent scolded Showalter for not supporting baseball's stance. (After five months out of the game, Howe too was rein-stated, by an independent arbitrator.)

In 1991 Vincent sent a cogent letter to all major league teams warning about the use of illegal drugs including, specifically, steroids. He said any player possessing such drugs would "risk permanent expulsion from the game." He threatened a fine of $250,000 to any club that covered up such drug use by its players. The letter was clear, smart, powerful and well ahead of its time. It is difficult to imagine that the steroid era would have continued on quite so rampantly, and done the damage that it has done, had baseball remained under Vincent's watch.

Vincent believed he was a moral arbiter for the game. At times it seemed he believed he was *the* moral arbiter. He banned chewing tobacco in the lower minor leagues. He tried to strong-arm through a realignment of the National League. He assumed a level of power, in labor relations particularly, that troubled many in the game. A Bill Gallo cartoon in New York's *Daily News* near the end of Vincent's reign depicted him wearing a crown inscribed with EMPEROR VINCENT, and a chest pin that read ONE MAN RULE.

Nor did Vincent seem particularly concerned with finding ways to in-crease revenue for the game. He had not handled things to the owners' liking in a 1990 labor dispute, and with player salaries escalating and crucial long-term television issues in the balance, the owners began to lose faith that Vincent would properly represent them in their battles with the players' union.

On Sept. 3, 1992, the owners gathered in a hotel in Chicago and during a four-hour meeting about the commissioner's fate, passed a no-confidence resolution by a vote of 18-9-1, urging Vincent to resign. Four days later under heavy pressure, Vincent did just that, making public a measured but unrepentant resignation letter in which he defended his actions and his views but said he would step down because he believed that the toxicity between himself and the owners was not, as he wrote, "in the best interests of baseball." He added: "A fight based solely on principle does not justify the disruption."

Vincent did retain strong support from a minority of the owners, and also in public opinion. One person who came to Vincent's defense, speaking from Florida, was Pete Rose. "I just wonder, what do they want as the commissioner?" Rose said of the owners. "Do they just want a figurehead and they want to make all the decisions? If I thought he wasn't going to show compassion and good judgment and be fair, I would wish he would leave tomorrow. But I can't get myself to believe that about Fay Vincent."

Vincent has always liked that some observers refer to him as the "last commissioner," with the implication being that those who followed him in the job would be beholden to profits rather than to the game.[4] Vincent titled his 2002 autobiography, *The Last Commissioner: A Baseball Valentine*. (It's a highly readable book, full of pearls.) He still loves the game and knows it well, and he has remained at once a gadfly and a voice of conscience on many issues in baseball: steroids and revenue imbalance, and the antitrust exception, and quite often gambling, which he sees as the single greatest threat to pro sports. He has not softened on Rose in the least. Anytime Pete steps in it in public, Vincent will pounce. "He is really a bad guy," says Vincent. "He is a man without a moral compass."

Vincent lives, during the warmer months at least, in a fine large house on a fine leafy street in a part of Connecticut where argyle socks never go out of style. He reads and he writes and he is often asked to speak.

---

4 Around the time that Vincent was ousted and Selig ushered in, White Sox owner Jerry Reinsdorf said that baseball needed someone who would "run the business for the owners, not the players or the umpires or the fans."

He has good friends and he watches baseball and he lives an intellectual life. His daily routine continues to be informed by an event that occurred more than half a century ago; the single event that, along with his years at Hotchkiss, has so profoundly shaped him in tangible and intangible ways.

During his freshman year at Williams, Vincent lived on the third floor of a dorm, in a suite with several friends. One December day one of those friends, pranking, locked Vincent into his room. Vincent was 18 years old and to his (and his father's) pleasure had played well in freshman football that autumn.

Vincent had the idea to escape his dorm-room lockdown by climbing out onto a narrow ledge and inching along it to the window next door. On the ledge, though, he lost his footing. He fell 40 feet, striking a metal railing before landing, on his back, on the ground. The impact paralyzed him, as he writes in *The Last Commissioner*, "from midchest down." The life Vincent had known was over and a new one had begun. These many years later, while leaning on his walker or while kneading his stockinged feet, he will say that he views his walk on the ledge as an error in judgment and blames only himself.

Vincent told the story of his fall to students at Williams as part of a 2008 talk he gave on the nature of failure and success. He was not, at the moment of telling the story, talking about his position on Pete Rose, although he might have been. For when he finished describing the drop off the dorm-room ledge, Vincent added this:

"What we learn in life— I'm now 70—is there's a certain ruthless sense of honesty about life. And that is that when you make a mistake you pay."

Chapter 18

Petey

FOR HIS first professional tryout camp, at old McBride Stadium in Richmond, Ind., June of 1985, Pete Rose Jr. wore a T-shirt that read COBB BUSTER on the front and CHARLIE HUSTLE on the back. The Reds were auditioning free-agent prospects and though Petey was only 15, too young to officially sign, the scouts said that, for the heck of it, they'd like to take a look at him anyway. He had short red hair and plenty of freckles across the bridge of his nose. Karolyn had driven him the 60 miles from home.

It was a day of partial sun and partial cloud, and during the tryout Petey hit a single in three times up during a simulated game. He also went in hard on a slide into second base, taking the fielder by surprise. "I'm going to the major leagues," Petey told reporters there, using "when" rather than "if." Karolyn contributed her own scouting report, suggesting that her son had desire equal to his father's and had talent even greater.

He tore it up in the American Legion that summer, batting .390 as the youngest player on a club that reached the district finals. He went with a Cincinnati all-star team to the town of Marion, Ohio, to play in an amateur World Series, and at night when some of the boys, pumped to be out on their own, blared Van Halen and the Fat Boys loudly in the rooms of the motor lodge and hung out of bathroom windows smoking cigarettes, Petey was out front in the parking lot, under the yolk-yellow light of a lamppost with a baseball bat, working on his swing.

He played third base and first base, and he started as a sophomore at Oak Hills, and he kept hitting the hell out of the ball. He wore number 14. Petey loved the ball field but school itself he "hated," he said—"Except gym and lunch and girls"—and when he found himself academically ineligible to play on the team in his junior year, he knew this was not a development that would anger his father. "Petey can hit," Big Pete said with a grin upon introducing his son to Nolan Ryan that year. "But he can't read."

When Big Pete talked with Petey at the ballpark, which was about the only place they saw each other, he was clear about what kind of education mattered most. "You get a Porsche if you hit .400," Big Pete said after Petey learned to drive. "So long as you play the right way and you're always on time." After the game, the two Pete Roses went different ways.

The kid kept his head in the game, picked up nuances beyond his years. Slow wheels and all—he had the same gait as his dad but was more plodding. "I'm a mule," Petey said—he could backdoor slide around a tag like a professional. One year in the American Legion World Series he caught a pitcher off guard and became the first player to steal home in the history of the tournament. As a senior at Oak Hills he was named MVP.

Four years, tops, he'd be in the big leagues, he said then, and so when he slipped to the 12th round in the '88 draft, which is where a good-hitting kid with little speed and a sketchy glove might go, he wasn't about to sign on the cheap. Especially with his father in his ear. Rather than commit—the Orioles had drafted him—Petey went out that summer and helped Budde Post No. 507 win it all in the American Legion, batting .440 on the season, .463 in the World Series. His risk had paid off. In September, Baltimore gave him a $21,000 signing bonus, which was about what a fourth-rounder might have gotten in those days.

Soon it would all begin, Petey's wrenching and unparalleled odyssey through the minor leagues, but first he would spend 10 late-winter days in Florida living with his father. Big Pete gave him batting clinics and looked at his stroke and they talked about two-strike hitting and subtle differences in breaking balls, those kinds of things. Near the end of that time together, Big Pete told Petey by way of some parting advice that he should grit his teeth when he came to bat and Petey, in response, took off his ballcap and wrote with a marker "grit your teeth" on the underside of the bill. Neither the son, who thought he knew all there was to know about what it meant to step onto a baseball diamond as Pete Rose's son (that the name might make him a bright target for words, for taunts, for fastballs high and tight), nor the father understood just how hard and for just how long Petey would indeed be clenching those teeth, as a way to hold himself in, to bear what was his to bear and to play baseball for another day.

PETEY HARDLY knew what was happening that summer of 1989. Mostly, he saw it all collapsing around his father in the news. Unnerving. Disorienting. Baseball was deep into its investigation of Pete Rose, a mission that would reveal him as a gambler, a tax cheat and a defiant liar, and that would lead to his banishment from the game. With all the attention upon him, Big Pete kept changing his phone number. To speak to his father, Petey had to call Reuven Katz, who would get hold of Big Pete. Of course a lot of people were calling Katz that summer. Must be, Petey figured when he didn't hear back, that his dad hadn't gotten the message.

He was 19 years old, one step into pro ball, playing home games in a Babe Ruth League park in Frederick, Md. When Rose Jr. came to bat grown men would stand and holler things loud enough that you could hear from centerfield to both dugouts: "Your papa doesn't look so great now, does he Rose? Fucking loser!" At more than one ballpark, fans waved dollar bills at Pete Jr. Karolyn drove out and came to some games and tried to drown out the hecklers. "Give it a ride, Googy!" she'd yell. Googy was what Karolyn and Pete called Petey when he was small.

He didn't hit much in Frederick and was sent down further still, to low-A Erie (Pa.), where the noise from the stands never stopped, people yelling out gambling taunts when he came up: "Three-to-one you'll strike out, Rose!" And the media was everpresent too, all the time looking for more out of Petey. The team finally had to forbid reporters from asking him any more questions about his father. Midsummer, Orioles management suggested he should take a couple days off to clear his head. Pete Jr. didn't want the break. "Go home and sit on my butt?" he said. "Thanks, but no."

Grit your teeth.

He made $1,000 a month and drove to scruffy Ainsworth Field with his roommate Arthur Rhodes—the good and fast friend he made that crazy year—and despite the nightmare of his father's disgrace, Rose Jr. provided for himself a measure of hope that summer. He batted .276 in 58 games for Erie, exactly one point less than his father had hit playing for Geneva in the same New York-Penn League three decades before. The younger Rose, it was noted, had a bit more pop in his bat than his dad had shown back then. *Baseball America* named Rose Jr. the 8th best prospect in the 14-team league. National headlines said things like 2ND COMING OF CHARLIE HUSTLE. "Anyone who works that hard has the potential to make it [to the majors]," an Orioles player development man, Roy Krasik, said.

Still, Pete Jr.'s small success could not compete with Big Pete's spectacular unraveling; always the events in Petey's world were small details on the broader canvas of his father's life. Big Pete's spiraling fate—in particular his being locked up for tax fraud—gave the hecklers unlimited ammunition. They couldn't get to Rose but they knew where his son was. "How much have you got on the game?" Pete Jr. would hear as he dug his left foot into the back of the box. Or chants of "I-R-S, I-R-S" as he ran out onto the field. As if the father and the son were one. The managers he had—old baseball guys like Wally Moon, Bobby Tolan, Fred Kendall—winced and shook their heads because they'd never heard a kid treated the way Pete Rose Jr. was treated by the fans. They wrapped their arms around him as best they could and stood with him in solidarity when the reporters circled around.

His batting average sputtered—down to .232 one year, .217 the next, then .253, .218. The Orioles traded him to the White Sox's system, and the White Sox let him go to Cleveland, and then he came back to the White Sox again. Class A ball all the way. He had some shoulder trouble, and his arthritic knees had already started to ache from time to time, and the men inside the game, the same men who had let him fall to No. 295 overall in that 1988 draft, believed that their suspicions were confirmed. For all his worthy effort, Pete Rose Jr. wasn't adapting against pro pitching. He got out in front too much at the plate, he was too aggressive, like he was pressing. You couldn't walk the guy, he wanted so badly to put his bat square on the ball. People began to wonder when he might stop hanging on. "He'd make a fine manager, you know," folks said even then.

"The bottom line is that I'm playing baseball," Rose Jr. said late in 1994, "and all the people who ask how much longer I am going to give it are still doing nine-to-five jobs. If it means staying in A ball for the next 10 years and then on the 11th I get called up to the big leagues, I'll play 10 more years."

He was at Prince William then and his manager, Dave Huppert, talked about Rose Jr. in a way that managers and teammates often did. They would say that he was dedicated as few players are. That he could be hard on the field but was softer off it. That sometimes he seemed too sweet and sentimental to be his father's son, and that at other times he had a bristle that made him seem exactly that. He was the guy to think of ordering a cake for some bench player's birthday. He was the guy, whatever his batting average at the time, that the team wanted up when a runner needed to get knocked over from second to third. The chip on his shoulder—truly, the block of timber that sat there—was implicit and understood in all that was said and observed about him.

"He has a chance to become a pretty good hitter," Huppert said. "He just needs a break. He changed this team around when he came with his hard work and effort. His attitude rubbed off on a lot of guys."

Petey tried everything to get a longer look, to move himself up, even going to spring training as a White Sox replacement player during the strike in 1995 ("When you're stuck not getting playing time in A ball . . . " he said in explanation), which, of course, provided new grist for anyone eager to lash out at him from the stands. He bulked up, downing protein shakes and swallowing supplements, so that the media guides that put him at 6' 1" and 180 pounds were 20 pounds light, at least. He added a little uppercut to his swing. And if he came to bat 500 times in a season, he heard something from the stands 500 times, the announcement of his name a catalyst for derision. When on a Thirsty Thursday promotion in some bush league town in North Carolina the two-for-one beers made their presence felt, the joke would always be on Petey.

Grit your teeth.

And then, nine seasons in, nine years just about exactly since he'd signed on with the Orioles, it happened. Having made it into the Reds organization, and up to the Double A Chattanooga Lookouts, Rose Jr. had that season of dream—"I saw myself in the big leagues," he said to team-mate Toby Rumfield after being jolted awake on the bus. "I saw myself!" He sprayed line drives, smacked tough pitches over the wall, drove in runs like no one else on the team. It all led to the phone call received by Pete Rose Jr. in Chattanooga at 5 p.m. Aug. 29, 1997. A Friday.

"We're calling you up," Reds general manager Jim Bowden said on the other end of the line. Just a few days earlier the Reds had announced that they were not planning to add Rose Jr. to the team, but the fans had been so indignant and made such a ruckus that the team changed its plans. Bowden told Petey to be in Cincinnati for the Labor Day afternoon game, Sept. 1. There would be a uniform and a place in the starting lineup awaiting him.

IT WASN'T the .143 batting average nor the nine strikeouts in 14 Reds at bats that charted Rose Jr.'s baseball future. No one could be judged on so brief a trial. "Not 14 at bats not 100 at bats, not 200," says Bowden. "Our baseball people evaluated him over years, not on those four weeks."

There was a day in Pete Rose Jr.'s fleeting major league career when he looked at the stat line and saw his batting average at an even .400. In his fifth at bat, pinch-hitting against Pirates' righthander Jason Schmidt in the bottom of the sixth inning, Rose Jr. lined a 2-and-2 pitch into rightfield for a single. He scored on Pokey Reese's home run, fac-toring into an 8–6 Reds win. That second—and what would be final—career base hit ensured that if his father was first in hits among all major leaguers, at least he, Pete Jr., would not be last.

"It was a good feeling," he says now. "I hit the ball on one hop to Jose Guillen in rightfield, went down and made the turn at first. That guy had an *arm* and he threw a seed to second base. But guess what. When I got back to the dugout after Reese's home run, one of the coaches started telling me if I'd hustled more out of the box I might have made it to second. I thought he was joking. The fastest guy in either league couldn't have made it to second base. Then I realized he wasn't kidding. Just part of the deal."[1]

He started only the one game, played the field in only three. "I was told that he didn't figure in our long-range plans," says Jack McKeon, who had taken over as Reds manager midway through that 1997 season. "The idea was to give him a look, but not all that much playing time. We had other guys we wanted to get in. What I remember about the kid was how hard he was working, trying to do everything he could do with a very limited opportunity."

Twenty-eight days. One big league September. There was a road trip to Philadelphia where the old grounds crew and the stadium workers came around to greet him. (He got one at bat in the four-game series, lining out to rightfield.) In a game against the Pirates on Sept. 6, Pete Jr. gloved a ground ball at third base and threw across to Eduardo Perez, playing first. Rose to Perez went the play; like old times in Cincinnati.[2] Later in that Pittsburgh game he threw a ball away, leading to a couple of runs. On another afternoon, during batting practice, Reds shortstop

---

[1] Guillen played his final game in the majors in 2010, but years later big leaguers still swap stories about his arm. One of Guillen's uncorkings—on April 27, 1998, from the rightfield warning track to third base, on the fly, to cut down Colorado's Neifi Perez— was in 2011 named "the most unbelievable throw of all time" in a package produced by the MLB Network.

[2] Rose Jr. had also played for the Reds in spring training that year, five months earlier. In that exhibition game, against the Rangers in Port Charlotte, Fla., Pete Jr. played third base, Eduardo played first base, and Davey Concepcíon, another son of a Big Red Machinist, played shortstop. Aaron Boone, brother of then Reds' second baseman Bret Boone, played second base and Stephen Larkin, Barry's brother, was the DH. "The Rangers weren't happy," Eduardo recalls. "They were saying how it was like an insult or a charade or something. They had a good lineup—Will Clark, Pudge Rodriguez, Mickey Tettleton. Only thing is, that day the charade won." In a 10–7 final, Pete Jr. homered, singled and made a few plays. "I knew I had it in me," he told *The Columbus* (Ohio) *Dispatch*.

Barry Larkin started calling Rose Jr. the Hit Prince. After the season's final game—he played a few innings at first base, scored a run in an 11–3 win—Petey left a few things in his locker, figuring he'd be back.

The Reds cut him in October.

Big Pete griped on the radio, saying Petey hadn't gotten a fair shake. But then it turned out that Junior, who after the release came back to the Reds on a minor league deal, couldn't stick at Triple A Indianapolis either. The Pirates picked him up, sent him to *their* Triple A team, then when he struggled let him go after 28 games. Now each season meant a new start, a bolt of optimism, another dead end. He played in the Phillies' system for a while, then in Chattanooga again. Canada. Mexico. Petey turned 30 years old. He turned 32. Thirty-three. Big league teams stopped calling. Even keeping him somewhere down in the organization didn't make sense anymore, not when the spot might go to a younger guy with a promising future.

Petey grit his teeth and found work in the Independent Leagues, teams like the Joliet (Ill.) Jackhammers, Lincoln (Neb.) Saltdogs, Long Island (N.Y.) Ducks. He had Bud Harrelson as a coach one year. Clubs like that could always use a name such as Pete Rose Jr. to put a few more people in the seats. And teams at that level could use his bat. One season in Winnipeg he hit .344. Still, the hecklers hollered from every grandstand in every town.

His father published his as told-to book, *My Prison Without Bars*, admitting he had bet on baseball. Petey asked the P.A. announcers to introduce him as PJ Rose for a while—as if he could hide—but the name didn't feel right to him, and he went right back to Pete Rose Jr. One season he refused to sign any autographs; before long he was signing them again.

Petey did not harden, even if there might have seemed to be a shell around him. Each time he came to a new club—sunglasses on, the Rose jaw right there—some teammates treaded gingerly, assuming Pete Jr. would be aloof and arrogant. Soon, though, that perception would disappear, and Petey would become a team leader, the glue. During pregame and postgame and the time in between, he was always one to talk, banter, loosen people up. He'd stay for hours in the locker room after the final out, dissecting the day's at bats, treating players with stories from his childhood and about things his dad once did. The Hit Prince.

And yet. *Grit your teeth.*

As a kid Petey used to hear his father say, "Playing baseball is the easiest way in the world to make a living." For him maybe. The $30,000 salary that Pete Jr. had earned as a Double A player now seemed a luscious sum. Independent leagues might pay $2,000, $2,500 a month over a short season. Petey ate peanut butter and jelly sandwiches six days a week. He crashed at friends' houses to save some cash. He turned 34. Thirty-five. Thirty-seven. Thirty-nine. No one had ever led a baseball life like his.

How do you *do* that? How do you sustain such a life, a life that by now included a wife and two young children, earning that kind of money in that kind of itinerant career? How do you shake off the credit card debt? The bus rides? How do you play on through the pain in your knees, ankles, hips? How do you bull through the disappointment? How do you hold on to hope, year after impecunious year?

THE FIRST time Pete Jr. saw Shannon Tieman they were both in kindergarten. Cincinnati, mid-1970s. It may be that she was wearing a red shirt; that's how he recalls it, anyway. In the sixth and seventh grades Shannon and Petey talked with one another sometimes. In high school he asked her on a date. He took her to Skyline Chili. She had long brown hair and a smile like Sunday morning and she was way smarter than he, as he'd known for years. They decided after high school that his going out on the road to play pro baseball was not something that would pull them apart, but rather would hold them closer together. Shannon arrived to stay with Pete Jr. in 1991 (he was 21 years old and playing at Sarasota) driving an old, white Sentra. "She had one bag and all the rest shoes," says Pete Jr.

She made chicken parmesan sandwiches, enough to last a few days, and they ate them sitting on the floor. They slept together on a mattress coarse as canvas. She came to games and growled at the hecklers. Between innings he looked for her in the stands and smiled when their eyes met. Over time, Shannon's parents became like second parents to

Rose Jr. Quieter, of course, and with other values than he had known at home. They came to see him play, and Pete sometimes worked for Shannon's father during the winter. Shannon kept traveling with Pete Jr., to Hickory, Prince William, South Bend, Birmingham, Nashville, through the call up to the major leagues and back down again. Along the way, in 1995, they married. In '99 Shannon took a full-time job and since then she has worked at a bank and in marketing and in advertising, all around Cincinnati.

For a number of years after the wedding they lived with Shannon's parents. Their son, Peter Edward Rose III was born in 2004, and two years after that a girl, Isabella Marie, both of them growing beautiful, impish, cute. In the baseball off-season, Pete Jr. changed the kids' diapers, strolled them to the park, drove them to preschool and picked them up. Shannon went in for her nine-to-five. Then spring training would come around again.

"Not once in all the time of my career, not once, did she say to me that she thought I should do something else," says Pete Jr. "She has supported me like a steel beam. We have had amazing times together, and she has also been there for me to cry on. I have needed that. All of the things she does—wife, friend, mom. None of this is possible without her. She has been the world to me. It is hard to do what I am doing. And it is really hard to do what she is doing, I know that."

In 2003 the debt got so deep that they filed for bankruptcy (among their listed assets: a signed Pete Rose baseball, $75) and then, three years later, Shannon sat in a Nashville district courtroom as Pete Jr. was sentenced to jail. According to the charges, *United States of America* v. *Pete Rose Jr.*, between 2001 and '02 Pete Jr. did, "knowingly and intentionally possess . . . [and] distribute a liquid mixture containing Gamma-butyrolactone (GBL), a controlled substance." He pleaded guilty. He says he took GBL to help him fall asleep because at times those bad knees, the throbbing heel, the whole grinding circumstance of his life, kept him lying awake staring at another ceiling in another motor lodge.

GBL, though, does other things. It causes the body to produce growth hormone. It can help build muscle. The drug was another strand in the sprawling web of baseball's steroid era. Pete Jr. took GBL before and for years after it was declared illegal in 2000. If the drug could help him hit a few more home runs, drive the ball the way he did back in 1997 at Chattanooga, well, then … When Pete Jr. was taking GBL his weight got up near 250 pounds.

Pete Jr. cooperated with the prosecution from the outset, and the judge believed the evidence showing that the "distribution" part of the charge was a little misleading, that it really boiled down to his simply buying some for himself as well as a few teammates. The fact that scores of players all across the game were taking drugs like GBL and that it was in the heart of a tainted culture was not overlooked. Petey was contrite and torn-up, that was obvious. What ate at him more than anything was not even the prospect of being locked away, but that, as he said in the courtroom, "I am not making the Rose name proud, and that is my fault." He saw no irony in his words. By the book, Pete Jr. could have gotten 20 years for what he did. A more typical sentence was around 24 months. The judge gave him 30 days in a county jail.

Shannon did not blink when Pete Jr. told her that when he got out of that Boone County cell (where some days he would spend all but an hour in isolation, never having a weight to lift or a bat to heft, though he would swing a laundry bag sometimes), he was planning to go right back into baseball. Soon after his time began, he called Dave LaPoint, the manager of the Bridgeport (Conn.) Bluefish, from jail looking for work and found that the Bluefish had a place for him on the team. His second game back he hit a three-run homer.

He batted .299 that season and over the next two years, over 962 at bats playing for LaPoint (now managing the Long Island Ducks), Pete Jr. hit .314 and knocked in 190 runs. Alongside former major league All-Stars—Edgardo Alfonzo, Carl Everett, Danny Graves, Jose Offerman—Rose Jr., as LaPoint recalls, was always "the heart of the team, the guy who made us go." The others regarded him with surprise: *Twenty-eight days in the Show? That's all the time you got?*

"There he is, 38 years old, and some nights he could hardly get around, his knees were that bad," says LaPoint. "He'd lie on the couch in my office icing until 15 minutes before game time, then he'd limp out there. And on every one of those days, and I am convinced of this, he was sure he would get back to the major leagues. He would say, 'I could give a team a little lefthanded pop off the bench, I play a couple of positions. Hey, my dad played in the big leagues until he was 45.'"

When Pete Jr. talked the same way with Shannon, she supported him then too. Always. *Sure, sweetheart, plenty of big league teams need a hitter like you.* She kept saying that right up until, and even beyond, his last minor league at bat, when at the age of 39 years, 10 months, he was let go by the York (Pa.) Revolution. Petey didn't quite retire—he never officially did—but just said he would take a little time off, rest the knee, help around the house, go watch his son's Little League games, chase his daughter around the couch. Be a dad.

All through the years Shannon understood that there was nothing to say but what she said, truly nothing else to do. No matter how tough it seemed, no matter how tight the money got. She was there from the very beginning, grade school on the West Side, and she saw with open eyes what it meant to be Pete Rose's son in Cincinnati. She understood, with an intimacy that few others ever could, the reach of his father's ascent and the depth of his father's fall. She understood that there were things that should be said between Petey and herself, and things that were better kept inside.

Shannon understands, just as Karolyn Rose understands, and Eduardo Perez understands, that all of Pete Jr.'s love for the nuances of the game—the striding up to the batter's box, the squaring up of a fastball, the way a ground ball cuts through the grass, the knocking of infield dirt off your hip, the moment of noticing that a pitcher's arm has dropped just this much late in a game, the heavy stick of pine tar—that all of that is wrapped up with his trying to find his way to another love. And that Petey's unending dream of making it to the major leagues, no matter the cost to get there, is wrapped up as well in another dream. And that it has never been entirely clear, not to anyone, where it is in Petey's life that his father ends and the game of baseball begins.

Chapter 19

Truth, Reconfigured

A S PETE ROSE began his life in baseball exile, his central concerns—as might be expected for a man who has lost his primary livelihood, has become troubled by debt and has been accustomed to a certain style of living—revolved around his finances. All the steady money he'd ever earned had come directly from baseball or, by extension, from his own commercial appeal. As he once told Denny McLain at a card show, "I get up and do Pete Rose every day."

He lived in Florida with Carol and the kids and presided over the investor-run Pete Rose Ballpark Cafe in Boca Raton, a sprawling family-menu place with a TV in every booth, a deep stable of coin-op video games and Pete himself as a lure for customers. He hosted a radio sports talk show in the evening, working inside a glassed studio from which he could see the diners and they could see him. Calls came in to the show on all kinds of sports topics and from all over the country—a guy from Anchorage, a woman from Pennsylvania, a kid from down the road in Boynton Beach. Pete had verve and humor and opinions and good guests. Some callers would go off topic and tell Pete that by the way he would always be a Hall of Famer to them.

Pete had a stake in the gift shop, which was stocked with big league apparel and trinkets, along with all kinds of Rose-related collectibles—autographed balls, bats and baseball cards. You could buy clothes (caps, jackets and pants) with "Hit King" woven into them, garments that Pete himself often wore around the place. He'd stop by your table for a quick greeting or to join in with a "Happy Birthday" chorus for some Little Leaguer out with his folks. The Ballpark Cafe established itself as a lively, crackling place, much like Pete himself. One time Tommy Harper showed up unannounced after so many years and Pete threw his arms around him in the parking lot and they didn't talk about the banishment at all.

At card shows he could earn $30,000 for an afternoon's work, and he got hired for other private appearances as well. His golf game was better than it had ever been, which helped when he made celebrity appearances.

Pete's brother Dave was around then, working for Pete as a cook in the cafe's kitchen and achieving local notice for his soups and his spinach dip and for the chili he crafted in the Cincinnati style. Dave had been playing golf a lot too, and when he was asked, in 2013, to describe the best day he'd ever had in the 65 years of his boyhood, youth and adult life knowing Pete, this is what he said: "It was the 1990s and Pete was banned from baseball and I was working for him at the Ballpark Cafe. We played golf a lot in the morning. I'd go with Pete and make up a foursome. I couldn't play that good at first but I stuck with it—I'd get out there and practice on my own—and I got myself a whole lot better.

"Around that time a casino in the Bahamas had put together a golf tournament, like a Pete Rose invitational. It attracted a lot of high rollers. Well, Pete had seen how my golf game was coming along and he said to me, 'Would you like to come there and be on my team?' I said sure—everything was all paid for by the casino, you know. So we get down there, me and my wife, and a limousine picks us up at the airport. They gave us a little suite up on one of the hotel floors that you needed a special key to get onto. They had these rooms set up with food and drinks and if you wanted a drink or anything anytime you just had to call and they brought it free. You know, the whole nine yards.

"The night before the tournament they had a reception, some cocktails and whatnot, and Pete comes up to me and says there has been a change. 'I'm not going to be on your team. They want me to play with a couple of guys from New York.'

"I said that was fine. I didn't mind who I played with. I ended up with a guy who made his money selling and leasing motor coaches. Terrific guy. The tournament was set up as a scramble of course, and I was the D player in our group. But I played my ass off that day and, well, long story short, we won the tournament! It was $750 apiece and it was Pete's job to give out the checks. When it came time to give me mine, Pete made a joke like he wasn't going to give it to me. Man, that was fun, he was all joking and stuff but I could tell that he respected me for winning that tournament. I remember being really, really happy."

PETE HAD long been a fan of professional wrestling—the shtick, the theater, the absurdity, and the huge noisy crowds that are drawn to it— and in the spring of 1998 at the age of 56 he made his pro wrestling debut, hired as a guest ring announcer for Wrestlemania XIV at the Fleet Center in Boston. He came out wearing a tuxedo to big applause, but then immediately turned against the crowd. "The last time I was here we kicked your ass!" he said, going on to describe Boston as the "city of losers" and invoking the names of Bucky Dent and Bill Buckner, players associated with painful Red Sox collapses. Boos and shouts rang out from the seats.

And then, abruptly, the lights fell and fire exploded and out from an arena tunnel—"straight out of the mouth of hell" as a television announcer bellowed—came the character of Kane, an enormous and sinister figure clad in spandex and with long sweaty locks draped in front of his allegedly disfigured face. The organ music was deafening and dirge-like and beside Kane strode a pale, fleshy manager wearing a suit and named Paul Bearer. When Kane climbed into the ring Rose stared in mute terror, helpless as Kane picked him up, turned him upside-down and with his signature pile-driver move, "tombstoned" Rose headfirst into the mat. Pete lay motionless before being wheeled off on a stretcher as the crowd remained in frenzy.

That same year in Cooperstown, the Hall of Fame established a new research center and named it in honor of the late commissioner, A. Bartlett Giamatti. "It's the perfect way to recognize and perhaps fix for all time at the Hall of Fame the name of my husband," said his widow, Toni. A plaque went up in Giamatti's name and a painting of him was hung on the wall.

Rose got hired again for Wrestlemania XV a few months later, this time scripted for him to seek revenge by dressing in disguise as the San Diego Chicken and ambushing Kane from behind. The result: another emphatic tombstoning of poor Pete. The whole enterprise seemed ignominious to many, perhaps—and among baseball's literati, Rose was roundly lampooned—but not at all to Pete. "I would let them throw me into the stands if they paid me enough," he said of the wrestling promoters.

Rose's devotion to money, to making it and showing it off and keeping it from the IRS, traces far back. In exile, as ever, Pete remains among those people for whom cash is always king. Eduardo Perez, Tony's son, remembers being at the Roses' house in Cincinnati in the 1970s, playing Monopoly with Petey when both boys were less than 10 years old. They had amassed stacks of the game's colorful bills and when Rose came into the room, a spot of shaving lather still on his cheek, Petey called out, "Hey, Dad, look at all this money we've got!" as he and Eduardo giggled and fanned it out. "So Pete says, 'Oh yeah?'" recalls Perez, "and then he goes into his room and comes back out with a $1,000 bill. He said, 'Well I've got this. And it's real!' We all just cracked up."

In the late 1980s, while Rose was managing the Reds, his former teammate Jim O'Toole visited Pete at his home in Plant City, Fla. "We had just played a ball game against some younger guys as part of a fantasy camp," says O'Toole. "I asked Pete if he had a cold beer. And he said, 'I've got something better than that. How about some cold cash!' And he reached into the refrigerator and pulled out stacks of bills. I think he'd won a Pick-Four or something."

Charles Sotto, the longtime memorabilia dealer who has been a friend and associate of Rose's for many years—he was interviewed about his relationship with Rose for the Dowd Report and still organizes events for him in Cincinnati—may have said it best when he remarked not long ago, "Pete doesn't have a gambling problem. He has a cash problem."

Certainly Pete believed that for him gambling was no sickness. In a lukewarm attempt to appear reconfigured after his banishment, he attended some Gamblers Anonymous meetings and heard the people there talk about having gambled away their mortgage or their rent and describe themselves as suicidal. Pete just knew that that wasn't him. An addicted gambler, in his eyes, was someone who "can't go to bed with a dollar in his pocket" without having bet it on something.

"One of our screening questions when we are deciding what treatment someone might need, is to evaluate whether gambling is doing harm to their lives. If it is, that's a problem," says Dr. Timothy Fong, a codirector of the UCLA Gambling Studies Program who has treated numerous sports figures. "Another sign that someone has a gambling compulsion is if they repeatedly lie about it or hide it."

Rose presents an unusual case. He didn't hide his gambling at the horse tracks or dog tracks (he tried to hide his *winnings* sometimes, to be sure, but not the fact that he was there and betting), nor did he care how it looked when, in his exile, he did paid events at casinos or moved his radio show from Florida to Las Vegas now and then. (Rose discussed point spreads and betting lines with callers all the time.) People squawked and tsk-tsked about his behavior, but the way things looked to others never mattered much to Pete. He had a living to make.

Yet there was no question, of course, of the profound damage that gambling had done to his life—a specific type of gambling. Throughout the 1990s he continued to deny, fiercely and often scornfully, that he had ever bet on baseball. He denied it to his closest friends and to his family. He denied it on CNN to Larry King. He denied it to reporters who came by the restaurant. He absolutely did not bet on baseball, he said, and anyway the baseball investigation wasn't fair. How could they have put a strike-force guy like John Dowd on a ballplayer? How could they have relied on testimony from all those untrustworthy guys who went to jail? How could Giamatti say that he believed that Rose had bet on baseball when the banishment agreement explicitly stated no finding on that issue? Rose said what he always said: that the only real mistake he made was picking the wrong crowd to hang out with. For that and his other minor peccadillos, he said, he deserved to be forgiven.

He put it this way: "If I was a cokehead, I'd still be managing the Cincinnati Reds. But I bet on some football games, so I'm out of the game. I'd hate to think I wouldn't go to the Hall of Fame because I bet on *Monday Night Football*."

In the opinions and arguments of many—and still Rose generated reams of copy and hours of debate; and still he commanded heavy discussion each summer on induction weekend; and still write-in votes appeared, and were discounted, on a score of Hall of Fame ballots each year—Rose's plight was hitched not simply to the sin he committed but also to his lack of remorse or acknowledgement. There were still those who believed Rose's denials, the willfully blind, but many others, especially among those closest to the game who might have influenced his fate, did *not* believe his denials and were vexed by his defiance.

This was a decade in America, a nation chock full of men and women granted second acts in their public lives, when a mayor of Providence (Buddy Cianci) was reelected after being convicted of assault and a mayor of Washington, D.C., (Marion Barry) was reelected after being caught on videotape smoking crack. It was a decade in which pitcher Steve Howe, a seven-time violator of baseball's drug rules (a cokehead, as Rose might have said), came back with great success for the Yankees. Baseball, like America, was predisposed to forgive and to embrace. Rose had picked the wrong crime to commit, yes—though it was not football betting as he claimed—and now it was clear that he was choosing the wrong path to redemption. As Jack Lang, the baseball writer and Hall of Fame voter said, summing up the sentiment, "If he admitted his crimes, I think there would be a public demand he be eligible for the Hall."

Rose might have done it so easily. With a few words of humility, of honesty, with an uncomfortable press conference or two, he might have changed course and pulled a raft of moralizers (and baseball executives) toward his side. Instead it seemed that he was not abiding by the code that Harry Rose had implicitly preached—that of owning up to one's failings and of owning one's sins. To all appearances, Pete was not taking responsibility for what he had done.

And yet, through the wider, deeper lens, he *was* taking responsibility. However conscious or not his intention, Rose was by his rigid stance choosing the life of exile, depriving himself of a chance not just at the Hall of Fame but also—and this was what really mattered to him in those years—to get back into baseball as a manager or coach. He was Socrates in the *Apology*, refusing to bow to the accusers and the dicasts who would seal his fate, unwilling to extend a conciliatory hand, bound almost smugly to his own version of the truth even at great cost to himself. There would be no compromise.

And so he beat on. Whenever the details of his banishment were brought up and rehashed, Rose stuck to his story. "I bet on football," he said. "I'm the one who called the bookmakers and made the bets." But still when it came to his betting on baseball there was always an explanation to counter what the evidence implied, always the noting of an errant detail or an irrelevant gap in logic. "They also said I bet the same amount on every game, $2,000. But you can't bet two dimes on baseball games because every game, from what I'm told, is different," he explained to *Playboy* magazine in the spring of 2000. It was always some kind of denial: The betting slips weren't real and it was someone else who had written them and Dowd had not caught him in any lies. No matter what had gotten them there on that dark night, it was Daisy Buchanan behind the wheel of the car.

He remained on the outside, unbending, and so was finally claimed by the ruthlessness of the truth, paying for his mistakes by the life that he led. "Did he *want* to be forgiven? Did it matter to him?" asks Pete's brother Dave. "I don't know."

———————————

ROSE RACED speedboats for a while in the '90s, steering a boat that could get up to 100 miles an hour and that flew high through the air off the waves. ("Absolutely awesome," he said.) He dabbled in horse breeding with a friend from Kentucky, went to the stock sale at Keeneland, invested in a couple of mares, had a winner at River Downs. Rose ran into a little more IRS trouble along the way in those years, leading to a tax lien of more than $150,000. He played nine holes of golf first thing in the morning most every day and he flew here and there for paid appearances and he got his regular rest.

"People say, 'Wow, you were with Pete Rose, you traveled to shows with him. That must have been a wild time,'" says Warren Greene, who represented Rose in his business dealings during the Florida years. "But, really, it was pretty boring. It was do the event and go back to our rooms early and watch sports."

In 1997, with his marginally reconfigured life—men such as Gioiosa and Janszen and Bertolini had long since disappeared from view—and with excitement building around his son Petey's major league stint as a Red, Rose applied for reinstatement to acting commissioner Bud Selig. The Cincinnati City Council convened and passed a resolution "expressing the sense of [the] Council that Pete Rose should be reinstated to the game of baseball and immediately made eligible for induction into the Baseball Hall of Fame" and sent it, signed by mayor Roxanne Qualls, to the commissioner. Others were less enthusiastic about Pete during that time. A car dealer in Florida, irked that Rose owed him about $10,000 after stiffing him on an appearance related to a car purchase (Pete had sold him a white Porsche), would write to Selig too. The car dealer didn't want Pete in the Hall. As he later told Selig, and explained to *The Cincinnati Enquirer*: "I'm dead-set against it because Pete doesn't conduct himself in the upstanding manner that you'd expect of a Hall of Famer."

Everybody had something to say, people weighing in from all over on whether the ban might be lifted. Selig, though, never even gave Rose a hearing. He said at the time he could not do such a thing to Giamatti's legacy, not with Rose still denying betting on the game, still disputing baseball's findings. Selig was close to Giamatti and recalled well the heightened and harried summer of 1989. He said he believed the Rose case "literally" broke Giamatti's heart.

The next March, when Pete went to Reds' spring training to watch Petey prepare for a season at Triple A, one of the team's front office guys asked him, impromptu, to say a few words to the minor leaguers assembled on the field. Pete cracked a few jokes to the young guys, talked a little hitting. "It was like having Bill Gates stand up in your computer class," said Petey afterward. The short address was enough to draw an investigation from the National League and, at Selig's direction, earn the Reds a stern and public reprimand. Even a little bit of Pete was against the rules.

So it was surprising to some (and either thrilling or troubling to others) when, in 1999, as baseball joined with MasterCard to initiate a fan ballot for an All-Century Team of major leaguers and Rose was voted onto it, that Selig said Pete could take part in the celebration. Certainly the people at MasterCard were pleased by Selig's decision, certainly greater attention would be drawn to the event. Standing alongside the rest of the team's living members, Rose would wear a Reds cap and be on the field in Atlanta—his first moments on a major league field in more than 10 years—when the All-Century Team was introduced and honored before Game 2 of the World Series between the Braves and Yankees. John Dowd, no longer in baseball's employ, chafed. "It's like inviting Willie Sutton to a bankers' meeting," he said. Baseball, through Selig's right-hand man Bob DuPuy, told Dowd to pipe down, that such matters were not his affair.

Pete killed it in the media tent before the game (he had missed an earlier press conference because he'd been doing an autograph signing at a casino in Atlantic City), and when he was introduced during the pregame event, an ovation thundered out of the stands for 55 seconds, longer and more energized than any other received by any player that night. Longer than the ovation given to Atlanta's hometown home run king Hank Aaron. "I said, 'Hank, you throw out the first ball here once a month. They're tired of seeing you,'" Rose said later.

When that cheering had died down and the ceremony had wrapped up and the game's first pitch neared, Rose was interviewed by NBC reporter Jim Gray, a live broadcast. The two men stood on the grass in foul ground and behind them the grounds crew worked the field for the game. Pete gushed that the fan ovation had been "heart-stopping, heart-stopping, man" before Gray came with his first question, asking Rose if he would be willing to "admit that you bet on baseball and make some sort of an apology to that effect."

"I'm not going to admit to something that didn't happen," Rose said, a tension taking hold of his face, and then he quickly got back to thanking the fans and saying that he was "just a small part of a big deal tonight." Gray, though, did not let go. He talked about the "overwhelming evidence" against Rose and wondered why Pete would have signed the agreement if he hadn't bet on baseball. Rose, no stranger to the line of questioning, grew testy and questioned Gray's accuracy and also said that he had not heard back from baseball regarding his reinstatement application. "That guy surprises me," Rose said of Selig. "It's only been two years, though, and he's got a lot of things on his mind."

And still Gray pressed at why Rose would not make an admission, and the entire friction-filled interview—nearly two and a half minutes on air—was spent this way and many of the good feelings of the moment and of Rose's brief but historic return to his element were drained away.

Phone calls inundated the switchboards at NBC affiliates across the country for an hour and then two—so many viewers angry at Gray for jumping Pete in that way, at that time. Gray, they complained, had been selfish to taint a long-awaited night of celebration by turning it into a rude hassling of the man. Dick Ebersol, the head of NBC Sports, later responded that Gray was an exceptionally fine journalist but Ebersol did allow that the interrogation of Pete might have gone on too long.

Ebersol then followed Gray onto the field before Game 3 of the Series in New York and during the pregame, Gray went on the air and apologized to "baseball fans everywhere" for the timing and persistence of his questions. He said he was sorry if it "took some of the joy out of the occasion." The Yankees won that Game 3 in the bottom of the 10th inning on a home run by Chad Curtis and moments after that ball cleared the fence, Gray stood beside the hero, microphone in hand. "Tell us about that pitch," Gray said.

"I can't do it," said Curtis. He explained that as a team the Yankees had decided that, "because of what happened with Pete we're not going to talk out here on the field." And he walked away.

The Jim Gray interview was another moment in the trajectory of Pete Rose's fate that, much like the decision by the synod at the Hall of Fame to take Pete's prospects out of the hands of baseball writers, won support for Rose. People saw unfairness and this created sympathy where otherwise there might have been none.

Really, for all his aggressiveness, Gray was simply mystified, as others were, as to why if Rose truly wanted back in the game he wouldn't try the tack of honesty. Perhaps even at that time, more than a decade of denial after the fact, an admission and an appeal for forgiveness might have moved the needle on Rose's reinstatement effort, might have been an olive branch to the game. Rose's coming clean could have changed things entirely, or maybe not. But in any case, it seemed then, telling the truth certainly couldn't hurt.

Chapter 20

His Prison Without Bars

ARLY EACH January the Hall of Fame announces its new inductees, creating a burst of energy around the institution and the game. Great players are celebrated, water-cooler debate ensues over who got in and who missed out and, all in all, induction-announcement week sends a warm current of base-ball through the heart of the cold, diamond-less winter. On Monday, Jan. 5, 2004, one day before the official (though much expected) revelation that pitcher Dennis Eckersley and 3,000-hit club member Paul Molitor had been elected, Jeff Idelson, then a vice president at the Hall of Fame and now its president, turned on the morning television shows hoping to find some talk about the incoming class. What he saw on *Good Morning America* was indeed about baseball and Cooperstown: There was Pete Rose discussing his new book, *My Prison Without Bars,* in which, plain to see on page 123, he admitted for the first time that he had, while managing the Reds, wagered on baseball. On the cusp of a crowning week in their public and athletic lives, Eckersley and Molitor had been rendered afterthoughts, or less.

"It was inappropriate and, frankly, yes, it was kind of annoying," recalls Idelson today of the timing of Rose's book. "But to me it was ultimately irrelevant to how I feel about Rose. I know that it was not irrelevant to everyone."

The fact that Rose, 15 years out of baseball and even longer into denial, would unleash his confession at this of all times of year led to ripples of disappointment. "It's unfortunate because this should be their day," said Hall of Fame chairman Jane Forbes Clark, referring to Eckersley and Molitor. As Molitor noted after the election announcement: "I answered questions for an hour yesterday but the only one that was used on the front page of *USA Today* was about Pete Rose."

Rose said in a statement that he "never intended to diminish the exciting news for these deserving players," and his camp of advisers suggested that the book's release date had been solely the decision of the publisher, Rodale—saying, that is, that even as the subject, nominal author, exuberant co-promoter and driving force of the book, Rose had no say in the book's unconventional publication date. Most baseball books come out in mid-spring, closer to Opening Day, but according to Steve Murphy, then Rodale's president, the plan to release *My Prison Without Bars* during Hall of Fame induction week had "been set for a long time."[1]

Segments for *Good Morning America* and an excerpt in *Sports Illustrated* had been coordinated for that week, and right away on Rose's website fans could buy autographed copies of *My Prison Without Bars* for $77.99. Personalized autographs ran the price to $99.99. Crowds of more than 1,000 people waited for hours in the January cold outside bookshops in both New Jersey and New York at Rose's signings (some 4,000 would turn out in Cincinnati) and the book shot to the top of *The New York Times* best-seller list. Most of the stories and discussions about the book mentioned that Rodale had paid a $1 million advance for the book.

Within the corridors of baseball power, the attention and the commerce led to a palpable distaste. In return for what he had done to base-

---

[1] Even nine years later, Warren Greene, who was one of Rose's representatives when *My Prison Without Bars* came out, maintained, straight face and all, that Rose "had no desire to have the book come out when it did. He would have liked it to be at a different date." Greene added, "I don't know why people got so upset with him about it."

ball, and then for his years of brazenly lying and of baselessly attacking the credibility of credible men, Rose was now reaping a payday, once again profiting at the game's expense. The book was a product of cold calculation on another front as well: After 2006 Rose, even if he were to be fully reinstated by baseball, would not appear on the writers' Hall of Fame ballots. He had played his final game in 1986 and by rule a player who is retired 20 years moves out of active eligibility and can only be inducted by a veteran's committee. As Fay Vincent noted in *The New York Times* that week—he wrote an op-ed in which he compared Rose's book, not favorably, to St. Augustine's *Confessions*—if Rose's public admission were to lead to a quick reinstatement, there was still time for him to get onto the baseball writers' Hall of Fame ballots for a year or two of voting. In the '04 election, Rose had received 15 write-in votes, bringing his 13-year total to 230 and further solidifying him, by an order of magnitude, as the most written-in Cooperstown candidate of all time.

Although Bud Selig would not comment on Rose's book nor say anything about its potential impact upon Rose's reinstatement chances ("The commissioner will take all of this into account," said Selig's deputy, Bob DuPuy), it was clear that Rose's carefully orchestrated confession was not yielding the intended results. Not at all. Rather than inspire support for his reinstatement, *My Prison Without Bars* had reinvigorated those who wanted to keep him out. Later in the week that the induction announcement and the book's release collided, Rose's friend and former teammate Mike Schmidt—who in previous years had acted as a liaison between Selig and Rose—was interviewed by the Associated Press and asked how he thought the book might impact Rose's chances for getting back into the game. "It doesn't look good, it's taken a turn for the worse," Schmidt said. "It is a sad thing . . . I hope the commissioner is reserving judgment. I've heard some of the worst references about Pete."

MY PRISON WITHOUT BARS is a strange burlesque of a book, an occasionally engaging romp and a tour de force of spin. Very little can truly be taken at face value. A Rose first-person account written with a former television actor, Rick Hill, the book feels most of all like an extended alibi, a series of events framed and reframed to put Rose in the best possible light. There are some attempts at humor (an extended fart story, for example, and a joke about Jewish people eating lox, told twice) but the book is devoid of irony. The reader gets a sense of what he is in for during an early passage that speculates on the possibility that Rose suffered from attention deficit hyperactivity disorder as a child, a condition which, the text observes, has been "genetically linked to gambling in adults." This ADHD section relies almost entirely upon the testimony of "David E. Comings, M.D.", who gamely suggests that the "entire Rose family is a geneticist's dream." (!) What's more, based on what he has heard about Rose's mom and dad, Dr. Comings feels comfortable declaring that Pete was genetically "destined for greatness . . . as well as tragedy." (Somewhere Mendel rolled over, Richard Dawkins scratched his head, and the field of genetics research pressed on.)

Dr. Comings, further considering Rose's childhood personality, also advances the notion that, "In fact, Pete Rose is not unlike Einstein, who flunked English but excelled in math." Furthermore, the doctor might have added, the young Rose was not unlike Mahatma Gandhi in that he too sometimes went about barefoot.

Rose gets around to his mea culpas (The biggie, near the end: "So let's leave it like this. I know I fucked up.") but they are invariably qualified, and braised with *tea* culpas throughout. A kind of schoolyard finger-pointing emerges as a staple of *My Prison Without Bars*. In one extended and mercilessly disjointed passage Rose muses about the many people in the history of America who have been involved in "questionable activities." He mentions Elvis, Rock Hudson and John Belushi and then veers over to the rumored bootlegging activities of Joseph Kennedy Sr., leading Rose to guess that Kennedy "might have had some partners on the payroll from the political world, which would have made him one helluva lot smarter than me. Come to think of it—that's probably why he never got caught! Maybe if I had enlisted the help of the mayor and the governor my life would have turned out differently." Yes, maybe.

"I'm not trying to make excuses or shift the blame," Rose writes amid his attempts to make excuses and shift the blame. We learn not only that Rose's unique life circumstances propelled him toward gambling, but also broad physiological details about his dopamine levels and the "impulse disorder" that might have made it impossible for him to "distinguish between sports when it came time to place his bets." (Dr. Comings again.) When, in yet another strategic tactic, Rose absolves gambling as a victimless crime, it seems unclear whether he realizes what a victim he himself has been.

Prison is all dodges and feints. Although Rose writes that the Dowd Report "had more goddamn holes than Swiss cheese" he spends a large portion of his book plodding through and admitting to all the significant charges that Dowd laid forth. Rose hammers energetically (and mockingly) on some dates and nuances that Dowd may have gotten wrong, and he makes outraged allegations (relying on a few facts and a lot of exclamation points) of the supposed bias against him in the whole investigation. But in terms of the central issues and many of the specific events that Dowd outlined in his report—namely that Rose had been involved with all manner of unscrupulous men and, mainly, that he had bet heavily and often on baseball and on his very own Cincinnati Reds—well, Dowd's case proved about as solid as a hunk of petrified Gouda.

"He pissed on me all those years, denied, denied, denied and then in his book he admits to everything," says Dowd. "Well, not everything. He still made a mistake. He said that he didn't bet while he was a player. But he did."

There was something else that Rose did not get quite right. Or maybe he did, depending on which Rose you believe. About 14 months before the book's release, in the autumn of 2002, Rose had, through the intervention of Schmidt and Joe Morgan, been granted an audience with Selig at his office in Milwaukee. DuPuy was there, along with Schmidt and also Warren Greene. As Greene recalls, "Selig was wonderful in that meeting—thoughtful and eloquent. He would point to the shelves around him and say that whatever decision he made on Pete would be recorded in those binders for all time. He was upbeat but he was careful in what he said. I didn't hear any promises. Then we left the room, all of us except Pete and Commissioner Selig."

Rose had come to this meeting with a clear purpose: He was there, and Selig knew it, to tell the commissioner privately what he would later reveal, in his book, to the public. Rose and his camp believed that a confession might in fact deliver his reinstatement. "From talks we had had with Bob DuPuy we had the feeling that it could happen," says Greene. "But he often reminded us that the decision was not his, that he was just the number two."

In *My Prison Without Bars*, Pete describes his discussion with the commissioner like this. "Did you bet on baseball?" Selig asked, and Rose responded, "Yes, sir, I did bet on baseball."

Selig: "How often?"

Rose: "Four or five nights a week."

Selig: "Why?"

Rose: "I didn't think I'd get caught."

So there it was. And there, as well, was this: "four or five nights a week." In the aftermath of the book, that declaration became a point of fertile discussion, as well as concern. Why did Rose only bet that often? What information did he have that led him to lay off the Reds on other nights? And by not betting on certain games wasn't he sending a message to other gamblers—his bookies and the guys who ran his bets at least—that they should lay off those games too? (Not unlike Paul Hornung's decision in the early 1960s to stay away from wagering on certain Packers games.)

Most concerning of all: Did Rose manage a game differently when he had money riding on it than when he did not? Pete says no, and as yet no evidence has surfaced, neither from parsing his managerial moves, nor from his players' comments or recollections, to suggest inconsistencies in how he ran a game.

Neither did Dowd, even in the fullness of his investigation (nor the reporters who descended in its immediate wake) ever produce any indication that Rose's managing was influenced by his betting. Still, the questions around his betting frequency were troubling and the "four or five nights" comment did lend support to another Dowd charge, one that Dowd expanded on most pointedly in interviews outside of the report: That Rose had a tendency not to wager on the Reds when Bill Gullickson or Mario Soto were pitching. ("I didn't know that but it doesn't surprise me," Soto said when he heard that.) A few years after *My Prison Without Bars* came out, Pete backtracked yet again, saying in a radio interview that he had actually bet on the Reds *"every night* because I love my team." That has been his steady line ever since.

"The way that Pete has changed his story over time bothers some people," says J.D. Friedland, an investment banker who since 2012 has helped run Pete's autographing and other events in Las Vegas. "First, for a long time, he said he didn't bet on baseball at all. Then he said five nights a week. Then he said every night. So, what is he not saying now? Knowing him, I don't think that there is anything more there, but for some people it leaves an impression."

For pure reading value, *My Prison Without Bars*—the title, of course, refers both to Rose's incarceration at Marion and to his years of unfettered baseball exile—is not without virtues. It provides, for one thing, alternative spellings for the phrase "sumbitches" and the narrative at times reads quite well. There are some unfortunate misspellings (Pete's very own Sayler Park is called Saylor Park throughout; the Braves' Rico Carty becomes Rico Cardi) and details of significant events (the 1970 All-Star Game; the aftermath of the Jim Gray interview) are wrong, but those are small shortcomings. The book's undoing is that it never stops giving the reader the feeling of being conned—about what happened with the gambling, yes, and also about every event of controversy in Pete's life. After the initial burst of excitement sales of the book fell off dramatically.[2]

The self-serving tone, along with Rose's lack of remorse—he doesn't say that he is sorry so much as say that he is sorry he got caught—as well as, again, the harsh timing of the book's release, led to much strenuous

---

[2] Despite having a multiple-week bestseller, Rodale sold only about 20% of the 500,000 copies it had printed. The book helped raise Rodale's profile in the publishing world, but, given the large advance, *Prison* itself did not come close to making a bottom-line profit.

objection on the part of some respected baseball writers. As the *Rocky Mountain News*'s Tracy Ringolsby, a past president of the Baseball Writers' Association said, "The way this whole thing came out probably took some people who were on the fence and pushed them over. I think he hurt himself." Ringolsby, who had previously defined himself as "undecided," on Rose's Cooperstown worthiness, now said that he would not vote for Rose even "if he was the only person on the ballot."

Tom Powers of the *St. Paul Pioneer Press*, also ticked by *Prison*, wrote, "I hope Pete Rose gets reinstated so he can finally be put on the Hall of Fame ballot. I am looking forward to having the pleasure of NOT voting for him. What a jerk."

And Peter Gammons, a highly influential dean among baseball writers, wrote in an online column for ESPN that the book and Rose's behavior in the immediate aftermath of its release "have made me rethink my initial decision to vote for him." Gammons added, "Until Pete Rose proves to me that he cares about something other than Pete Rose, he does not have my vote."

It is a galling position, strange and misguided: A voter's preference turning on *this*? The real issue had been lost. Some baseball writers actually appeared willing to forgive, or at least to look past, Rose's betting on baseball if only he were to come clean in a manner that suited them. But excuse Rose's shameless me-first promotion? No. These voters had become interested in legislating a candidate's behavior. The argument against Pete Rose's being in the Hall of Fame, in other words, had devolved, now turning not upon his violation of a sacred baseball tenet, but rather on whether a voter *liked* the guy or not.

My Prison Without Bars creates a strangely circular effect. Rose's attempt to manipulate the reader is so crude and blatant that it can't help but inspire a level of annoyance, maybe even contempt. But to absorb his efforts more fully, to understand Rose's attempts, via the writer Hill, at humanizing himself, replaces some of that annoyance with a feeling of charity. Consider, for example, that Rose felt he needed to re-mind the public that he *did* in fact feel emotions. Or that in telling of LaVerne's passing in 2000 he says: "A death in the family is always a shock—especially when it's your mother." It is not at all comfortable to watch someone trying so hard to portray himself as something he's not.

What hits home by the end of the book, and what is reinforced by years of watching his public life, is the depth of Rose's limitations, how ill-equipped he is to answer the demands for humility, contrition and self-awareness that society asks of him. It is indeed enough to make you feel, if not empathy, sympathy after all. There remains something heart-breaking about the way Rose revealed himself at the time of his public confession—a man trapped like many men by his own pathology, trapped by his own delusions and denials. Indeed, a prison without bars.

Chapter 21

The Importance of Being Earnest

I N THE spring of 2012, a few weeks before the start of his 20th season in the majors, and about a month short of his 40th birthday, Atlanta Braves third baseman Chipper Jones announced that he would retire at season's end. Although he went on to have a solid year, eventually knocking in 62 runs in 387 at bats and helping the Braves reach the playoffs, he did not waver in his decision. His career, a flat-out marvelous career in which he batted .303, hit 468 home runs, made eight All-Star Games, won an MVP and a batting championship and brought late-inning crowds to their feet time and time again, was ending.

Jones's final weeks were marked by warm tributes, even on the road. The Marlins gave Jones a fishing rod before a game in mid-September. The Astros presented him with a Stetson hat. The Brewers gave him a gas grill and a year's supply of sausage. Jones received a Stan Musial jersey from the Cardinals, a surfboard from the Padres and an actual third base from both the Yankees and the Reds. The Phillies and the Mets—who were particularly victimized by Jones's heroics over the years—gave him pieces of artwork.

In Atlanta, where he had spent his entire major league career, the affection was naturally deeper and far more pronounced. During

Chipper's final homestand, groups of fans arrived in buses from outlying areas—including towns such as Bristol, W.Va., and Chattanooga—to see him play one last time. Georgia governor Nathan Deal declared Sept. 28, 2012 to be "Chipper Jones Day" throughout the state. For days on end, fans at the ballpark cheered him with standing ovations each time he came up, calling out in adoration and holding aloft banners reading things like: CHIPPER, ONCE YOU'RE GONE WHO'S GOING TO BE MY HERO? The last of these ovations came in Chipper's final game, the National League's do-or-die wild-card playoff game against the Cardinals in Atlanta.

The Braves trailed 6–3 with two outs and no one on base in the bottom of the ninth inning when Jones came up to face St. Louis closer Jason Motte. Even with the outlook bleak for their team, the fans rose and thundered once more for Jones. This now was the true farewell. Children held placards emblazoned with his number 10 and there were again homemade signs (CHIPPER THANK YOU FOR ALWAYS BEING AN ATLANTA BRAVE) and choruses of people calling his name. Before stepping into the batter's box, Jones raised his helmet high in acknowledgment. Even some of the Cardinals on the field applauded into their gloves. Then Jones said out loud "Let's go, baby!" and got into his stance.

On the sixth pitch from Motte, on a 2-and-2 count, Jones sent a soft line drive toward the middle of the diamond, breaking his bat on the hit. He came sharply out of the box as Cardinals second baseman Daniel Descalso moved to his right, backhanded the ball on a high hop and made a leaping throw to first base.

By this point Chipper Jones—40 years old and playing through some pain in his legs—had slowed to a halfhearted jog, giving in. This explains why he was well shy of first base when Descalso's throw pulled Cardinals first baseman Allen Craig off the bag. Craig fell to the ground as he caught the ball, but he still had time, from his backside, to kick at the base before Jones reached it. Umpire Mike Winters ruled, however, that Craig's foot didn't hit the bag in time; Jones was called safe and awarded an infield single. An Associated Press account later described him as "hustling until the end," but that's inaccurate. The only reason the play at first base was close at all was because Jones did not go hard down the line. Had he been running full-out he would have been safe the moment Craig got pulled off the bag.

A ground-rule double followed Jones's single, but the Braves' rally ended there and St. Louis won the game. That Jones got a hit in his final at bat will go down as a bit of happy trivia attached to an exceptional career. But what may be more notable, and more telling of a larger base-ball truth, is that in the very last of his 11,031 plate appearances in the major leagues, before a devoted and paying crowd of 52,631, the majority of whom had risen to their feet to see him perform, and with his at bat potentially representing Atlanta's last chance in an elimination playoff game, Chipper Jones, a certain Hall of Famer, did not find it incumbent upon himself, nor did he betray any inner desire, to run as hard as he could run to first base. Also notable is that no one observing the event seemed to find this striking or even unusual. None of the game's television announcers said a thing about it.

VERY FEW major league players, even among respected gamers like Jones, run as hard as they can on every play. It's just not done. "Guys do care and they play hard," says Keith Hernandez, a big league first baseman from 1974 through '90 who is now a color commentator for the Mets. "But 162 games is a long time. You play through injuries and you play through times when your legs are dead, and you have games when you just don't feel so well. The reality is that sometimes over the course of the season you have got to save yourself for the long haul. That's why it's so rare to find a player, anyone, who truly hustles on every play."

"Hustle" doesn't simply mean running out close plays. (That's called "playing baseball.") Rather, it implies a player giving maximum effort even when the chance for reward is slim: Bolting hard out of the batter's box and not slowing, even when you've hit a ball—a routine fly to center-field, say—that 99 of 100 times will result in an out. "Because that way," says the Reds MVP first baseman Joey Votto, "the one time that some-thing strange does happen or the fielder messes up, you will get the most

273

that you can get out of the play. It can be hard to do all the time, though."

It's also difficult to measure or quantify; hustling stories live primarily in anecdotes, not statistics, and that's also true of *nonhustling* stories, which tend to take on an even longer life given the way they irk fans and managers. In May of 2000, the Mets released outfielder Rickey Henderson, who was nearing the end of his 25-year career as the greatest base stealer and leadoff hitter in baseball history. For the second time in less than a year, Rickey had failed to run hard after hitting a ball that he thought would be a home run but instead landed in the park, forcing him to settle for a single when he should have had a double or more. (The first time he had reached second when he should have been at third.) "It's basically what everything is built on," then Mets manager Bobby Valentine said, explaining why Rickey's lack of hustle so troubled him. Rickey's otherwise glorious, first-ballot Hall of Fame career was pocked throughout by such lapses on the bases and in the field.

The Phillies' outstanding shortstop Jimmy Rollins and the Tigers' great hitter Miguel Cabrera are among numerous stars who have riled their team's faithful by not hustling, but this is a tendency that inflicts players of many talent levels and career-stages. A very small and randomly collected sample of incidents from the past few years include the Red Sox rookie Will Middlebrooks failing to run out a ball he hit that he thought was going foul but landed fair (he wound up with a single instead of a double); Yankees' veteran Andruw Jones leisurely approaching a ground ball in leftfield and perhaps costing the team a base (the Twins' batter reached second easily when he could have been thrown out) and a similarly nonchalant play by Rockies' centerfielder Dexter Fowler that allowed a Mets runner to go from first to third in extra innings. These things happen all across baseball, and often.

"My frustration grows anytime I see anybody not hustle," said Phillies manager Charlie Manuel after benching Rollins for having twice jogged to first base. "It grows [even] if I see the *other* team not hustle." When, in 2009, Mets rookie Fernando Martinez did not run out a pop fly that was dropped in fair ground by the Nationals catcher (Martinez was thrown out at first base) manager Jerry Manuel chose not to take Martinez out of the game but rather, as punishment, sent him back out to play rightfield so that he could feel the displeasure of the fans—who indeed peppered him with loud and angry boos.

An implicit contract exists between the fans and the players. A baseball game, like all sporting events, is naturally unpredictable. Whereas the Metropolitan Opera can pretty much guarantee that its diva will deliver a beautiful, buckle-bending aria, and the producers of a Broadway play can promise the same dialogue and plotline each night, a sports consumer receives far fewer assurances. A baseball team can't guarantee it will win on a given night. It can't promise that one of its players will hit a home run or make a great fielding play or pitch a great game. It can't guarantee the rain will stay away. So what *can* a team and its players promise to the people who have bought tickets or paid their cable premium to watch them play? What does the fan have the right to expect? "Effort," says Giants manager Bruce Bochy. "It has to be that. Players hustling should be the baseline minimum."

ROSE'S APPROACH to the game elevated not only his career, of course, but also the careers of many players around him, Hall of Famers as well as legions of less accomplished players. Rose's sprinting to first base after a walk was a piece of showmanship, a splash of needless panache. But there was nothing superfluous in the way he went after it when the ball was live. "If playing with Pete Rose did not inspire you to play the right way I don't know what did," says Doug Flynn, who was a part-time infielder for the Reds in the mid-1970s. "He ran out everything. I mean everything. Comebacker to the pitcher in the ninth inning of a lopsided game, Pete is busting it down the line."

On the summer day in 2005 that third baseman Wade Boggs went into the Hall of Fame, one of his postinduction interviewers steered him toward the notion of hustle—what it meant, and whether it was an aspect of the game that mattered to him. Yes, said Boggs, it did.

"When you watch a major league baseball game and when you see a guy not run out a ball or loaf after a ball and not go first to third or second to home because he's just trotting or something like that, it's disturbing," Boggs said. "I played the game one way. I gave it everything I had. It doesn't take any ability to hustle. I learned how to play the game by watching Pete Rose. Watching him play all those games and watching him on TV and do the things he did, inspired me to play the game at that level.

"I felt that if I disrespected the game by not hustling and not giving everything I had to give, it was a circumstance of cheating the fans. You're cheating the fans, you're cheating your teammates, and you're disrespecting the name on the front of your jersey."

Hustle traces to deeply rooted values in American life, the values of effort and sacrifice from which the country's narrative has so consciously sprung. It's not lip service. It's not irrelevant. It is part of how we see ourselves. The almost unimaginable perseverance required of pilgrims on the frigid shorelines of New England is echoed by that required of the pioneers who crossed into the feral regions of the West: a kind of primal hustle as a force propelling the American Dream. John Henry used two hammers when that was what it took. Baseball players are not settlers or steelworkers—survival is not at stake on the diamond—yet the game provides an open landscape onto which an ethos can be projected, represented, honored or not.

And so it is that a reverence for hustle constitutes a big portion of the affection that today's Yankees fans feel toward the team's aging captain, Derek Jeter; that Red Sox fans feel toward second baseman Dustin Pedroia and that fans in Washington, D.C., feel toward Bryce Harper, the balls-out Nationals outfielder. Harper was born in 1992— seven years after hit number 4,192, three years after the banishment— and he often talks about how he has modeled his approach to the game after Rose's.

We remember Babe Ruth for his prodigious power and his performance, Willie Mays for the thrill of his movement, Cal Ripken Jr. for his steadiness. We think of Sandy Koufax for his dominance, Mickey Mantle for his raw athletic talent. But there is only one player among the game's elite whom we remember primarily for his effort, for his unstinting commitment to playing the game the way that it seems meant to be played. Pete Rose, even with all those base hits and all those major league records (he holds 17 of them, and he can name them all), is known first for that devotion on the ball field, for day after day fulfilling his contract to the baseball-watching public, for adhering with an almost religious conviction to the core value upon which, as Bobby Valentine put it, "everything is built."

Chapter 22

Cooperstown, 2012

HILE THE Hall of Famers and other important baseball people tend to spend induction weekend at Cooperstown's sprawling Otesaga Resort Hotel, Rose has always found his own accommodations. In 2012 he and Kiana Kim and Ashton and Cassie stayed in Andrew Vilacky's two-bedroom apartment above the Safe At Home store. Whenever they would look down out the front windows before one of Pete's signing sessions, Main Street was already full of people crowded near the store entrance, many of them wearing Rose jerseys. "Wow!" said Cassie the first time she saw this. Trundling down the single flight of stairs a few minutes later, Rose quipped to Kim, "Can't beat the commute, babe."

The 133-room redbrick Otesaga opened more than 100 years ago and Hall of Famers have slept there or at its sister property, the smaller, nearby Cooper Inn, during just about every induction weekend there has ever been. You have to be an approved guest to get into the Otesaga on those days—the property's entrances are closely guarded and inside the scene is like a convention with various groups and sponsor reps and related VIPs on hand. People gather in the large formal dining room or in the area by the enormous wooden front doors. Out back, a spectacular terrace overlooks broad, immaculate green lawns and weathered oaks and glinting Otsego Lake, the Glimmerglass. Flower-print curtains and Adam chandeliers give the guest rooms an Edith Wharton look, and most everyone agrees that based on the unexplained footsteps that patter through the narrow corridors at night, the place must be haunted.

There can be an air of formality in the lobby and main rooms of the Otesaga, but things are a lot looser downstairs at the Hawkeye Bar & Grill (no jacket required) where gaggles of Hall of Famers inevitably wind up at the end of each day. You might find Rickey Henderson holding court at a table of 12, or come upon Phillies lefty Steve Carlton standing in the doorway of the marble-topped men's room talking about how to set up a batter for the kill. Tony Perez could walk in with one of his sons, inspiring Dave Winfield to bounce out of his armchair to say hello. The ballplayers greet one another the way old classmates do at reunions and they're prone to teasing one another and to losing themselves in "remember-when" conversations. Baseball front office types and team owners mill around with drinks in hand and over by where the rock and roll house band plays you just never know when you might see a 13-time American League All-Star like George Brett start moving it like he means it on the dance floor.

"If Pete came through the door," said Joe Morgan, standing near the bar and looking around the place, "I think everyone would stop what they were doing and go over and see him."[1]

But Rose and Kim were half a mile away, alone with the kids and not at all uncomfortable in Vilacky's place, with its renovated master bath and hardwood floors and the island in the kitchen. "It's a Manhattan-style apartment in Cooperstown," says Vilacky. Along with a stainless

---

[1] Not every Hall of Famer takes part in the late-night gatherings of course. Willie Mays, who is in his 80s and whose eyesight is considerably less than it was, stayed upstairs and received guests at certain times in his room. He had a small entourage close to him, including a couple of bodyguards, and there was some food out on the table. When people came in they were led to Mays's chair to be introduced or recognized. "It was like going to see the Pope," said one visitor after coming back down to the Hawkeye.

steel refrigerator and a handsome grandfather clock, he has also put in a couple of large flat-screen televisions, which Rose naturally made extensive use of. When he's not watching sports, Pete is the Fox News type. "The guy who invented TV? I love that guy!" Rose says.

Vilacky—lean, bright-eyed and years removed from his own tax fraud conviction—feels grateful to Pete for the happy business relationship they've had together in Cooperstown and also for the kindnesses that Rose has shown him, bringing Vilacky out to Vegas to stay with him in a palatial suite or taking him to a boxing match at the Mohegan Sun. "Someone like me can live like a famous millionaire," says Vilacky. "One time we were eating dinner at the Palm at Caesars Palace when Jamie Foxx came over. The first thing Pete said was, 'I'd like you to meet my friend Andrew and his wife Melissa.' To Jamie Foxx!" When Pete does an event in New York or New Jersey, Vilacky is sometimes the one who comes along to make sure things go as intended.

Rose's presence touches that Main Street apartment even when he's not there. Two seats from the old Veterans Stadium in Philadelphia, autographed by Pete, lean against one wall, and a corner of the living room has been given over to a metallic statue of Rose sliding headfirst. Near the front door hangs a T-shirt—also signed—that reads: HEY BUD TEAR DOWN THE WALL/GET PETE OFF MAIN STREET AND INTO THE HALL, as well as a baseball under glass. "To the great Pete Rose. Love him, hate him, you can't ignore him" the ball says, and it's signed, "Reggie Jackson. Mr. October."[2]

Perhaps the most interesting piece of Roseabilia in Cooperstown stands not in Vilacky's apartment but just a few doors down, on display for the paying public at the Heroes of Baseball Wax Museum. Strange, whimsical, and, yes, a little creepy, the museum features a hodgepodge of about three dozen life-size wax figures spread among its three floors—

[2] Vilacky also has some non-Rose items, including a photograph of him and his business partner Tom Catal with Mickey Mantle that's framed along with a golf scorecard. It's inscribed, "To Tom and Andy: I can't believe I only won $20, you lucky assholes. Mickey Mantle."

replicas of Satchel Paige and Ted Williams, of George W. Bush throwing out a first pitch after 9/11, of Wade Boggs on the back of a police horse after winning the World Series; of characters from the movie *A League of Their Own*. Rudy Giuliani's here and Judge Kenesaw Mountain Landis and a ghoulish-looking Joe DiMaggio dressed to pins and descending a staircase in front of an equally ghoulish Marilyn Monroe in furs. The wax figure of Rose bears no facial resemblance to him whatsoever but you know who it is by the old-style Reds cap and the pinstriped vest uniform number 14. The figure stands at a podium on a stage and behind it a simply drawn sign announces "National Baseball Hall of Fame Induction Ceremony." Benches have been set up in front of this scene and visitors to the museum can sit, gaze toward the podium and talk about what Pete might say up there if he ever did get the chance. More people do this than you might expect.[3]

NOW THAT Cooperstown has so heavily given itself over to the memorabilia and tourism markets—now that McGown's hardware is long gone from the corner of Pioneer and Main, and the Church & Scott pharmacy has moved out to State Highway 28 and even the town's lone Little League field has been wiped away to make room for more visitor parking—enterprising merchants face a challenge to distinguish themselves among the glut of competing shops. Joe Cannata, a retired NYPD captain moved here in 2008 to run Shoeless Joe's, a store

---

[3] This wax display conjures a scene that was reportedly envisioned by some members of the staff at the Hall of Fame. In 2004, when *My Prison Without Bars* came out, several older inductees, notably Bob Feller and Robin Roberts, had reiterated their objections to Rose and made clear they would not attend his induction ceremony were he ever to have one. According to a *Hartford Courant* article by longtime baseball writer Jack O'Connell, a Hall of Fame official told him, " . . . we have imagined a ceremony where 200,000 people stare down at [Hall chairman] Jane Clark and Pete." Meaning that the stage would be devoid of any other Hall of Famers, and also that such a prospect was not something the Hall was keen on. It's a telling comment for another reason: the guess of 200,000 attendees. That would be Rose all right; the largest crowd ever at an induction ceremony was 82,000 to see Tony Gwynn and Cal Ripken Jr. go in in 2007.

now bulging with uniforms, old signs, autographed balls, photographs and other keepsakes.

In 2012, partly because of his shop's proximity to the Hall of Fame—it's about a Texas leaguer away—and partly because of his background in justice and partly because of his increasing indignation that steroid users are being considered for Cooperstown induction, Cannata established a kind of public antishrine in a small, old landmarked building that stands in the weedy lot behind his store. He calls it the Hall of Shame. Admission is free and items are primarily to look at and consider, but not to buy. Cannata encourages his Shoeless Joe's customers to go 'round and take a look. "Sammy Sosa is back there," he'll sometimes say. When people express surprise (*Sosa? Here? Today?*), Cannata insists, yes. What visitors in fact find is a grinning, life-size cardboard cutout of Sosa in his Cubs uniform. "I told you he was back there," Cannata will say. "He's fake. Just like his records."

The Hall of Shame pays sarcastic homage to those players who, in Cannata's view (and in the views of millions of others), cheated the game or, more relevantly, cheated the fans. Most conspicuous are the players linked to performance enhancing drugs—Mark McGwire's and Barry Bonds's rookie baseball cards are framed on the wall, for example, as is a photo of Rafael Palmeiro at the 2005 Congressional hearings on steroid use in baseball. (Palmeiro famously wagged his index finger emphatically during his angry denial that he had ever done such drugs and then a few months later—*D'oh!*—tested positive.) A copy of the Mitchell Report, the 2007 investigation that connected dozens of ballplayers to performance enhancing drugs, rests in a binder, available for visitors to thumb through.[4]

Cannata also features players of other disrepute, including those con-

---

[4] The question of how to render the steroid era has faced other baseball collectors. At the remarkable Green Diamond Gallery in Cincinnati, owner Bob Crotty has hanging above a "memorable moments" wall the jerseys of Bonds, Sosa, Palmeiro, Alex Rodriguez, Roger Clemens and several others. He says they're up there to represent "the black cloud that hangs over baseball," and he has run out of room for new additions. The jersey of two-time offender Manny Ramirez, for example, hangs elsewhere. "These guys," says Crotty pointing up at the black cloud with a laugh, "these are just the founding members."

nected to the 1985 cocaine trials such as Tim Raines, the former Expos All-Star who carried vials of cocaine in the back pocket of his uniform during games, out of fear, he explained, that they might be found if he left them in his locker. To be sure that he did not break a vial, Raines added, he usually slid headfirst. "That one gets me most of all," says Cannata. "Talk about drugs having an impact on the game! This guy is getting support on the Hall of Fame ballot"—through the class of 2013, Raines, with his 808 career steals, 1,571 runs scored and .385 on base percentage has received at least 22% of the vote in each of his six years of eligibility— "and yet Pete Rose isn't even on there?"

Not surprisingly, Rose appears in Cannata's Hall of Shame as well, although he along with former outfielder Jose Canseco, whose 2005 whistle-blowing book *Juiced* revealed the names of numerous steroid cheats, is presented in a different light, alongside the portion of the museum that Cannata has devoted to "True Kings" like Hank Aaron and Roger Maris, baseball's most prominent home-run record holders before performance enhancing drugs came along. Cannata sees Rose and Canseco as having done, on balance, more good than harm for baseball. When Kiana Kim visited the Hall of Shame during induction weekend of '12—for a *Hits & Mrs.* scene that never aired—Cannata pointed out a framed, classic photo of Rose scuffling with Bud Harrelson on the field in 1973. "Oh, I've seen that picture a million times," Kim said, although never, she added, "in a setting like this."[5]

Rose's Hall of Fame worthiness has come under renewed discussion with the emergence of steroids in the game and into public awareness,

---

[5] Kim has made it her business to understand Pete's plight and the circumstances around his banishment, though she's sometimes misinformed on the details. "He did not get banned for gambling, you know," she said to me. "They couldn't find anything! He got banned because he hung around with undesirables. Later he admitted to the commissioner that he bet, but at the time he got banned they didn't know that at all." Wait, all Pete did to get kicked out of the game was hang around the wrong kind of guys? "Yes, that's what did it. I've talked about this with Pete a few times." When you ask Kim whether she has ever had a chance to look over the Dowd Report herself, she says, "Not really."

and comparisons sharpened when Roger Clemens and Bonds—both among the most accomplished players in history—appeared on the Hall of Fame ballot for the first time in 2012, eligible for the class of '13. Neither received anything close to the needed number of votes (they finished eighth and ninth, respectively, in the balloting), and for the first time in 17 years the baseball writers did not elect anyone at all to the Hall of Fame. Other steroid-linked players such as Palmeiro and McGwire have appeared on the ballot several times and also not come close to election. Sosa, also on the ballot for the first time for the class of 2013 and officially eighth alltime with 609 home runs, received a vote on less than 13% of the ballots. Still, all of those players have had a fair chance; Bonds and Clemens may yet get in.

Steroids were never an option for Rose—"It's too late for me," he told a Reds trainer as the drug began to proliferate in the mid-1980s—and whatever the impact of the widespread amphetamine use in baseball that Rose participated in, those stimulants did not grossly transform player production, wreak havoc on the record book and distort the day-to-day product on the field. Steroids have. Rose, who is often asked his views on steroid users, has adopted varying attitudes. At times, even as recently as 2013, he has referred to Alex Rodriguez as his favorite player (he has also had A-Rod programmed as a "favorite" contact in his mobile phone) and has suggested that players such as Bonds and Clemens should indeed be inducted into the Hall of Fame.

But Rose has also cast sharp aspersions, saying he could only imagine what men such as Babe Ruth and Roger Maris would think to know that "guys came along and cheated their way past those records." When in 2013 new information surfaced about a lab in Florida that allegedly provided performance enhancing drugs to Rodriguez and numerous other active players, Rose implied that the punishments—mostly 50-game bans, aside from A-Rod's—were not nearly enough. "I was a first offender too when I lied to baseball and I've been suspended 24 years," he told *The Huffington Post.* "And I did nothing to dicker with the integrity of the game of baseball." When asked to weigh the sin of his betting against that of ingesting steroids he added: "To all the young kids out there I'd say don't do either one . . . but if you do the one that I didn't do, you have a good chance of hurting your body in the long run."

At the same time that baseball has, over the past decade, adopted an increasingly strong stance against performance-enhancing drugs, its resistance to its teams having an affiliation with gambling interests has softened. The Yankees installed the Mohegan Sun Sports Bar just above Monument Park at their new stadium. (Though of course there's no gambling in the bar, the Mohegan Sun is a prominent casino in Connecticut two hours northeast of Yankee Stadium.) The Tigers invite guests to their MotorCity Casino Hotel Champions Club at Comerica Park. The Braves, the Dodgers and the Brewers feature casino presences along with several other teams—including, yes, the Reds, who have prominent ads for Cincinnati's downtown Horseshoe Casino on the outfield wall and in the stands. When the Mets opened Citi Field in 2009 they did so with Harrah's on board as a "signature partner" and with its Caesars' Club restaurant as a core attraction. (Harrah's, remember, runs a large sports book, taking in millions of dollars in baseball bets each year.) One "fan experience" promotion consists of a package in which a bus leaves postgame from Citi Field headed to Caesars' Atlantic City; fans also get a $10 credit for the slot machines in the deal. Signage at Citi Field advertises lasvegas.com.

The clear and enormous danger of Rose's baseball gambling lies less in its own crude execution and more in its implications. "The Pete Rose case represents the larger issue of gambling's prevalence in America," says Fay Vincent. "It is always out there and it is a real threat to professional sports, which tells you why a commissioner has to keep such a hard line against it." The crux, as ever: Gambling can lead a player (or a manager, or a referee) to intentionally influence the outcome of a game in order to benefit a wager. A player might try to lose. And while fans will continue to pay to watch games played by athletes engorged by drugs, folks are not likely to stand for games that are not on the level. Those are for the WWE crowd.

As unsettling as it is to imagine an active major league player deeply involved with baseball betting, a *manager's* involvement may be even more ominous. A corrupted manager—for example, one who might want to throw a game as a way to help erase a personal gambling debt—would have ample opportunity to make lineup and strategy decisions that work to undermine his team.

Even if a manager only wagered on his team to win, he might be swayed to give that short-term gambling interest precedence over his team's long-term needs. Theoretically, for example, in the mid-1980s Reds manager Pete Rose might have called upon an already overtaxed relief pitcher to try to win a particular game rather than preserve the pitcher for the long haul of the regular season. While this may seem a trivial baseball subtlety to those outside the game, it's a real issue on the ground. So it should be pointed out that Rose had a lefthander in the bullpen, Rob Murphy, who in 1987 and '88 appeared in 163 games, the most in the National League. Murphy was effective (he had a 3.06 ERA over that time) but not remarkably so. In '88, for example, he went 0–6. And he did appear suited to heavy use; after being traded to the Red Sox and later pitching for the Cardinals, Murphy continued to rank near the league leaders in game appearances.

"The idea that Pete might have overused me or overused some other pitcher I was in the pen with, I never saw that at all," says Murphy. "I'd just about say it is a ridiculous idea. I wanted to pitch and there were a lot of situations that called for me to come in and get a couple of outs. If anything I wanted to pitch even more times than I got in." Murphy, who's involved in thoroughbred breeding, is still in touch with Pete. "Early May I know I might get a call," says Murphy. "Pete will want to talk about who I like in the Kentucky Derby."

Even aside from Murphy, there's no indication, neither through game logs nor player testimony, that Rose's betting influenced how he managed. But it could have. Speculation, sure. Evidence? Not yet. Rose himself, not surprisingly, says wagering had no impact on his managing—although there's always the possibility that his stance will change. If there is enough money to be made, as even those closest to Rose will tell you, Pete can change his mind on just about anything.

Of all the ways one might characterize the differences and similarities between Rose and those players known to have used performance enhancing drugs, the Hall of Shamers as it were, at the bottom line it comes to this: Rose has been banished for the incalculable damage he might have done to the foundation of the game. Steroid users are reviled for the damage they actually did.

———————

IN 2009, a special and unexpected visitor stopped by to see Rose at his table on induction weekend: Sparky Anderson. The two had been on uneasy terms ever since Rose's fall—Sparky couldn't get over Pete's brazen lying—and had not spoken in many years. As Anderson approached, frail but still vital at 75, a smile broke over his creased face, and then a mock scowl. When he got to Rose he took off his baseball cap and, holding it by the bill, thwacked Rose back and forth about the head, muttering no-goods at him all the while. "He knocked my cap sideways!" Rose later said, laughing. It was the scolding of a boy who had strayed, a what-am-I-gonna-do-with-you! display of benevolent pique. Anderson had come into Rose's life less than a year before Harry died, and he had known the kid for nearly 40 years; Sparky's wife Carol had been after him to bury the hatchet with Pete for years. "I owed him that visit. He played his heart out for me," Sparky said later to friends at the Otesaga.

People around Rose say that for the rest of that day, after Sparky had chatted for a while and then left, and the tear between them seemed suddenly, miraculously mended, Pete was in an exceptionally light mood—easier and more forgiving than usual, with all of his ebullience coming through.

About a year after that Cooperstown exchange, on an August after-noon in 2010, Rose and one of his steady associates, the memorabilia dealer Charles Sotto, drove out from Los Angeles to visit Anderson at his home in Thousand Oaks. Sparky was thinner still than he had been in Cooperstown, smaller it seemed in every way, and his chalk-white hair was yellowing at the sides. Although the day was not at all cool, he wore a jacket inside the house. Sparky and Pete sat at a table and drank iced tea and told each other stories they both already knew—about the Big Red Machine, and Anderson's own playing career, and Pete's hit record and about so many people they had known in the game that had once been everything to both of them. Sparky had some trouble hearing Rose, had trouble at times deciphering the rapid, Roseian chatter-scat that had once been part of the soundtrack of his life. That was O.K., though, because Pete did not mind repeating himself for Sparky.

They phoned former Reds coach George Scherger and left messages on his voicemail—Sparky and Pete calling. *Together!*—and they took a few snapshots standing side-by-side in the kitchen. And when, five or perhaps six hours after pulling in, Pete and Sotto finally got up to go so that Sparky and Carol could eat their supper and Rose could get back to L.A., Sparky came to the front door and stood there watching them go.

Six weeks after that visit to Thousand Oaks—and six weeks before the November morning when Sparky quietly passed away—Rose officially returned to the ballpark in Cincinnati. The Reds had invited him to commemorate, before a Saturday night game on Sept. 11, 2010, the 25th anniversary of his 4,192nd hit. On the big screen, they aired video of the Ty-breaking at bat and the pandemonium surrounding it and then a recorded message played through the stadium: Pete's voice recalling that night and hailing his teammates and thanking the fans who "made everything possible . . . made everything what it was." The sky was clear and the evening sun still shone.

Rose was driven out in a cart from the bullpen, traveling in foul territory along the rightfield line until he signaled to the driver, "Here, this is fine." The cart stopped and Pete lumbered out and began to walk—oh, maybe 90 feet or so—from the outfield toward first base as the crowd rustled and cheered, the hooting increasing when Pete neared the bag and, once there, raised his right leg and stomped his foot hard upon it. Home again. Cries of *"Peeete! Peeete!"* came out of the stands and then a spontaneous chant *"Hall of Fame! Hall of Fame! Hall of Fame!"* Former teammates of Rose were on the field that night, and Reds executives and Pete Jr. along with little PJ who, when he saw his grandfather out there and heard all the cheering, jumped his cue (What did the boy know? He was five) and ran out of the Reds dugout to clap his arms around Rose's waist.

More than 36,000 turned out to the park that night and the Reds beat the Pirates 5–4.

The whole scene, this particular Cincinnati homecoming, almost never happened. The Reds organized it and Bud Selig gave the O.K., but at first Pete said he couldn't make it to the ballpark for the ceremony that night on account of having committed to do a paid dinner appearance in a ballroom at the Hollywood Casino over in Lawrenceburg, Ind. The casino operators said that was absurd, that *of course* Pete should go and appear at the Great American Ball Park and that he could just come over to the casino afterward. They would just push the start time back, the customers could wait.

And would he still collect his check, the full amount? Pete wanted to know, making sure to get a guaranteed yes.

The purpose of the casino dinner was a roast of Rose, and teammates came up one by one to give him a zing: Tom Browning, George Foster, Tony Perez, Ken Griffey Sr. . . . About 500 people were in the room, seated at round tables of 10 or 12. Petey took the microphone briefly and made a crack about his dad's retro-chic clothes. At one point the lights dimmed and a clip aired of Rose singing in the old Aqua Velva commercial.

Then Pete himself got up there. By now the night was nearing its end and the coffee cups were half-full on the tables and the wine had been drunk. Everyone's attention was right up front on Pete, this being the moment they had all really come for. Rose zapped Perez (for his unusual use of English) and Griffey (for his batting style) and he told the one about the time Petey had phoned him from the minor leagues, battling through an 0-for-22 stretch, to ask his father the best way to get out of a slump. And Rose answered, "How the hell would I know? I've never been in a slump. Call Concepcíon."

Not only was Pete Jr. there, but Tyler Rose as well. Maybe what happened next was because those two were in the room (it was so rare to have his sons together) and maybe it was also because of the aftereffects of the celebration at the ballpark that night, and having so recently seen Sparky in the condition he was in, and also having those teammates in the room around him, but what happened next, to everyone's great surprise, is that Pete broke down. His voice did not simply waver or crack, he began to sob, much as he had standing on first base 25 years ago that night.

"I was covering this dinner, and it was kind of standard stuff," says John Erardi, *The Cincinnati Enquirer* reporter, "but then Rose started to lose it and that really got your attention. It felt completely unscripted, completely sincere and very powerful. I had covered Rose for more than 25 years and hadn't ever heard him like that."

Rose told the room that he finally understood what it meant to "reconfigure" his life. He said, "I disrespected baseball." He looked at Perez—calling him, "like a brother to me"—and apologized directly, and also apologized to the other teammates from the Big Red Machine. "I'm a hard-headed guy," Rose choked out. "But I'm a lot better guy standing here tonight . . . I guarantee everyone in this room I will never disrespect you again." He said, as he fought to get his composure, that he wanted his legacy to be of someone who "came forward" and added, "I love the fans, I love the game of baseball, and I love Cincinnati baseball."

Before that night, even in the years after he'd made his admissions in *My Prison Without Bars,* Rose had talked about his gambling with a kind of swagger, that familiar screw-you defiance. "It was like, 'Yeah, I bet on my team every night to win! So what? I'm a winner!' " says Greg Rhodes, a longtime Reds team historian. But this was completely different. Something had come over Pete. As Browning puts it, "We saw a man humbled that night. Pete was definitely humbled and he was ashamed. You could see inside him and with the way Pete usually is, that was not something any of us expected."

Browning and Erardi, Perez and Rhodes, and other people around the Reds had similar thoughts in the days after that night, a few questions they would discuss among themselves. Was this the kind of apology everyone had been waiting for? They wondered. When word got back to baseball's leadership about how contrite Pete had been up there, would it matter? Would Bud Selig think anything of it at all?

EVER SINCE taking on the commissioner's role, replacing Fay Vincent more than 20 years ago, Selig has been caught in the middle when it comes to Rose, straddling a line. As owner of the Brewers, he had been on the Hall of Fame board that, in 1991, voted to deny Rose his appearance on the writers' ballot. Selig cared a good deal about Giamatti and he has no tolerance for a manager doing the things that Rose has done. The commissioner has been asked about his position on Rose, publicly and privately, many hundreds of times, and he has never suggested that he would bend on Rose's permanent ban. But he has listened to Rose and his advocates, and also, in recent years, to an informal whisper campaign from the Reds. ("There's a hope on our part that maybe when Selig leaves office [after the 2014 season] he might pardon Rose on his way out," one member of the team's brass told me.) And Selig has, through his office, feuded with Dowd, sought to muzzle him from talking about the Rose case. Selig let Rose participate in events such as the All-Century Team and the 4,192 celebration at the Great American Ball Park, because he knows that a chance to embrace Pete Rose is something that some fans want.[6]

"Selig has been pretty good when it comes to Rose," says Vincent, "but he has also shown a lack of conviction. One problem with Bud is that he does not like to get booed, and that has an impact on his choices. When he lets Rose onto the field, when he does not enforce the rules, then what do the rules mean?"

Selig came to Cooperstown for the 2012 inductions, as usual, and on

---

[6] In September of 2013, Rose was also permitted to take part in a multiday event at the Reds ballpark, surrounding the unveiling of a sculpture of Joe Morgan. The occasion included two on-field reunions of the Great Eight—the position players Johnny Bench, Tony Perez, Joe Morgan, Pete Rose, Davey Concepcíon, George Foster, César Gerónimo and Ken Griffey, who formed arguably the strongest lineup in baseball history in the mid-70s. It was the first time they had all been together, Morgan said, "since the last day of the '76 season." For a time the Reds weren't sure whether Rose could participate, but Morgan has a long and amicable relationship with Selig and he appealed to the commissioner directly. "I saw him in Cooperstown on induction weekend, and I said, 'I need for Pete to be able to be on the field with me for this,' " says Morgan. "And he said O.K." There were restrictions however. While the other seven alumni were free to go into the Reds clubhouse or to linger in the dugout, Rose was not. He was led carefully to the specific places he needed to be—the base of Morgan's sculpture, the press room, the tunnel leading onto the field—and he was not to stray. Another of the commissioner's clear conditions for allowing Rose to take part, the Reds say, was that Rose, under no circumstances, was to be given a microphone on the field.

Sunday morning he was standing near the entrance of the Otesaga about to get into a car to take him to the induction ceremony when Larry Christenson, Rose's former teammate, spotted him. "I went over and asked, 'Would you listen if Pete were to come and talk with you again? Would you be open to talking about him getting back into baseball,'" says Christenson. "I tried to make a quick case for it." But Christenson says Selig did not give an answer. He smiled, shook his head and politely put up a hand before getting into the car.

A couple of hours later, Selig stood on the broad outdoor stage at the induction ceremony, reading, as is the commissioner's charge, Barry Larkin's newly created plaque. "Smooth-fielding steady-swinging short-stop whose dynamic defense and all-around play sparked his hometown Reds," Selig read. There were 44 Hall of Fame players seated behind him, and more than 18,000 fans sprawled out on the great lawn before him, on folding chairs, blankets, coolers. It was a bright and very hot day, and though the stage was well-shaded in an elaborate clamshell, out on the lawn people slathered on sunblock and fanned themselves with paper fans and occasionally poured bottled water over their brows.

The Hall of Famers had come out one by one, introduced by the deep-voiced broadcaster Gary Thorne and then Larkin's daughter Cymber had sung the national anthem. First Vicki Santo had accepted a Hall of Fame plaque on behalf of her late husband Ron, and she delivered a beautiful speech about the way Ron played third base for the Cubbies and the diabetes he had battled, and his deep love for the game, which especially came through during his broadcasting years. Then Johnny Bench had gotten out of his chair and to please the many Chicago fans out there donned a pair of thick-rimmed eyeglasses and pulled on a Cubs jersey and done his Harry Caray impression.

It was Larkin's turn next.

"A 12-time All-Star, he totaled 2,340 hits and 379 stolen bases in 19 seasons," Selig continued. He read the plaque inscription right through to the last line: "He batted .353 in the 1990 World Series, guiding Reds to four-game sweep of Oakland A's."

Amid applause and cheers, Larkin came to the dais in his suit, officially the 45th Hall of Fame inductee on the stage. He thanked Jane Forbes Clark and Jeff Idelson. He thanked his wife Lisa and his parents, Robert and Shirley. He thanked his daughters and his siblings and other members of his family, and then he started to talk about growing up in Cincinnati, about going to Moeller High and rooting for the Reds in the 1970s, and going on to play baseball at the University of Michigan. To pay tribute to the many "influential people of Latin descent" who had guided him and befriended him along the way, Larkin spoke for several minutes in Spanish.

Larkin gave thanks all over the place—classy—and called out many people specifically. The crowd cheered and clapped at the names they recognized. Sparky Anderson. Bo Schembechler. Rod Carew. Tony Perez. After the dozens of passing mentions Larkin began to deliver his first extended anecdote of the afternoon. He said, "I played with some monumental figures in the game of baseball and I want to acknowledge a few of those guys." Larkin paused and you could hear a few rowdy yelps come out of the crowd and someone shouted the name.

"You know it," Larkin said. "Pete Rose. 4,256 of them. That's right." The fans really roared then, all those people who had made the trip from Cincinnati and had been out for hours in their replica Reds jerseys on their folding chairs beneath the sun.

Larkin spoke about how Pete helped him through some "very rough times as a young player," and then he told this story from his first major league game, when Pete was managing the Reds and Larkin had arrived late after some travel troubles and was without any of his equipment. "Pete's walking out of his office and he looks at me and says, 'Larkin, it's your first day in the big leagues and you're already late.' And I go, 'Skip, I don't have anything.'

"So he laughs, we share a few minutes, he asks me, he says, 'You got any bats, gloves, anything?'

"I'm like, 'No I have nothing.'

"He's like, 'Well, what size bat do you use?'

"I go, 'Whatever size you use, Skip.'

'How about your shoes, what size shoe you wear?'

"'Those Mizunos, they look like they'll work.'

"He says, 'All right, here you go.' So I take it.

"It gets no better than the first day of the big leagues, playing for the hometown team. Pete Rose, my manager, I've got his bat, I've got his shoes."

After the game, Larkin went on, after he'd pinch-hit and driven in a run with a ground ball, and finished speaking with the media in the clubhouse, "Pete walks over to me and says, 'How was that?' I said, 'That was awesome, man.' He talks to me about growing up in Cincinnati, he talks to me about the opportunity to represent the hometown, the responsibilities of being a Red, how to conduct myself in a professional manner. He spends, like I said, about a half an hour with me and finally asks me, 'It feel good in your hand, that bat? Those shoes, they feel good on your feet?' I was like, 'They are awesome.' He's like, 'Good. Give them back.' I said, 'What?' He said, 'Your stuff will be here tomorrow, give me my stuff back.'"

Some of the players on the stage cracked up, *Yep that's Pete*, and the crowd on the lawn laughed too. Larkin said how he had been planning to take that bat and those shoes home with him and keep them forever, but Pete was a step ahead of him. "I just want to thank Pete for the opportunity," said Larkin speaking now in more general terms. "His words of wisdom and his support and him talking to me all the time. Thank you, Pete Rose. I love you, man."

It was right about then, not yet three o'clock on a Sunday afternoon, July 22, 2012, with the Hall of Famers listening to Larkin's speech and some chuckling at the stories and some applauding and others not, and Selig sitting with that neutral look on his face, listening, and the crowd out there on the hot, clear day in Cooperstown, whooping for Pete and calling his name, 1.1 miles from the plaque gallery at the Hall of Fame, it was right about then that you could get a sense, a realization, that maybe this right here was as close to a Baseball Hall of Fame induction ceremony as Pete Rose will ever get.

Chapter 23

Petey

O N WEEKENDS sometimes, when Petey was still in Bristol, Shannon and the kids would drive the 300 miles south from Cincinnati and spend a few days with him as he managed the team. Petey and PJ would play catch on the field—each clad in black-and-white number 14 Bristol Sox uniforms—and in sudden, playful moments Petey would break off and start chasing Isabella down the foul line. During games, Shannon and the children would sit together in the front row beside the dugout, clapping and cheering and calling out encouragement to the players by name. Afterward, PJ would come into the locker room and change next to Pete Jr., the two of them pulling their jerseys over their heads at just the same time. PJ was seven years old and, says Tim Hayes, the *Bristol Herald Courier* reporter, "It looked like the kid had just finished managing the game too."

Petey says that one of the many reasons he has stayed in baseball so long is so that PJ could have moments like this. "It's not the big leagues, but it is still baseball. It is still the same game with a lot of the same routines. I wanted my son to experience this, to get what I got."

When Pete Jr. and Shannon started talking about having children, in the early 2000s, he determined, and she offered no resistance, that their first son would carry on the name, Peter Edward III. "It is the greatest name in the world," says Pete Jr. "And now there are three of us." At the same time they decided that the boy would be known as PJ from the start. Not Pete or Petey or Pete Jr. Just PJ. The reason being, Pete Jr. explained then, "So that he does not have to go through what I've gone through."

The Bristol Sox are perennially a dreadful team. Since bringing home the Appalachian League championship in 2002, the Sox have produced only one winning season and over Pete Jr.'s two years the club was especially unsuccessful, going 43–90. As fans there have come to accept, the mission in Bristol—as well as for the Great Falls Voyagers, the short-season A ball team in Montana where the White Sox assigned Petey in 2013—is not to win games but to develop talent. These are often competing goals. Bristol's team is typically laden with players young even by Appalachian League standards and the White Sox, more so than many organizations, move their prospects quickly through the system. As soon as anyone starts to play well, they are gone, pulled up a level or two. Rose Jr. often gets to deliver the good news.

"We've decided you're not going to make your last start of the season," he told Todd Kibby, a tall lefthander with high strikeout numbers, in late August of 2012. Kibby looked surprised, then hurt. Rose Jr. waited solemnly for effect, then blurted: "That's because you will be pitching in Kannapolis!"

Managing in a developmental league, Pete Jr. can't freely strategize, or have any real control over many of the machinations of a game. The idea is to give the young players exposure. You almost never walk anyone intentionally in these leagues, and you rarely pinch-hit. A relief pitcher gets summoned in to a game not because Rose Jr. thinks he can get the next guy out, but in accordance with an innings-pitched plan devised by White Sox player development heads. The concept is something that Pete Rose Sr., who spent less than three seasons in the minor leagues and whose evaluation of just about everything hinges upon who comes out on top, cannot quite grasp. "How is your bullpen shaping up?" Pete Sr. might say when Petey calls him. Once after the doormat BriSox improbably swept a doubleheader in the summer of 2012, Pete Sr. called and said "Two in a row! They're going to make you manager of the year!"[1]

For Pete Jr. reaching the major leagues as a manager is something "I know I can do and will do. It's part of me. I can relate to a player and help him through something, a slump or what have you. As for running a game, well, my dad always taught me that if you watch a game of baseball, really pay attention to all that's going on, then it will tell you what to do. The game makes the decisions for you," Pete Jr. says. "It is the same game here as in the majors. It's just that in the big leagues you make more money and more people see you. When I get up there, my wife can quit her job, and my family can come with me wherever I am."

The White Sox have used Rose Jr. as a coach at Triple A Charlotte in the spring and summer months before Bristol's short season begins, and he has left his impression there as well as in Bristol. The circumstances around Pete Jr.—his roots in the game, his history, his perseverance—confer upon him a particular kind of valor among baseball men. Buddy Bell, the White Sox vice president and assistant general manager (that is, Pete Jr.'s boss), sees in the manager what he years ago saw in the boy and in the player. "He is respectful of the game and the people around the game and he has got a crazy passion for it," says Bell. "We all have it but Petey seems to just have a little more. You see how he talks to the kids, how he teaches the game. . . . He and his dad are similar—great teammates, generous teachers and all about baseball."

Patrolling the field before games in Bristol, Petey often carried a taped-up black fungo bat resting on his shoulder. A tool of his trade. At the end of the bat one afternoon hung a small baseball glove (truly tiny, smaller

---

[1] Although Rose Jr. embraces his role in developing players—"Anytime a kid moves up you feel a little lift, like you've helped the organization," he says—he can have a hard time stomaching the losing himself. Firm but controlled with his players, accessible and plainspoken in his tutorials, he is not one to suffer nonchalance or incompetence. After one lethargic Bristol loss in 2012 he locked the field house door and lit into the team, then made the players run laps around the field. During a game against Johnson City, Rose Jr. got ejected for arguing a blown call at first base. "It's not the first time and it's not going to be the last time," he said.

than Joe Morgan's), lending Rose Jr. the look of a country boy carrying a tree branch with a kerchief tied as a sack on the end, and wrapped in that kerchief some clothes, a harmonica, worms for bait. Even in his 40s, Pete Jr. still has plenty of Opie Taylor in him. Although he says that he is getting "a little big" to go by "Petey," other coaches call him that all the time. The little glove, which he later used while playing catch with Greg Briley, Bristol's hitting coach and a former big leaguer, belongs to PJ. "It's new and I'm breaking it in for him," Pete Jr. explained.[2]

Now country music strums out of the sound system at Boyce Cox Field as Pete Jr. swats fly balls with the fungo bat, calling out to the Bristol outfielders and telling them where the throw should come in. His left knee, the worse of the two, is lightly wrapped. The country songs tell about long roads and busted trucks, hard times and belief in better ones, songs about America.

Pete Rose Jr. does not blame his father for the difficulties of his own life, not for all the heckling he endured, nor for the baggage attached to his name; not for any of the things that have made his minor league journey so much harder than it might have been. He does not blame his father for the fact that the two of them couldn't be together in the club-house at Pete Jr.'s major league debut in 1997. Long before that debut, as Pete Jr. recalls now, Pete Sr. "sat me down and told me that he had bet on baseball and started to say he was sorry. I cut him off. I said, 'You don't need to tell me you're sorry. We all make mistakes.'"

For years after that conversation—and it was rare, almost unprecedented for his father to open up to him in such a way—right up until Pete Sr. officially came clean in 2004, Pete Jr. did not betray his father's guilt. Gambling, says Petey now, was never a problem in the years that his father and mother lived together, and his father has never spoken to him about the trouble to which gambling might lead.

---

[2] In the 2012 Bristol game program, incidentally, Petey's personal biographical sketch was comically wrong. His wife's name appeared as Linda, the information about his children and where he attended school was way off. A list of his father's statistical achievements, however—and this was also included in Petey's bio—was spot-on.

Through his early childhood memories, and then later ones from the time in Philadelphia and when Pete came back to Cincinnati and then later still as the father and son began in brief and fitful attempts to make up for the time that was forever lost, his father's sins—of neglect, mainly, of indifference—are for Petey forgotten and forgiven. "I am the only one he ever threw batting practice to," Rose Jr. might volunteer. "No one else can say that."

He regards the parameters of his life as a gift—*the greatest name in the world*—and he does not ever take his father's name in vain. ("He is an incredible mentor, and the best part about it is that he's my dad.") The fact that as a boy and a younger man he resented his father's distance (for example, lamenting his father's absence during his early years in the minors by saying, "It's hard to catch him. He's always playing golf") now seems to Pete Jr. the product of youthful ignorance. He says that these days he speaks to his father "all the time." He is keen to the extraordinary opportunities that he received by being Pete Rose Jr. Sometimes, talking about his father, he will call him the Hit King throughout a conversation.

It is true that Pete Sr., even as he leads a life in Las Vegas and California, has in recent years attached himself more firmly to Pete Jr. and his family. Rose is in his 70s, after all, and the grandchildren have a softening effect upon him. Isabella and PJ call him Papa. He will come to Cincinnati and show up at one of PJ's ball games—the boy plays baseball, football and basketball—or take him to a Reds game at the Great American Ball Park, or to see a WWE Raw event when it's in town. Or the two of them, PJ and Papa, will sit together on the brown couch in the den of Petey and Shannon's home on the West Side, watching baseball on a flat screen. Papa doesn't stop talking about what is happening in the game. "Like how he did it with me," says Petey. Shannon and Petey have in their kitchen cabinets a stack of leftover plastic cups adorned with the logo from Pete Rose's Ballpark Cafe in Boca Raton and Papa and PJ might drink iced tea out of them as they watch. This is a side of Big Pete that Petey says he wishes everyone could see.

"He's just a normal dad, and I am just a normal son," Pete Jr. likes to say. "The only difference is that my dad has more hits than your dad."

When Petey gets to PJ's little league games—or to Isabella's, as she has begun playing too—he watches not from behind home plate like most parents but from far down the leftfield line. And at times seeing PJ out there in his uniform pounding his tiny glove in the field or stepping into the box, a talented little hitter, becomes more than Petey can stoically bear.

"What are you crying about?" Shannon will ask him. And for Petey it is too much to explain exactly what he sees and feels: all the promise and the memories; what really was and what might have been; Sept. 11, 1985; fatherhood; the fears of a life manqué. He cannot get all that out, or any of it, and keep his calm. He is given to crying, he allows; he gets emotional. So he will simply shrug his shoulders and raise a hand, pointing out toward the scene blurred now in front of him—little PJ Rose swinging a bat on a neighborhood ball field, West Side of Cincinnati—and say to Shannon, "Look."

Chapter 24

Where He Belongs

P ETE ROSE says he really can't remember when he began spending so much time in Las Vegas, when he first got an apartment there, or how the city evolved from a place he would visit sometimes for a payday and into the primary source of his livelihood. It all happened long after he'd moved to Los Angeles. For a while, beginning in the late 1990s, Pete had commuted between his home in Florida, doing his radio show out of the Ballpark Cafe, and L.A., flying out for a few days a couple times a month to his house in Sherman Oaks with Carol and the kids. Then the Cafe in Boca Raton wrapped up, the investors going on to other things, and Los Angeles became home.

The point of the move to L.A. was to help give their daughter Cara a real shot in show business. Carol had begun putting Cara into beauty pageants by age 4, and by the time she was 11, Cara had been acting for years under the name Chea Courtney. She'd done a few TV commercials, made a few appearances on the sitcom *Ellen*, played a recurring character for half the 1999 season on *Melrose Place*, landed a gig on the daytime soap *Passions*. "I'd love to do a movie in which I'd get to sing and dance and wear cool clothes," she said in 2001 when she was 12. Part of the reason she used a stage name rather than her own Cara Rose was so that when she went on auditions people didn't spend the whole time asking about her dad, Pete.[1]

Tyler, five years older, played basketball—he was tall and thin, his mother's son in that regard—and Pete came to his high school games. Tyler was good, though not a star (he would later play at Glendale Community College) and Pete wasn't shy about calling out from the sidelines, questioning a referee's call or encouraging Tyler to be more aggressive. Pete also sometimes went along with Carol on Cara's acting gigs—such as when she shot a scene for the hit television drama *Judging Amy*, a show whose ensemble cast featured Marcus Giamatti, Bart's son.

"I saw Rose on the set a few times," Giamatti says. "And I also saw him once at the Y in Hollywood—I think he'd taken his son over there to play basketball. My father had been dead for more than 10 years, but people still asked me about Rose when they heard my name. It still wasn't easy. And, honestly, it still isn't easy today. Each of those times that I saw Rose I had a similar feeling. Part of me wanted to go over and shake his hand and introduce myself. Look him in the eye. Another part of me just wanted to punch him in the mouth. But I knew what my father would have told me to do: He would have said that I should walk away. So that's what I did."

LAS VEGAS just made sense for Pete. He could drive there in four hours from L.A. and he'd done radio shows and appearances there for years. He knew the ropes. He *got* the place. In Vegas, and perhaps only in Vegas—to which people come from every state and status of the United States with their wallets open, and where customer turnover is so high—there was

---

[1] Though a movie opportunity did not arise and Cara has not continued to find roles in television, she has maintained an artistic side. She has taken intensive voice lessons and under the name Cara Chea posted a catchy, original pop song, "Never Know" on the independent music site Reverbnation.com. A Myspace music page on which she goes by "Ms. Rose" also features seven other original songs, titled: "Move On," "I'm Alone," "The Way I Am," "Broken," "Contradiction," "OhMioDio" and "In Darkness." In 2010, as Cara Rose, she produced for a film class a one minute, 23 second horror short called *Nolan: The Evil Gnome* in which Pete appears, fleetingly, as a coroner.

money to be made, day in and day out, perpetually selling his signature and himself. Good money.

For nearly a decade, before and after his marriage to Carol dissolved, Rose has held a regular gig at a Las Vegas memorabilia shop; most recently that has been at a store called The Art of Music in the Mandalay Place shopping area, where he sits and signs, five-hour shifts, at least 20 days a month. "He's guaranteed $3,500 a day," says J.D. Friedland, the co-owner of Hit King Inc., which employs Pete and organizes the signings and some of Rose's other ventures. "If he sells more than $10,000 worth of merchandise in a day, he starts getting a bonus percentage. It's good business for him, and good business for us. Pete is terrific. He always wants to work. We'll say, 'Why don't you take a couple of days off?' And he'll say, 'What for? What am I going to do, go sit on a beach somewhere?'" Hit King Inc. and Rose recently extended their contract, for the fixed wage and the guaranteed minimum days per month, through 2017.

Rose makes money in other ways too, through speaking engagements and private appearances, or doing the occasional advertisement. For $5,000, you and a few friends can have dinner with him at the Palm in Vegas. Good steaks, plenty of side dishes, and Pete, all meal long, being Pete. Brides-to-be like to give that dinner to their oncoming husbands as a bachelor's party gift. All told Rose might earn between $1 million and $1.5 million a year.[2]

---

[2] Away from the signing table, Rose "sightings" in Las Vegas are legion, stories swapped by the common man. This person saw Rose stepping off an escalator and got him to sign an old Phillies game program. That one asked Rose for an autograph in the parking lot and he instead wrote down his hours at Mandalay Place. Another person spotted Rose at a slot machine—truly rare; it's not Pete's game—and took a photo with him. Someone else came upon Rose trundling along in the evening after work, the fedora on his head and a bag of takeout in his hand. One time Pete was walking around a hotel lobby in a purple velour jogging suit; another time in silk pajamas. Etc., etc. You hear tales tall and true and wonderful. Like this: "I was with some friends in a nightclub in Vegas, about 2008, and a midget walked in," says Kevin Wassong, a media executive in his mid-40s from New York. "Behind him came a normal sized guy and then behind him another guy who was absolutely huge, like a Sumo wrestler, tall and maybe 400 pounds. It was bizarre. And they were all wearing tuxedos! I looked again and realized that the middle guy was Pete Rose. We were like, what the F?"

Pete's garrulous self, his off-color humor and buddy-boy irreverence, works perfectly at his signing table in Las Vegas. Customers, in town for a lark, are up for exactly what Pete provides. Rose gets asked about winning the World Series and playing in All-Star Games (Ray Fosse still comes up a lot) and his hitting streak of 1978. He has stories, it seems, from whatever U.S. city a customer is from—a story about a teammate being caught in a hotel there *in flagrante*, perhaps, or about a game he won there with a bunt in the ninth. He'll tell you about the frowsy post-game locker room, and he'll look at you and ask where your kids go to school. Sitting there chatting while watching a newly purchased ball or jersey or photograph being inscribed, the customer feels, and this isn't necessarily a false feeling, that he is getting a real piece of Pete.

Many customers, perhaps most, ask Rose about the Hall of Fame and whether he thinks he will ever get in. The conflict clearly lends him a cachet, the lure of the unresolved. That people see him as tainted—the outlaw hero—or as the victim of an injustice adds an attraction he would otherwise not have, something beyond his being the Hit King. Most retired baseball stars benefit greatly in the marketplace after getting into the Hall of Fame: Their autograph becomes more coveted, their time more valuable. Their profile is raised. In Rose's case, however, it is not in any way clear that being inducted in Cooperstown would increase his demand. "I don't think it would, actually," says Steve Wolter, a Cincinnati memorabilia collector who bought, among numerous other bits of Roseabilia, the bat that Rose used on the night of hit 4,192, as well as the bright red Corvette he received. "Pete's unique that way."

If anything, being inducted might, some collectors say, work *against* Pete Rose as a commodity, might take away the edge. "Yeah, not being in the Hall of Fame—I guess that's my shtick!" Rose once said to me, laughing.

Not surprisingly, Rose gets along famously with the employees, gofers and hangers-on at the venues where he signs. A few years ago he was working his table at the Field of Dreams store at The Forum Shops at Caesars Palace (I sat beside him, interviewing him as he worked) when a bleached blonde and conspicuously endowed woman in her early 20s swept in. She came right up to Rose, bent down and hugged his neck.

The woman had formerly worked in the mall, but now she was just coming in to visit. She wore a white tank top with no bra in the air-conditioned room, creating a happy diversion for some of the men waiting in line to get with Pete.

She hung around for awhile, lamenting a broken cellphone and a problematic boyfriend, and after some chat and advice—"Sure, you could move to a new town, honey," Rose said, "but for a girl who looks like you, every town is the same town"—Pete took out some cash and asked the woman to go to one of the mall's betting windows and put something down for him on a horse race at the Hollywood Park track in Los Angeles. As soon as she left, Rose turned to me and said, "Do you see those boobs? She won them in a fake orgasm contest. . . . A $5,000 boob job that she won for faking an orgasm!"

Set up on a table to Rose's right was a television showing those races from Hollywood Park. It was an unremarkable Thursday at the track. This was not a significant race card, but rather the daily fare that appeals only to a devoted lover of thoroughbred horses or to an avid gambler; a telecast decidedly for the bettor. All the odds relating to the upcoming race—each horse's win odds, as well as the odds for exactas, trifectas, daily doubles, Pick-Sixes and other exotic bets—ran continuously across the bottom of the screen.

Rose kept an eye on the TV. Now and then he would break from signing and use his cellphone to call, he said, a trainer at Hollywood Park and see if there was "anything going on." Then he'd reach into the front right pocket of his jeans and pull out a thick wad of $100 bills. He had more than 40 of them when the day began. Counting out five or six bills, Rose would call over one of the Field of Dreams employees—or his visiting Morganna—and say something like, "Go get me the 4-6 exacta box in the third race." The employee would go out to place the bet, then return with a ticket and give it to Rose.

And then, as he continued to sign autographs and to engage the public, that third race at Hollywood Park would go off. Rose's eyes would drift to the screen; he appeared interested, but not rapt. The 4 horse won. The 3 horse rallied down the stretch to place. The 6 horse showed. Rose had missed a heavy return—thousands of dollars—by about a length.

Rose didn't say anything or show emotion, but rather went on signing and keeping up his banter. After a few minutes he said to me quietly, "That back end always gets you. That 6 horse, he just slipped out."

Rose didn't try to hide his gambling. Not from me—a working journalist with a notebook—not from the workers in the store, not from the customers crowding near him. He bet on the horses throughout the afternoon (on five races in all) and he did so the way another person might unwrap and chew a stick of gum. There was no hesitancy, no shame, no fuss. This was simply something he did, that anyone might do. Much later, at the end of our time together that day, although I had not asked, Rose said to me suddenly: "That's all the betting I do, you know. The horses, maybe a little something else here or there. No more betting on other sports or baseball though. I'm done with that."

Whatever the object of the wagering may be, the lure of it, the habit, remains strong. When in 2011 Hit King Inc. moved Rose from Field of Dreams to The Art of Music, his daily walk from the parking lot to the store led him directly past a sports book. About a month into the new gig, Kiana Kim called Friedland and complained. Pete was bringing home less money than he had been, she said, and he had told her it was because he kept putting down a little something extra when he passed the window. Rose does not tend to hold on to his cash for long.

This is why when Hit King Inc. pays Rose it first puts money into an account to cover Rose's monthly expenses: the apartment in Las Vegas, his car lease (he's always got nice wheels), the L.A. house he stays in with Kim, a little something for his son Tyler, who is often around The Art of Music store in Vegas. Rose takes what might be described as an allowance out of what is left. "He has people who depend on him and this way all his bills are taken care of first," says Friedland. "Pete understands that that's how it needs to be. If he suddenly had a million dollars in his bank account it would be gone by the end of the month. That's just how he is."

Rose has also had government bills to pay, namely hefty liens from unpaid back taxes over the years—a reported sum of nearly $1 million for taxes between 1997 and 2002 alone. Says Friedland, "I think Pete would be very happy if he still owes money to the IRS when he dies."

Doesn't it all make sense? Didn't Rose's way have to lead to Las Vegas, where people act how they want to act and say what they want to say, their peccadillos overlooked and their sins, of course, forgiven? It is a city disarmed and transparent—everything out on the table, anything goes—even as it harbors the consequential secrets of so many lives. Las Vegas may be steeped in fabricated glitz, with its fake Venice and its fake Eiffel Tower, but it is also brutally honest. You win, you lose, you go home. Vegas has a ruthlessness not unlike that of the American Dream itself, and it has a duality not unlike Rose's: through all his openness, something hidden—something, finally, else. There is always the other side of Pete that Dave Rose and Pete Jr. have lived with all their lives, and that some in the clubhouse recognized. *Nobody will ever know him completely. Can't know him.*

It cuts both ways, as Las Vegas does. Rose may be given to lies, to stretching a story, to saying one thing one day and another the next, but there remains an unassailability in the way he lives his life, stripped bare, busting his ass to first base or on his latest autograph shift no matter who is hooting at him. Take me as I am. Pay me.

Pete Rose will never be a man to whom cardinal virtues can be ascribed, and yet in the impression he leaves and in the essence of what he projects, he may be one of the few honest people that you will ever meet.

AN EXECUTIVE at HBO Sports put it this way in the summer of 2013: "Rose is an asshole. You work with him and at the last minute he's always asking for more money, or saying that some guy of his has to be flown in first-class. Rose always needs something extra." (Partly because of his demands—often arrogantly issued—and partly because of access issues, HBO canceled its plans for the Rose documentary it had begun working on in 2012.)

Rose is known to haggle doggedly over his appearance fee (he can get up to $25,000 for a full night's event) but he is also known for delivering far beyond what was agreed upon. He'll stay longer, shake more hands, swap more stories, sign a few extra items, never act as if he is being imposed upon. With a few standing exceptions—he won't sign something that disparages Major League Baseball or Bud Selig, and he has refused a female collector's repeated requests to write above his signature "Thanks for the greatest night of my life"—Rose, for a price, will write just about anything next to his name. In 2005, at a collector's request, he began writing on baseballs, "I'm sorry I bet on baseball, Pete Rose." (In other words, as the wags had it, he finally had the balls to say he was sorry.) That spawned other inscriptions, Pete all the while japing his sin. "I'm sorry I shot JFK," he'll sign. Or "I'm sorry I screwed up the economy." He will write that he was the first man on the moon.

In 2012 Rose began shopping around his original version of the five-page document that banished him from the game. He and his people had a price in mind of about half a million dollars, and he first offered it to private collectors. "But what if baseball reinstates you someday?" asked Green Diamond Gallery owner Bob Crotty. "What will that do to the value?" And Pete said, "I'll put it in my will that you get the reinstatement letter too." Eventually the document went on the block through Goldin Auctions, drawing a high bid of about $250,000—not meeting the reserve price. No sale.

Meanwhile, Rose has offered autographed *copies* of that banishment document (for $500) through his website, and he has also sold signed editions of the Dowd Report—even, at times, from a table in Cooperstown. Profit-driven stunts like these have been the source of heavy hand-wringing from baseball moralists (one sample headline from *The Sporting News* read in part, PETE ROSE: DIGNITY STILL FOR SALE), yet even Dowd can't help but chuckle at the chutzpah. "He's just signing that fucking thing and selling it! The fucking report that ruined his life!" Dowd says, shaking his head gently, his smile refusing to leave.

Rose, you know, is in on the joke, living in a landscape scarcely dotted by sacred cows. Filming a scene for his 2009 movie *Brüno*, Sacha Baron Cohen tried to punk Rose, bringing him in for an interview during which, due to an alleged furniture delivery snafu, they had to sit on "chairs" that were actually men on all fours. Later Brüno (portrayed by Cohen) ordered up a smorgasbord of sushi, which was wheeled in, arrayed on the prone body of a large, naked and hirsute man. Bruno started to tell Rose about the choices. "There is yellowtail just above the navel . . ." But Pete stopped him and said, "The only problem is that it's all got hair with it. I don't eat hair."

The scene didn't make it into the movie; the point of such skits, obviously, is to zap an unsuspecting victim, but Pete, though he didn't reveal it until the end, had caught on early to the prank, stayed in character and played along.

He was winking then and he is winking today when he signs a baseball "I'm sorry I broke up the Beatles" and he was winking way back in September of 1969 when Dennis "Wildman" Walker hopped out of the stands and ran onto the Crosley Park field to shake Pete's hand in the middle of a game. "Your ass is grass, man," Rose said to Wildman. And after Wildman was taken to the jailhouse and posted bail, he came back the very next day and waited for Rose outside the ballpark. "Would you sign it for me Pete?" Wildman asked, holding out his bail form. Pete, of course, did.

Rose was winking—and, yes, taking another payday—when in 2013 he and Kiana did a TV ad for a local furniture place in Cincinnati. ("I really like this Lane sofa," Rose says, while seated in a reclining chair.) And he was winking in '04 when he put on a tuxedo and gelled his dyed red hair and delivered an acceptance speech, lauding the professional wrestlers around him, upon being the first celebrity inducted into the WWE Hall of Fame.

Rose weighs more than he should, maybe 50 pounds too much, and he does not exercise with the regularity or the vigor that he might. He's had some health issues here and there—a heart murmur in 2012—but Pete Rose is very much alive, and very happy to be so. "What would I have been if I wasn't a baseball player?" he mused to a fan at his table in Vegas not long ago. "I don't know. I wouldn't have been a scientist, I know that." He is in his 70s, deep into the strange and sometimes cartoonish evensong of his life, and he is out to make what he can while he can, always ready to embrace another day of doing Pete Rose.

THE HOUSE on Braddock is still there, its facade and its sloping grounds largely unchanged. The little street is crudely paved and just below it, on River Road, heavy trucks wheeze and jounce noisily along. The man operating the Anderson Ferry these days, Paul Anderson of northern Kentucky, believes he is related to the original Anderson who started it all, though he is not sure exactly how. The front porch from where La-Verne Rose cast her line and caught her fish in the flood of 1937 remains, refurbished but intact.

"Nah, we haven't changed much about the house," says Johnny Flemming, who was born in 1990 and says he has lived at 4404 Braddock Street all his life. "I know a lot about what happened here. My mom told me some, and other people, the neighbors." Johnny's a smoker, thin as an infield rake, and he has a job doing maintenance at a Radisson hotel. Part of the narrative of Johnny's life is that he lives (along with his mother and sister) in the house where Pete Rose grew up.

"We used to have a Doberman Pinscher and he would never want to go on that stair, you know where Rose's father fell down and died," Johnny says. "He always had to kind of go around it, try to avoid it. It's weird but I believe in things like that. You feel the ghosts in the house. One night the television kept changing channels by itself; we didn't even touch it."

Johnny was in the seventh grade when *My Prison Without Bars* came out in 2004 and on the Thursday a few weeks later that Rose came to do a book signing at the Media Play a few miles north in Western Hills, Johnny skipped school. He woke before 5 a.m., he says, to go and get in line at the store and he brought with him five copies of the book. Johnny stood with hundreds of others for hours and when he finally got in front of Rose, sometime after the signing session officially began at noon, the kid took a deep, nervous breath and told him where he lived.

"No shit!" Rose said. And though the line was long and the people in it were antsy, Rose spent several minutes with Johnny, gripping his hand and asking about the house. "Is that sewer cap still out back?" Rose asked. Johnny told him yes it was and told him also that he'd once found in the bramble at the side of the house a tin dog tag with the name LAVERNE ROSE on it. Johnny said that the broken rear window had never been repaired—the same window that some folks in Cooperstown had, at the time that Rose was chasing Cobb, inquired about getting shipped to the Hall of Fame as true Americana evidence of Pete's rascally, ball-playing youth. "That window is history!" said Johnny. And Rose said, "Aw, I broke the thing with a basketball, anyway."

Johnny told Rose how he himself wore number 14 in Little League, to pay homage, and he told him how in fact he saw the name ROSE just about every day, as it remained crudely but permanently carved into the siding of the house, a remnant from decades past. Johnny wondered if maybe this was an early Pete Rose autograph of a sort, but Rose laughed and said he didn't remember how the name got there.

"It must have been me who carved our name in the house," says Dave Rose. "Pete wouldn't have wasted his time on something like that." Dave says he hardly sees Pete these days. He will call Pete's cellphone and leave a message—Pete rarely picks up—but the message might not be returned. Occasionally Dave runs into someone at the Pit Stop Barbeque & Grill outside Indianapolis where he now cooks, who will say, "Hey, I saw your brother in town the other day!"

"It's kind of embarrassing when someone else is telling you he's been around and you didn't know," he says. "Pete might come to town to see a Pacers game when Kobe or LeBron are in town—and he came in for the Indy 500—but then he'll leave right away. I get it. I know he's real busy. I love him. I'm proud of him. I only wish I could see him a little more."[3]

On summer nights Dave likes to go with his girlfriend Rita to watch the Triple A Indianapolis Indians play, especially when there's a two-for-one ticket special. They can sit by the rail along the leftfield line for $11. Dave often wears a Reds cap with Pete's signature on it, and he'll

---

[3] During the filming of TLC's *Pete Rose: Hits & Mrs.*, neither Dave nor his older sister Caryl—whom Dave talks to just about every week—were ever even mentioned. You might have thought Pete was an only child. "That's because he knows if they get me on camera, I'll steal the damn show!" Dave says with a laugh.

clap loudly at a play he likes, calling out, "That's fundamental baseball!" He and Rita draw looks—they're an interracial couple—and that might lead to a double take, to a ballpark fan registering Dave's mien and his rounded chest, noting his ballcap and hearing the timbre of his voice and so coming over to ask, "Are you Pe—"

"Dave Rose," he'll answer putting out his hand, and he and the fan will wind up talking about Pete.

Dave can at times be hard to track down himself, for a day or even two, and his old friends in Indy, Jim Luebbert and Greg Staab, say they live with a lingering fear that they will find out that Dave has slipped off the rails once again.

Pete goes to ballgames too, Reds games, a few each season. He'll sit in a suite or a box and if he is shown on the big screen, the crowd roars. Because of his ban Rose still can't go anywhere at the Great American Ball Park beyond where an ordinary fan might go—no clubhouse, no dugout, no field. Still, he's in regular contact with several Cincinnati players, including Joey Votto, the team's star. Votto credits his relationship with Rose for helping him to maintain his intensity over the season's grind. "He reminds me never to give away an at bat," Votto says. "He has said things that help keep me focused."[4]

Right next to the stadium, the Reds have their own Hall of Fame, a cleverly curated, two-story museum that traces the team's long, rich history. The team has been inducting members—voted in either by fans or baseball writers—since 1958 and the inductee roster now consists of 75 players, three managers and three executives. The Hall's public FAQ sheet includes the question, "Is Pete Rose eligible for the Reds Hall of Fame?" And the answer, "No. Rose is not eligible for the Reds Hall of Fame (or for the National Baseball Hall of Fame) because he is on baseball's ineligible list." Naturally, the team could have set its own eligibility rules in any way it wanted, but "in the spirit of cooperation" as the

---

[4] In July of 2012, Rose got wind that Votto had missed a team workout and immediately sent him a chastising text. Votto, Rose says, texted right back, apologetic, and explained that he had missed the workout only because he was having surgery on his knee.

museum's curator Chris Eckes puts it, chose to follow Cooperstown's lead.

Even without being inducted, Rose is well represented among the exhibits at the Reds Hall of Fame in Cincinnati, most appealingly in a bronze life-size statue of him cavorting on the field with seven other members of the Big Red Machine. In 2007 the team unveiled a special exhibit there to honor Rose—displaying game-used jerseys from as far back as Western Hills High, along with baseball cards, photographs, significant bats and balls from his career and so on. The Reds invited Rose to the exhibit's opening and, after agitating unsuccessfully to get paid ("Which part of 'We are celebrating and appreciating your career,' did you not understand?" a Reds executive said to him in denying the fee), Pete finally accepted. He asked for a guest pass for Steve Wolter, the memorabilia collector, and for Arnie Metz, the old Reds maintenance guy who used to go with Pete to the track.

Pete Jr. drove over to that exhibit opening too—this was in March, before the minor league baseball season had really begun—and he brought PJ, who was not yet three, and the Roses made their way together through the museum, stopping at a permanent exhibit that has become a visitor favorite: a wall made up of 4,256 baseballs, one for each Rose hit. The wall borders an open stairwell that looks out through large windows to where left-centerfield used to be in Riverfront Stadium before it was torn down in 2002. The area there has been planted thick with roses, all of them red save for a single white rose bush marking the spot where Rose's 4,192nd hit fell to earth. In the airy stairwell an endless loop of the radio call of the hit, the broadcast by Reds greats Marty Brennaman and Joe Nuxhall, plays overhead. A museum employee will tell visitors that they are welcome to stand in the stairwell—just as Pete, Petey and PJ did that day—and to look out at the Rose Garden and listen to the radio call for as long as they might like.

Chapter 25

The Sand Lot Kid

SINCE THE spring of 1964 a bronze sculpture has stood prominently on the southern side of Main Street in Cooperstown, just at the entrance to the parking lot for Doubleday Field. The sculpture, set on a thick bronze base and mounted upon a marble block, is a slightly larger-than-life figure of a barefoot boy wearing overalls and a brimmed farmer's hat. He is standing in a hitter's stance, gripping a knobless bat, the barrel just above his right shoulder, and he's staring ahead. The man who sculpted it, Victor Salvatore, worked from a studio in nearby Springfield Center, N.Y., and he died at the age of 80 in '65. The name of the sculpture is *The Sand Lot Kid*.

This is one of the true landmarks in the village, ideal as a meeting and gathering place. Throughout busy days on Main Street, passersby slow down to stroll around the sculpture, looking at it from all sides. Others sit on the edge of the marble block, setting down their drinks on the bronze base. A kid might put a foot up on the statue to tie his shoe, and mothers have been seen changing diapers there. The tops of *The Sand Lot Kid*'s feet have been worn shiny from people rubbing them for luck.

Postcards of the sculpture sell in many Cooperstown shops, and the Kid, slightly shaded by sidewalk trees, is among the most photographed images in town. He seems to evoke a long-ago but not so distant time, when the ballfield behind him was grazed by cows and kids would race down to the Glimmerglass and hurl themselves into the water after a hot day of chores. When the maquette for the piece was first received by the Hall of Fame in 1944 (it was envisioned as a tribute to commissioner Landis, who had recently died) an acquisition committee described the sculpture as serving to "symbolize the interest of boys throughout the country in the national game."

We don't know who the Sand Lot Kid is, of course, whether he is gentle or ornery, a farmer's son or a drunk's, whether he is lazy or industrious, whether he is pagan, indifferent or devout. Perhaps the skin on his hip beneath his trousers has been shredded by a basepath slide. Perhaps he's late for supper. Perhaps he has a girlfriend in the lot watching him hit. All we know about the boy, true in 1944, in 1964, in 2014, is that he is in his stance forever, his bat in hand and awaiting the pitch, and each person who looks at *The Sand Lot Kid* can make of him what they will.

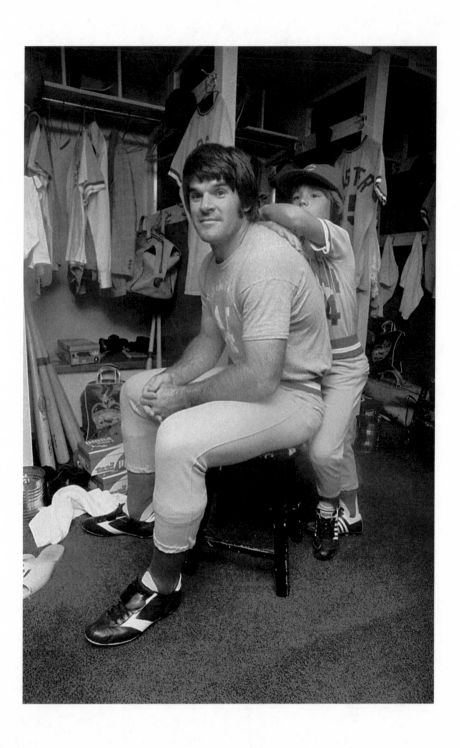

The Rose boys: (left) Pete with young Petey in the Yankee Stadium locker room at the 1977 All-Star Game; (top) with brother Dave during a ballpark visit in 1980; (above) with father Harry in Cincinnati, 1960s; (right) with Pete Jr. (Petey) in Chattanooga, 1997.

Acknowledgments

NUMEROUS PEOPLE, from various and disparate walks, helped me in my reporting of this book—in large ways and in small. They should be acknowledged, and thanked, for the time they spent with me, for the details and the insight they provided. To start: Pete Rose Jr., David Rose and Karolyn Rose. As well as Caryl Schnebelt.

In Cincinnati (and thereabouts) there was Bob Crotty and Bob Castellini Jr., Jeff Ruby and Steve Wolter. Also John Erardi, Greg Rhodes, Chris Eckes, Wayne Lyster, Kevin Manley, Mike Shannon, Jim Bowden, Dennis "Wildman" Walker. And out of the West Side in particular: Greg Staab, Jim Luebbert, Charles Parsons, ferryman Paul Anderson, Johnny Flemming (and Miranda), Ray Hassard and Lonnie from Braddock Street.

In Cooperstown (and thereabouts) there was Bill Francis, Jeff Idelson, Tom Heitz, Jim Gates, Joe Cannata, Brad Horn, Ted Hargrove, Andrew Vilacky, Tom Catal, Ken Meifert, Craig Muder, Freddy Berowski and the mayor, Jeff Katz.

There were ballplayers, past and present, who gave their time, and managers too. Among them, alphabetically: Buddy Bell, Johnny Bench, Kurt Bevacqua, Bruce Bochy, Wade Boggs, Greg Briley, Lou Brock, Tom

Browning, Jay Bruce, Steve Carlton, Marvin Chalmers, Larry Christenson, Doug Flynn, John Franco, Steve Garvey, Billy Grabarkewitz, Greg Gross, Tommy Harper, Billy Hatcher, Tommy Helms, Keith Hernandez, Dave LaPoint, Stephen Larkin, Jack McKeon, Denny McLain, Paul Molitor, Joe Morgan, Rob Murphy, Dan Neville, Phil Niekro, Steve Nikorak, Claude Osteen, Jim O'Toole, Dave Parker, Eduardo Perez, Brandon Phillips, Lou Piniella, Cal Ripken Jr., Jerry Royster, Mike Schmidt, Art Shamsky, Joel Skinner, Chris Speier, Rusty Staub, Andy Tomberlin, Joey Votto, Dave Winfield, Robin Yount. And also the umpires Ed Montague and Doug Harvey.

I was helped by Bill Giles in Philadelphia and Tim Hayes in Bristol and Larry Mileo in Long Island and by the encyclopedic Bob Hoie. By Phil Pepe and Bobby Brown. Also John Thorn, Rick Wolff, Roger Kahn, Hal Bodley, Maureen Marion, Josie Johnson, Tom Williams, Rita Crenshaw, Tom Villante, Mark Schraf, Nate Hubbard, Richard Berman, Jack O'Connell, Debbie Boggs, Paul Janszen, Suzi Elliott and Matt Cline.

Some public relations directors were very helpful, including the inimitable Pat Courtney at Major League Baseball and the commissioner's office. Also the excellent Rob Butcher at the Reds and his colleagues in trade: Greg Casterioto (Phillies), Jay Horwitz and Ethan Wilson (Mets); Joe Jareck and Mark Langill (Dodgers); Tommy Viola (Charlotte Knights); Bob Beghtol (White Sox); Melody Yount (Cardinals) and Matt Roebuck (Marlins).

Out of the land of TV there was Joe Lavine and Steven Stern, Mark Scheibal, Shannon Martin, Laurie Goldberg, Alon Ornstein and Gabriela Tavakoli.

From around Pete, there was J.D. Friedland and Charles Sotto as well as Dan Goossen, Warren Greene and Joie Casey.

Also, for other important perspectives: John Dowd and Fay Vincent, Kevin Hallinan, Joe Daly and Terry Dinan. And Marcus Giamatti.

My research was aided greatly by Amy Gresham in Cincinnati, as well as by Brian Powers at the public library there. The translating work done by Kathrin Perutz was invaluable.

Some people spoke with me and asked not to be mentioned by name. To them, a silent and grateful tip of the cap.

Although Pete Rose did not sanction or facilitate this book, he engaged with me at the times when I got myself to wherever he was, and also by telephone. I interacted and spoke with Rose on various occasions and in various milieus, including Cincinnati, Cooperstown, Las Vegas and New York. I also spoke with Kiana Kim in person and by telephone.

This book, to its great benefit, was supported and aided from the outset by Andrew Blauner, a literary agent, and a man, with the clear eyes and the good sense that anybody would be lucky to have on one's side.

I and this book were fortunate as well to have had the attention of the excellent David Bauer, an editor of grace, grit and simple wisdom.

Cheers to Elizabeth McGarr McCue—diligent, meticulous, smart—who made sure that fact was fact and nothing but, and contributed as well her own worthy perspective. I don't know how anyone, anywhere gets anything done without Stefanie Kaufman, who kept this particular ship sailing and on course with her intelligence and diplomacy. Kevin Kerr's subtle and reasoned work as a copy editor bettered this book time and again.

At Time Home Entertainment thanks to Jim Childs, Joy Bomba and Tom Mifsud, and to Michele Bové for her special and fine attention. Also thanks to Richard Fraiman and Terry McDonell, who believed in this book from its first lines, and at *Sports Illustrated* to Stephen Cannella and Chris Stone. Thanks to the photo-taking of Erick Rasco and the photo-selecting of Cristina Scalet and to the creativity of designer Stephen Skalocky.

These lights never dim: Sonya and Maya—my inspirations and revelations for this work and for so very much more. And finally, this book does not get written, nor does this life get led, without Amy, the harbor and the horizon. No thanks, in any words, would be enough.

Kostya Kennedy
New York
2014

Selected Bibliography

BOOKS

Bench, Johnny and Daugherty, Paul. *Catch Every Ball: How to Handle Life's Pitches.* Orange Frazer Press, Wilmington, Ohio, 2008

Birdsall, Ralph. *The Story of Cooperstown.* The Arthur H. Crist Co., Cooperstown, N.Y., 1917

Browning, Tom and Stupp, Dann. *Tales from the Cincinnati Reds Dugout.* Sports Publishing, New York, 2012

Chafets, Zev. *Cooperstown Confidential.* Bloomsbury USA, New York, 2009

Cook, William A. *Pete Rose: Baseball's All-time Hit King.* McFarland & Company Inc., Jefferson, N.C., 2003

Dowling, Jerry. *Drawing Pete!* Edgecliff Press, Cincinnati, 2008

Durocher, Leo and Linn, Ed. *Nice Guys Finish Last.* University of Chicago Press, Chicago, 2009

Giglierano, Geoffrey J. and Overmyer, Deborah A. *The Bicentennial Guide to Greater Cincinnati: A Portrait of Two Hundred Years.* The Cincinnati Historical Society, Cincinnati, 1988

Erardi, John. *Pete Rose 4,192.* The Cincinnati Enquirer, Cincinnati, 1985

Fitzgerald, F. Scott. *The Great Gatsby.* Charles Scribner's Sons, New York, 1925

Fleitz, David L. *Shoeless: The Life and Times of Joe Jackson*. McFarland & Company Inc., Jefferson, N.C., 2001

Giamatti, A. Bartlett. *A Great and Glorious Game*. Algonquin Books of Chapel Hill, Chapel Hill, N.C., 1998

Guilfoile, Kevin. *A Drive into the Gap*. Field Notes Brand Books, Portland, Ore., 2012

Gutman, Dan. *Baseball Babylon*. Penguin Books, New York, 1992

Harrelson, Bud and Pepe, Phil. *Turning Two: My Journey to the Top of the World and Back with the New York Mets*. Thomas Dunne Books, New York, 2012

James, Bill. *Whatever Happened to the Hall of Fame?* Fireside, New York, 1995

Jones, Louis C. and Duncan, Richard S. (Photog.) *Cooperstown*. The Farmers' Museum Inc., Cooperstown, N.Y., 2006

Kashatus, William C. *Almost a Dynasty: The Rise and Fall of the 1980 Phillies*. University of Pennsylvania Press, Philadelphia, 2008

Kennedy, Caroline. *A Patriot's Handbook*. Hyperion Books, New York, 2005

Kimball, Roger. *The Long March: How the Cultural Revolution of the 1960s Changed America*. Encounter Books, San Francisco, 2000

MacWatters, Robert C. and Jones, Mark S. (Illus.). *The Fishes of Otsego Lake*. Biology Department, State University College, Oneonta, N.Y., 1980

McLain, Denny and Zaret, Eli. *I Told You I Wasn't Perfect*. Triumph Books, Chicago, 2007

Mersch, Christine. *Delhi: Cincinnati's Westside*. Arcadia Publishing, Charleston, S.C., 2005

Plimpton, George and Kinsella, W.P., et al., and The National Baseball Hall of Fame. *Baseball As America: Seeing Ourselves Through our National Game*. National Geographic, Washington, D.C., 2002

Plato, *The Apology*. Lexington, Ky., 2012

Powell, Lyman P. (Ed.). *Historic Towns of the Western States*. G.P. Putnam's Sons, New York (The Knickerbocker Press), 1901

Randall, Stephen (Ed.), and the editors of *Playboy* magazine. *The Playboy Interviews: They Played the Game*. M Press, Milwaukie, Ore., 2006

Reisler, Jim. *A Great Day in Cooperstown*. Carroll & Graf Publishers, New York, 2006

Rhodes, Greg and Erardi, John. *Big Red Dynasty*. Road West Publishing, Cincinnati, 1997

Ridley, Matt. *The Origins of Virtue*. Penguin Books, London, 1996

Robinson, Frank and Stainback, Berry. *Extra Innings*. McGraw-Hill, New York, 1988

Rose, Pete and Garagiola, Joe. *The Pete Rose Story*. The World Publishing Company, New York and Cleveland, 1970

Rose, Pete and Hertzel, Bob, *Charlie Hustle*. Associated Features Inc., New Jersey, 1975

Rose, Pete and Kahn, Roger. *Pete Rose: My Story*. Macmillan Publishing Company, New York, 1989

Rose, Pete and Hill, Rick. *My Prison Without Bars*. Rodale Inc. U.S.A., 2004

Sandel, Michael J. *What Money Can't Buy: The Moral Limits of Markets*. Farrar, Straus and Giroux, New York, 2012

Searcy, Amy (Ed.) *Stories That Must Be Told by the People of Sayler Park, Ohio*

Shannon, Mike and Hannig, Scott (Illus.). *Hutch: Baseball's Fred Hutchinson and a Legacy of Courage*. McFarland & Co. Inc., Jefferson, N.C., 2011

Smith, Ken. *Baseball's Hall of Fame*. Grosset & Dunlap, New York, 1958

Towle, Mike. *Pete Rose: Baseball's Charlie Hustle*. Cumberland House, Nashville, 2003

Spatz, Lyle (Ed.). *The Team That Forever Changed Baseball and America: The 1947 Brooklyn Dodgers*. University of Nebraska Press, Lincoln, Neb., 2012

Thorn, John. *Baseball in the Garden of Eden: The Secret History of the Early Game*. Simon & Schuster, New York, 2011

Vincent, Fay. *The Last Commissioner: A Baseball Valentine*. Simon & Schuster, New York, 2002

Vincent, Fay. *The Gift of His Example: George Van Santvoord of Hotchkiss*. The Hotchkiss School, Lakeville, Conn., 2012

Vlasich, James A. *A Legend for the Legendary: The Origin of the Baseball Hall of Fame*. Bowling Green State University Popular Press, Bowling Green, Ohio, 1990

Warhol, Andy. *The Philosophy of Andy Warhol.* Harcourt Inc., New York, 1975

Weber, Nicholas Fox. *The Clarks of Cooperstown.* Alfred A. Knopf, New York, 2007

White, Bill and Dillow, Gordon. *Uppity: My Untold Story About the Games People Play.* Grand Central Publishing, New York, 2011

Workers of the Writers' Program of the Works Progress Administration in the State of Ohio (American Guide Series). *Cincinnati: A Guide to the Queen City and its Neighbors.* The Wiesen-Hart Press, Cincinnati, 1943

Xenophon; Tredennick, Hugh and Waterfield, Robin (Trans.). *Conversations of Socrates.* Penguin Classics, New York, 1990

NEWSPAPERS, MAGAZINES AND WEBSITES

American Record Guide; *Associated Press*; baseball-almanac.com; *Baseball Prospectus*; baseball-reference.com; *The Boston Globe*; *Bristol Herald Courier*; *Bristol Sox game program*; *The Chicago Daily News*; *Chicago Tribune*; *The Cincinnati Enquirer*; *The Cincinnati Post*; *The Cooperstown Crier*; *Daily News* (N.Y.); *The Daily Star* (Oneonta, N.Y.); *The Evening Independent* (St. Petersburg, Fla.); *The Freeman's Journal* (Cooperstown); *Glendale News-Press*; *Las Vegas Review-Journal*; *Los Angeles Times*; *Memories and Dreams, The Official Magazine of the Hall of Fame*; *New York Post*; *The New York Times*; *Newsday* (N.Y.); *The Ottawa Sun*; *Playboy*; *The Philadelphia Inquirer*; *The Post-Standard* (Syracuse, N.Y.); *Reds Report*; reverbnation.com; *The Sporting News*; *Sports Illustrated*; spruillhousemusic.com; *The Tampa Tribune*; *Vanity Fair*; *The Washington Post*; weebly.com; *Yahoo! Sports*

OTHER PUBLISHED SOURCES

Transcript: *Before the Grand Jury of Cook County, In the Matter of the Investigation of Alleged Baseball Scandal,* September 28, 1920. 1:00 o'clock p.m.

Criminal Docket for Case #3:05-cr-00152-ALL. From U.S. District Court for the Middle District of Tennessee (Nashville Division)

Report to the Commissioner: In the matter of Peter Edward Rose, Manager, Cincinnati Reds Baseball Club, 1989. John M. Dowd, Esq., et al.

Blumenreiche Handelswege Ost-westliche Streifzüge auf den Spuren der Fabel Der Skorpion und der Frosch. Deutsche Vierteljahrsschrift für Literaturwissenschaft und Geistesgeschichte, Volume 85, 2011. By Arata Takeda

AUDIO AND VIDEO

Advertisement: *It's Morning Again in America*; CD: Baseball Voices: *Marty Brennaman: Voice of the Reds* (Hall of Fame Series); DVD: *The 1975 World Series*, Games 1 through 7 (MLB DVD); Movies: *4,192: The Crowning of the Hit King* (2010); *Brüno*, deleted scenes (2009); *HU$TLE* (2004); *The Crying Game* (1992); *Mr. Arkadin* (1955); *Natural Born Killers* (1994); Television: *Star Trek: Voyager*, "Scorpion," May 21, 1997

Other: *Gaudino Dialogues*, 2008, by Williams College

PHOTO CREDITS

Opposite table of contents: Neil Leifer; pages 316–317 (clockwise from left): AP; Courtesy of Dave Rose; Bill Frakes; Bettmann/Corbis; Last page: Peter Kramer/NBCU Photo Bank/Getty Images

Index

About the Author

KOSTYA KENNEDY, an assistant managing editor at *Sports Illustrated*, is the *New York Times* best-selling author of *56: Joe DiMaggio and the Last Magic Number in Sports*, winner of the 2011 Casey Award and runner-up for the 2012 PEN/ESPN Award for Literary Sports Writing. He lives with his wife and children in Westchester County, N.Y.

www.kostyakennedy.com